HARPOON VENTURE

HARPOON VENTURE

by *Gavin Maxwell*

Introduction by Stephen J. Bodio

THE LYONS PRESS

Guilford, Connecticut
An imprint of The Globe Pequot Press

This book is dedicated with gratitude to the nine whose generous enterprise in 1945 made the adventure possible.

The Lyons Press is an imprint of The Globe Pequot Press.

Printed in Canada

Originally published by The Viking Press, 1952.

10 9 8 7 6 5 4 3 2 1

The Library of Congress Cataloging-in-Publication Data is available on file.

ISBN 1-58574-370-4

CONTENTS

APPENDIX

ILLUSTRATIONS IN THE TEXT

(Drawn by the author, unless otherwise stated)

But as to risings, I can tell you why.
It is on contradiction that they grow.
It seemed the best thing to be up and go.
Up was the heartening and the strong reply.
The heart of standing is we cannot fly.

—WILLIAM EMPSON

INTRODUCTION

If you say the name "Gavin Maxwell" to any reasonably liter-
ate reader, he or she will likely respond *Ring of Bright Water*. In
1961, this love letter to the wild west coast of Scotland and the
otters—I can't really call them "pets"—who lived with him there,
became an unlikely bestseller, making its author famous
overnight. *Ring of Bright Water* is a wonderful book, and like
most of Maxwell's books, a bit hard to classify in any genre.
Nowadays, Maxwell's books are usually considered "travel literature." But *Ring of Bright Water,* his fifth, wasn't, nor was this
one—his first and still one of his best.

Gavin Maxwell was born in 1914 to an aristocratic family that
combined high birth, Puritan rigor, and intellectual achievement.
In his youth he was interested in natural history and not much
else. At Oxford, his major was in "Estate Management." He
wrote and painted, went on an ornithological expedition to northern Finland, and went off to war. Although he became a major in
the Special Forces, he spent much of the war, as he was to spend
a good deal of his life, as an invalid. After the war, a lifelong
romantic fascination with the rugged coast of Highland Scotland,
still one of the world's wilder places, drew him there in his thirty-foot lobster boat. He was thirty-one years old, and looking for
something to do.

He hit on an idea that, even after he explains it, can still amaze
the reader with its crazed impracticality: He would outfit a fishing boat with harpoons and build a commercial fishery for the
basking shark on the Isle of Soay (which he bought) in order to
bring a useful industry to the depressed Western Highlands. The
plan was typically Maxwellian in that it combined romance,

adventure, and danger with contact with nature and an impulse to do good. It was also typical in that it cost an enormous amount of money, that all financial signals pointed to disaster, and that he leaped into it without really looking to see where he was leaping. Or as he put it, always honest in hindsight: "...when in November, I found myself a civilian I had finally made up my mind to experiment in commercial shark fishing. I had gone further than that: I had taken the first false step and bought a worthless and entirely unsuitable boat." As Mark Cocker would write in *Loneliness and Time,* his excellent book on English travel writers, *Harpoon Venture* "was inevitably a book about failure."

But what a book, and what a failure! All Maxwell's books are in part essays in autobiography, and despite their diverse subjects—the fishermen and bandits of Sicily, the now-vanished Marsh Arab culture of Iraq, otters, the brigand-lords of the Atlas Mountains, basking sharks and harpoons—his character remains as interesting as his interests. On the face of it, he is an unlikely macho hero, modest, introverted, sensitive, and impractical. He was often ill and suffered from (to use one list only) "synovitis of the right ankle, a duodenal ulcer and an enlarged heart." He had constant trouble with his circulation, which nearly crippled him in the sixties, and would die of lung cancer at fifty-five, perhaps because he habitually smoked eighty cigarettes a day.

On the other hand, he was a crack shot with rifle and shotgun, had a genius for taming wild animals, was utterly intrepid, and was a stoic in pain and disaster. Cocker characterizes him as "soldier, poet, journalist, portrait painter, conservationist, fisherman, writer..." Perhaps an even better glimpse of his character can be seen in his choice of books for the shelf on his harpoon boat *Sea Leopard:* "Eliot's *East Coker* was, I remember, stained by the damp green kiss of its green-covered neighbor, *Le Tamage des Peaux des Animaux Marins**; [poet Roy Campbell's] *Adamastor* rubbed shoulders with its avowed enemies, [critic Cyril Connolly's] *The Condemned Playground* and *Enemies of Promise,*

---

* Marine Animal Skin-Tanning

and next to them came Hogben's *Principles of Animal Biology,* Empson's *Seven Types of Ambiguity,* Huxley's *Evolution,* and *A History of the Whale Fisheries.* Technical works on ballistics and navigation alternated with tattered novels, of which Evelyn Waugh claimed seven out of twenty…"

Is this the library of an Oxford esthete, a man of action, or a biologist?

Maxwell was a spendthrift who would live for years in a cottage with no modern amenities, a bisexual who married, a man who could cry for an otter or a dog but who hated the not-yet-romanticized killer whale. He had a love affair with the poet Kathleen Raine and used a line from one of her poems as the title of his most popular book, though this sometime man of science also believed that her curse had led to the death of the otter hero of the same book. "Contradictory" seems an inadequate word for him.

He adventured through the islands for three years. The work was always exciting, but the shoreside part of the business refused to go smoothly. It took an incredible amount of time and money to design a reliable harpoon head, partly because Maxwell had an idea about how to design one that he would not let go, despite the fact in never worked. (He was still fiddling with new harpoon and gun designs when the whole concern went bankrupt.) His first boat, as mentioned, was useless. A plan for pickling shark flesh went awry; they didn't use enough salt and ended up with *sixteen tons* of rotting flesh. "It was alive, heaving, seething, an obscene sea such as Breughel might have conceived, alive as the sanctuary of Beelzebub himself, with a million grubs, twisting, turning, writhing, as though beneath that surface layer were the struggling bodies of all the wounded but resurrected dragons that we had attacked and that had escaped us."

They were only a little better at chasing his "dragons": "I was able to fire into him at almost point-blank range, the gun at maximum depression, and the gigantic expanse of his flank practically stationary below me. I had loaded with a slightly increased charge of powder, and I could feel the decks below me shudder with the recoil as the harpoon went squarely home. The shark reacted very quickly, tipping to dive almost in the same instant as the harpoon struck, and the tail rising level with the *Sea Leopard's* decks in a tremendous flourish. The tail was on a par with the rest of him; it seemed half as big again as any that I had seen. An average tail is about seven feet across; this looked to me like ten at least, and I bounded back from the gun as the flat of the tail slammed wetly on to the boat's side a foot below the gunwale. Then the shark was down under the water and the rope streaking out from the fair-lead at tremendous speed.

"I stared, incredulously, watching a thin trickle of smoke rising from the rope where it passed over the metal—the first time I had ever seen a rope running out fast enough to be practically catching fire. I was aware of Dan behind me, trying hopelessly to slow the rope enough to catch a half-turn on the winch, but the speed was too great for him to do anything. I was a matter of seconds before the heavy thump of the rope snapping off short at the iron ring to which it was tied—a three-inch yacht manila rope with a breaking strain of about two tons."

He learned to fix his particular problem by attaching the rope to a buoy rather than to a fixed point, a method I saw used in the New England tuna fleet in the late seventies. But the problems multiplied even as the money dwindled and the pickled flesh rotted. The *Sea Leopard* turned out to be riddled with dry rot. Another ship ordered as a replacement was wrecked on a rock, and by 1950 the Soay Island Shark Fishery, a venture of "almost unlimited derring-do," according to a contemporary newspaper report, was no more. But Maxwell had observed well, kept a diary and notes, and in 1951, published his history of failure in a critically-acclaimed book. It was not the last time he did that.

Today, it seems almost no one has read it; I'm not sure why. Perhaps it was the cover, the title (The English edition, *Harpoon at a Venture*, reads as vaguely less aggressive), the dust jacket copy. Are modern readers wary of explicit adventure, equating it with cheap machismo? Are they too sophisticated for sea stories? The deserved success of the Patrick O'Brian stories would seem to argue against both points, though maybe their setting in the remote Napoleonic wars absolves them.

To me, *Harpoon Venture* has a lasting appeal that is as complex as Maxwell's character. First, there's the sea; *Harpoon Venture* is one of the few great *modern* sea tales. I'll admit I'm an addict; I was born within smelling distance of the ocean to a mother whose people were mariners back into the mists of time. Though I live in arid regions today, I don't need even that smell to arouse painful nostalgia, just a few well-chosen words. But again, judging from the sale of O'Brian's saga, you don't need salty blood or an oceanside upbringing to feel that yearning.

There is the problem of the shark fishery itself: How would *you* go about inventing an industry? There is science, plenty of it, for the rationalist and the biologically-minded naturalist. Despite Maxwell's often professed dismissal of "machinery," there is enough fascinating material on the evolution of his harpoons to satisfy an engineer. (He has always admired and owned boats, expensive fast cars, and fine guns.)

And then you have the sheer grace of his writing, his powers of observation. So often, he will turn from his problems and observe passing beauty with the delicacy of a Buddhist poet: "A single gannet was fishing in the Sound of Soay; he rose in a spiral, snow-white against the dark sea cliffs, and descended arrow-like, vertically, to strike a small splash from the surface of royal-blue glass." Sometimes he mixes the lyrical and the mechanical; here's a description of fulmars: "Beside them in the air the gulls looked clumsy and inept, old-fashioned laundaulettes beside modern racing cars, their flight lacking grace and style by comparison... If there is enough breeze to make it possible, the fulmar takes off as does an airplane, with a short taxiing run on stiff outstretched wings that do not flap."

And sometimes all his skills come together in a perfect set piece, another kind of poem, like this miniature tragedy and its smaller dragons: "Everywhere were little dragonflies of a bright electric blue; they darted low over the surface of the water, soared and remained momentarily stationary, alighted gem-like and delicately poised upon the smooth jade-green of the water-lily leaves. One pair, joined in that brief embrace of the insect world which seems so pathetically improbable, alighted near me; there was a whirring rattle of wings, and they were swept away by a huge yellow-banded dragonfly. He circled me, carrying the struggling pair, and alighted upon a lily close by. He did not finish his meal, but flew away, leaving them dead but still joined, a spot of colour suddenly robbed of meaning."

***

Maxwell lost all his money in his "harpoon venture." He would go through his life restless and reckless, usually poor, living beyond his means, writing down his experiences as fast as he lived them to stay afloat. Once, uncharacteristically, he complained: "I work for increasingly long hours every day, working simultaneously on *The House of Elrig* and *Lords of the Atlas*, but with an ever growing sense of frustration—and, I believe, a growing petulance and ill temper... I felt like an aphis, immobile and solicitously kept alive in a cell by ants who tended me assiduously for my daily excretion of written words." It's a feeling most writers know but, as I said, it was not typical. Despite all his disasters, I think he was a happy man, more so than most. He had the trick of looking at things sidelong—"Everything askance, and it all shines on," as Thomas McGuane said in *92° in the Shade*. Maxwell turned his disasters into fine books, maybe art, even humor.

All Maxwell's books are worth reading, but this one has it all: the smell and heave of the sea, magical animals, Hemingway's weather. It's been out of print far too long. If you read it, I suspect you'll love it and know that Gavin Maxwell didn't fail.

——Stephen J. Bodio

HARPOON VENTURE

I

STEPPING-STONES TO ADVENTURE

This story begins in 1940. We were stationed in the South Metropolitan Gas Works on the riverside just below Blackwall Tunnel and opposite the East India Dock: a detachment of three officers and two hundred men as a nominally mobile anti-parachute column.

It was the third week of the Battle of Britain blitz, and we were tired and nostalgic. I had been doing a round of our extensive perimeter. The raid had been continuous throughout the night; at about three a.m. a single note had suddenly become separated from the welter of sound—a falling bomb almost directly overhead. It caused my Commanding Officer to say briefly, "This is our lot at last," as we dived for the nearest cover. The noise increased to a sort of gobbling roar, then the ground shook and shuddered, but there was no explosion.

"Another U.X.B.," he said disgustedly, "and a monster, by the sound of it. Someone'll have to go and look for that one as soon as it's light."

I went out an hour later in the uncanny quiet of the All Clear. The dawns were always the same in that brilliant September—cloudless, calm, with the silver barrage-balloons floating on a pale, radiant sky. I looked for the bomb-hole for a

3

long time without success. Everywhere were the rubble and confusion of former raids; the night before a paper factory had received a direct hit, and over a wide area its contents blanketed the ground and the rubble like dirty snow. I was on my way back to report failure when I turned into the church-yard, saw the great well shaft ten feet across among the grave-stones, and remembered with a sickening lurch of the heart that the crypt was in use as a shelter. I ran down the long wind-ing steps and struggled with the doors. As one burst open under my weight I was hit by a stifling wave of air so noisome that I retched even at its first impact. The temperature was that of a Kew hothouse, the stench indescribable. As I became accus-tomed to the dim light I saw that the stone floor was swimming in urine, and between the packed human forms were piles of excrement and of vomit. One hundred and twelve people had been in that airless crypt for seven hours. They were not anx-ious to be disturbed; abusive voices, thick with sleep, told me to close the doors. I had just time to open both wide before I was myself sick, helplessly and endlessly.

When I came in I went to my bedroom, which had been one of the make-up rooms of the Gas Works private theatre and was lined with mirrors. Coated with the dust of blast, I looked much like the publican whose corpse I had seen removed the day before from the ruins of his pub on the corner. I got a towel and went down to the communal shower-baths; took off my clothes and elbowed my way between two naked Guardsmen, one of whom stood ludicrously to attention. I told him with some embarrassment that it was unnecessary, but he remained as though he had not heard me. After a moment the corporal on my other side said, "You have to speak very slowly, sir; he comes from the Hebrides, and he doesn't understand very easily." I tried again more slowly; he relaxed sheepishly and went on soaping himself. I asked him from which island he came. It was a small island in the Outer Hebrides; I did not know it, but I had seen it from the sea, and the name and his soft speech brought a momentary vision of its low hulk dark against a harsh Atlantic sunset.

When I had dressed and gone up to the tiny windowless room which served us for anteroom and mess, my thoughts were far away. One of my brother officers was there reading a yellow-back. I said, "I've made a resolution. If I'm alive when the war's over I'm going to buy an island in the Hebrides and retire there for life; no airplanes, no bombs, no commanding officer, no rusty dannert wire."

"And no leave, and no friends, and no pay. But I'll join you. Let's look at a map."

Deep in a spirit of nursery make-believe, we spread a map of Scotland on the floor and, like children, lay at full length before it, propped on our elbows. We started at the north of the map and worked down. It took a long time; we found many places that we knew. I remember the atmosphere of the room vividly, and the comparison that my mind drew with the island pictures painted by my hyperactive imagination. In the mess it was stuffy and airless, for the only lighting and ventilation came from a skylight which had to be kept permanently blacked out. The room was lit by gas, whose constant hiss meant to me for a long time only Blackwall and blitz; now the louder hiss of Tilley lamps in boats and in crofts has overlaid that impression with more pleasant ones. There was an intermittent buzz of drowsy bluebottles, and the walls were spotted black with their remains. The room was tiny; my recollection is that we occupied most of it by lying at full length.

We spoke of Hyskeir, Rona, Canna, Staffa; in my mind were high-pluming seas bursting upon Atlantic cliffs and booming thunderously into tunnelled caverns; eider ducks among the surf; gannets fishing in deep blue water; and, landward, the scent of turf smoke.

After an hour there were rings drawn round several islands. I had drawn an extra red ring round the island of Soay, an island unknown to either of us, below the Cuillin of Skye. We were still playing at make-believe; Soay was my Island Valley of Avalon, and Avalon was all the world away. Presently the sirens sounded, and down the river the guns began again.

THE SECOND STONE

It was more than two years before I thought of Soay again. In 1942 I joined Special Forces and found myself stationed at intervals in their training area in the northwest of Scotland. Though it had crossed my mind several times that Soay was not far away, leisure was extremely rare, and it was not often that from the whole week we could call more than a portion of Sunday afternoon our own. But I made friends with the officer commanding a small yacht used in connection with our training, and on the first day of one of my leaves in 1943 he volunteered to take me across to Soay. It seems strange to me now that I can ever have had a first view a piece of land which became so integral a part of my life, but I remember that first occasion because it was uncomplicated by worry or responsibility, while there remained something of the mood of that dockland September three years before.

I remember that it was a blue day, hot and still, and that it was lit for me with something of the vivid anticipation that belongs to childhood. My companions, whose home the yacht had been in peacetime, were wholly delightful, and the yacht itself had the orderly comfort of a neat cottage. We sailed from Mallaig in the morning. The islands swam in a pale blue sea, Eigg and Canna and Rhum with white puffballs of cloud balanced above its peaks. There was not the faintest breath of wind, and the whole length of Sleat was mirrored in a still sea dotted with resting birds.

In a little over an hour we rounded the point of Sleat and headed due for Soay, on the same course that I was to follow times without number in all winds and weathers for four years.

At that distance the island was barely separable from the bulk of the Cuillins—one would have taken it for an insignificant promontory of low-lying land at the foot of their long plunge to the sea. The eye was held by the great mountain massifs—to the north the regular scree-covered upthrust of the Red Hills of Skye, opened by Loch Slapin; a little to the west the solitary dark peak of Blaven; and straight ahead the great splintered ridge of the Cuillin itself. Not even North Norway's Troll Fjord can compare with the hills of Skye as they open, peak upon peak, across those eight miles of sea from Sleat to Soay (photographs 1 and 2).

There was a groundswell now, the long, oily Atlantic swell that only the longest periods of calm can erase from Hebridean seas, but there was still no wind. The undispelled exhaust smoke lay white over our wake in a cottony trail, and the Red

Hills seemed to tremble in the heat like giant blanc manges.

We crept cautiously into Camus na Gall, Soay's east bay, the leadsman calling soundings from the bows. The yacht's captain, a stranger to northern waters, had the navigational guide in his hand, a long bleat of warning that makes one wonder at any stranger sailing the Hebrides without a pilot. At "By the mark, five," he gave the word to let go, and the anchor rattled out noisily into the stillness. We were perhaps a quarter of a mile out from the shore of the bay, a gravel-and-boulder shore with a dozen or more houses lined just above the tidemark, some slate-roofed and some of the older turf-roofed dwellings with rounded walls. Smoke came from a few of the chimneys, but there was no sign of a human being, nor did any appear as we lowered the dinghy and rowed shorewards. We pulled it up in a run that had been cleared of larger boulders, and still no one appeared from the houses.

I was anxious to explore as much of the ground as I could in the two hours allowed to me, so I left my companions and started up the rough path leading over the narrow isthmus to the west harbour. The path climbed steeply over a ridge of rock, from the top of which I looked across the neck of the island to the sea beyond. Almost joining the narrow inlet of the west harbour to the east bay where we had anchored was a freshwater loch dotted with white water lilies, and with a tree-covered island at its centre. The near bank was grown with oak, alder, and birch, whose bark shone silver in the sunlight; on the other side of the loch the hill that forms the east half of the island rose round and purple against a blue sky, the pink rock showing everywhere through its sparse covering of peat. The whole had a vibrant intensity of colour that I had never seen on the mainland.

I climbed to the top of the east hill, and from its four-hundred-and-fifty-foot height could look down over the western end of the island, some twenty-five hundred acres of moorland, with birch scrub and willows growing in its glens and about its numerous lochs. Beyond stretched the sea of the Hebrides, with all its islands spread dim and blue upon the horizon.

I had more than half an hour left before the yacht must sail. I made my way down through a wood of oaks to a small bay on the Soay Sound. The sun was hot on the red, sea-smooth rock. Six feet below me the tide lapped, a vivid intense blue, with the transparency of white sand and sea tangle two fathoms down. Here on the sheltered side of the island the swell was diminished to a two-foot rise and fall on the red rocks; the surface, mirrored and glassy, reflected the great bulk of the Cuillin a mile away across the sound. From everywhere on the island the Cuillin seemed towering and imminent, three thousand feet of bitter black rock rising stark and hostile out of the sea. Even then, in the heat of a still July afternoon, white tendrils of mist moved sluggishly among the heights and the glacial nakedness of the corries. Nearer, where the island ran out to a promontory, the water reflected the dense scrub of birch and oak; breaking the reflection, two black guillemots sailed in the water, small black-and-white birds with sealing-wax-red bills; through the ripples their splayed legs showed the same colour. Gannets were fishing in the sound, snow-white against the immense dark of the mountains: shaggy cattle were cropping the rushes nearby. The sound of their jaws, the low slap of the tide, and the hum of bees in the heather seemed only part of an immense and permanent stillness.

The cattle moved into the weedy shoal water, snuffling and

blowing; a calf backed in comic alarm from the jacket I had left upon a rock, his fringed baby face staring wonderingly from it to me.

This was the last time that I would ever see Soay as I saw it then, as an untroubled island with a single and beautiful face. When next I came to it I came as its owner, and the owner of all its troubles, internecine feuds, frustrations, and problems; when I go there now it is with a fierce and bitter nostalgia, and when I walk across that narrow neck of the island I can hardly bear to look at the azaleas that I planted by the path side.

When I returned to Camus na Gall the crew were waiting to embark. One of them had a fish box containing three large lobsters and a box of eggs. I asked him if he had bought them.

He shook his head. "They wouldn't sell anything, it being Sunday. That's why nobody came down from the houses—they're Seceders."

As we rowed back to the yacht he went on to tell me that he had had tea in one of the houses and had heard something of the island's troubles: its inadequate communications and transport, its decreasing population, and the absence of state sympathy. He added, "There seems to be a good deal of ill feeling between the families, and they mostly seem to be related. The people I was with seemed to think a resident landlord would do the place a lot of good."

THE THIRD STONE

I decided to buy Soay if I could do so at a figure that would show me, from rentals and feu-duties, the small rate of interest that I received from my invested capital. I entered almost immediately into prolonged negotiations with the owner, Flora Macleod of Macleod, and the island became my property about a year later.

But during the latter part of those months of negotiation I began to feel a growing uneasiness. My medical category made it probable that I should survive the war, and the spirit in which at Blackwall I had first thought of a Hebridean island, a mood in which rest and remoteness from struggle seemed all that was desirable when the war was over, had left me. The years of hard work and organization had become habit, breeding, as with so many others, a restlessness, an impatience with former interests and ambitions, and a desire for application and achievement. There was no clear way to the satisfaction of these cravings on Soay.

With the island were sold to me the salmon-fishing rights of its coast, a commercial bag-net fishery which had for some years been leased to Robert Powrie, owner or lessee of commercial salmon fisheries on both coasts of Scotland. But by an oversight his lease had been renewed for a further eight years during my negotiations, and the door to the only obvious work on Soay had been slammed in my face. Without the introduction of a new industry, it was difficult to see how the island could be developed or improved.

In the spring of 1944 I bought a thirty-foot lobster-fishing boat, in which I spent the whole of my free time. By this date the routine of my department was no longer six and a half days' hard work and a free Sunday afternoon. Instead, the work had become spasmodic and a little feverish; we would be asked the impossible, and for weeks on end would work all day and most of the night—then, without warning, we would find ourselves virtually unoccupied for an equal period. After D-day the work of our back room was practically finished, and there was little to do but to clear away the mess. But our department could not be closed until the trend of events on the Continent made it certain that we could be of no further use, and during the latter part of that summer we had to stay where we were, waiting and often idle. It was as though all the week-end leaves that we had forfeited for three years were restored suddenly and in aggregate; we could not spend a night away, but our days were for the most part our own. The weather was brilliant, hot and still, and whilst many were bitter not to be able to spend this unexpected idleness with wives and families, I wanted nothing but to be where I was.

Those brazen days I spent in my boat, exploring the coast and the islands from Mull to the narrows of Skye, slipping imperceptibly back into a world I had almost forgotten, dreamlike and shining. I used to visit the seal rocks and spend hours watching the seals; sit among the burrows of a puffin colony and see the birds come and go, unafraid, from their nests; fish for conger eels by moonlight; catch mackerel and lobsters; and for the first time I saw a basking shark at close quarters.

I had with me a Morar man, who looked after the boat for me; "Foxy" he was called, both by his friends and his enemies. He was a little over thirty then, fat yet enormously strong—I have seen him lift the back of a medium-sized limousine clear of a ditch onto the road—arms reaching almost to his knees, a massive boil-pitted neck, and a foul mouth as fluent in English as in Gaelic. His requirements were those of all mankind, though all, perhaps, a little magnified. He would have made a good guerrilla fighter in the Chouan tradition; not a leader, because it was difficult to keep his attention focused on any one thing for long. When Foxy started working he would do as much in an hour as three other men, but how many such hours there would be was always unpredictable.

That day we were returning from Glenelg. It was late afternoon; the sky was paling and the hills turning to deep plum, their edges sharp and hard, as though cut from cardboard. We were about a mile off Isle Ornsay Lighthouse, heading southward over a still, pale sea, when I noticed something breaking the surface thirty yards from the boat. At first it was no more than a ripple with a dark centre. The centre became a small triangle, black and shiny, with a slight forward movement, leaving a light wake in the still water. The triangle grew until I was looking at a huge fin, a yard high and as long at the base. It seemed monstrous, this great black sail, the only visible thing upon limitless miles of pallid water. A few seconds later the notched tip of a second fin appeared some twenty feet astern of the first, moving in a leisurely way from side to side.

It was some seconds before my brain would acknowledge that these two fins must belong to the same creature. The impact of this realization was tremendous and indescribable: a muddle of excitement in which fear and a sort of exultation were uppermost, as though this were a moment for which I had been unconsciously waiting a long time.

I could only guess at what was beneath the surface. In common with the great majority whose lives have not been lived in fishing boats, I had no idea what basking sharks looked like. Once, years before, I had seen them from the road bordering Loch Fyne, three great black sails cruising in line ahead—heavy with the menace of boys' adventure stories and shipwrecked sailors adrift in the Caribbean. I knew nothing of them, their size or their habits; to me all sharks were man-eaters. That was my state of knowledge as I looked at those two fins and guessed wildly at what must lie below them.

Foxy's knowledge, though not encyclopædic, was less sketchy than my own. He knew the name by which the fishermen called them—"muldoan," "sailfish," "sunfish," and the Gaelic name *cearbhan*; he knew that they played havoc with the herring nets; that their livers contained large quantities of valuable oil; that they were immensely powerful and could damage small boats; that long ago the people of the islands used to harpoon them from massed formations of small boats, to get a winter's supply of lamp oil. He assumed that they fed upon the herring shoals, because they were usually to be found where the herring were.

All this he told me as we closed in to the fish. I scrambled up on the foredeck and stood in the bows, hoping to see clearly what lay below the surface.

The first clear and entire view of a basking shark is terrifying. One may speak glibly of fish twenty, thirty, forty feet long, but until one looks down upon a living adult basking shark in clear water, the figures are meaningless and without implication. The bulk appears simply unbelievable. It is not possible to think of what one is looking at as a fish. It is longer than a London bus; it does not have scales like an ordinary fish; its movements are gigantic, ponderous, and unfamiliar; it seems a creature from a prehistoric world, of which the first sight is as unexpected, and in some ways as shocking, as that of a dinosaur or iguanodon would be.

At ten yards I could make out a shadow below the surface; at five, as Foxy slipped the engine into neutral, I could see the whole form clearly in transparent water. The body was brown, with irregular python markings upon it, a vast barrel that seemed to get steadily wider towards the incredibly distant head. The head was perhaps the most unexpected thing of all. The gills were by far the widest part, frill-like and gigantically distended. The upper jaw was a snout, the tip of which was now breaking the surface; the mouth was held wide open, and a child could have walked upright into that whitish cavern. As we began to sheer off, our wash slapped across the dorsal fin, and the shark submerged with a flurry of water about his tail.

Mounted in the bows of the *Gannet* was a Breda light machine-gun, which I carried to shoot up drifting mines, and also in the rather ridiculous hope of engaging a U-boat, since they had been sighted as near as Eigg. A Danish seaman had told me that a small launch, accurately handling a light machine-gun, could permanently damage the periscope and also command the conning tower if a U-boat surfaced, since it wouldn't waste a torpedo on so insignificant a target.

Foxy said, "Try him with the gun, Major."

When I had finished loading two extra magazines, the fin had reappeared, apparently stationary, and within a stone's throw.

We circled the fish widely and approached from astern— the technique we later used for harpooning. I waited until the fin was abreast of me and not much more than a yard away; the boat was almost scraping the shark's side. I fired thirty rounds in a single burst, straight into the huge expanse of the flank, and saw a mass of small white marks spring out on the brown surface. A great undulating movement seemed to surge through him, and near the stern of the boat the tail shot clear of the water. Its width was a man's height; it lashed outward away from the boat and returned, missing Foxy's head by inches, to land with a tremendous slam upon the gunwale of the stern cockpit. It swung backwards and hit the sea, flinging up a fountain of water that drenched us to the skin.

The shark was back on the surface in less than a minute. Six times we closed in; I had fired three hundred rounds into what was now a broad white target on his side. At the last burst he sank in a great turmoil of water, and it was ten minutes before the fin surfaced again. Now it seemed to me that he was wallowing and out of control, the fin lying at an acute angle. I thought he was mortally wounded, if not actually dead.

Foxy suggested that we should try to make fast to the fin with the *Gannet*'s boat hook. He stood up on the foredeck, and I steered him as close to the fish as I could. I felt the bows bump against the shark's body; then Foxy took a tremendous swipe with the full force of eighteen stone. I could see the hook bite deep into the base of the apparently helplessly rolling fin. There was just time for Foxy's triumphant shout of "Got the b——," then the boat hook was torn from his hands and those gorilla-like arms of his were waving wildly in a frantic effort to keep balance, as shark and boat hook disappeared in a boil of white water.

It was some time before the boat hook came to the surface; then, several hundred yards away, it shot ten feet out of the sea, as though scornfully hurled back from below. We did not see the shark again.

The fly-spotted room at Blackwall, one golden day on Soay, the mystery and excitement of that chance encounter at Isle Ornsay—these were the first stepping-stones across the ford; from them my feet went on inevitably to the next stone and the next, and when I turned to look back the stream had risen and covered them, and it was too late to return.

II

BEYOND THE FORD

I was intrigued by this first adventure, and it made me curious
to know more about basking sharks. It was only then that I began to understand that here was an unexplored field; an amazing blank upon the neatly, if superficially, filled-in map of the
world's natural history. Here was the largest fish of European
waters, a creature as large as any land animal in the world, and
yet virtually nothing was known of it.

The herring fishermen gave me a good deal of unrecorded
field natural history but left a thousand questions unanswered.
They seemed to agree that sharks had not been common in
Hebridean waters before the 1930s, but for some fifteen years
had seemed steadily to increase in numbers and regularity of appearance. They told me that the sharks arrived about the last
week of April, usually on favored herring grounds well inshore
on both sides of the Minch. The Soay Sound was said to be
one of their favourites. They were in evidence until September,
though there were some who said that they could not remember sharks in July, and others who said specifically that they
always disappeared from mid-June until mid-August, reap-
pearing on an apparently southward migration. One man told
me that in March he had seen a huge congregation in the open
Atlantic twenty miles south of Barra Head, "like a great fleet
of sailing boats." And it was in March that they were usually

reported off the Irish coast. Everything I was told about their movements built up a picture of a steady northward migration to the Hebrides in spring, and a southward migration in September, though there would be years in which the route of the autumn migration seemed to be round Cape Wrath and down the North Sea. Little has been added to our knowledge in that respect, and I have found no reason to change the original picture that I formed.

I do not think that any of the fishermen with whom I talked could tell me the food of the shark. Even now, after the wide publicity which the press accorded my venture, daily papers still report plagues of basking sharks "in pursuit of the herring shoals," and there are many fishermen who believe this to be true. In fact, the shark feeds upon the same food as the herring: small organisms in the water which in aggregate are called plankton. Some are larval forms of crustacea, others are mature but almost microscopic creatures, some are vegetable and some animal. The word embraces all minute free-swimming organisms in the sea, as distinct from those which are attached to, or crawl upon, the bottom. The stomach of a shark may contain as much as a ton of this material, a soft pinkish mass, very like shrimp paste in appearance and smell.

About the size of the sharks it was difficult to obtain agreement. "As big as the boat" was a common expression; the ring-net boats are between forty and fifty feet long. Some fishermen with wide experience claimed to remember individual fish much larger than this. This question is discussed in greater detail in Appendix 3; until many more sharks are caught and beached for measurement it must remain a vexing question. I am certain, however, that I have seen very much larger sharks than any I have ever caught.

The smallest shark that any of the herring men had seen was about six feet, which they assumed to be the young of the year. Then the astounding fact emerged: no one, no scientist and no fisherman, knew whether the young were born alive or hatched from spawn. Here was the largest fish of northern seas, the second largest fish in the world—the largest is *Rhinodon*, the whale-shark of the Pacific—and no one knew this elementary detail.

To the fishermen the sharks were a menace, to be avoided at all costs. They destroyed the herring nets, passing through them as an elephant would pass through a stretched sheet of muslin, and when the nets were mended the tear would reopen like a recurrently festering wound, rotted by the black glue-like slime from the shark's flanks and back. To a small boat the sharks were dangerous, and they also were apparently inquisitive; an inshore fisherman hand-lining mackerel from a dinghy would pull with all his strength for the shore when the black sail surfaced nearby.

Of scientific data there was practically none. Very few fresh specimens had ever been examined by any qualified person. The rotting carcasses occasionally washed ashore—and nearly all hailed as sea monsters (for the gills, being soft, decay first, leaving an apparently distinct and slender neck)—had in the past to be examined hastily between tides. I should guess, too, that the field instruments available to an unsuspecting marine biologist were inadequate for the dissection of a basking shark. Even a simple dismembering calls for axes, saws, and armoured gloves.

My curiosity led me to acquire two harpoons, which I carried in the *Gannet* in the hope of meeting another shark. They were the old type of whaling harpoon, intended to be fired

from the muzzle-loading whaling guns of the type we later employed—with entirely different harpoons—as our standard
equipment. I do not to this day understand how those harpoons
could be expected to remain in a whale under the slightest
strain. The tips were spear-shaped, much like a flat stone arrow-
head. There were no barbs, no holding surface to give the least
resistance to the harpoon's being withdrawn exactly as it had
entered; in fact, the rear edges of the arrow-blades were sharpened, as if to cut their way out more easily. Each harpoon was
about a yard long; the whole of the shaft was intended to fit
inside the barrel of the gun, with only the arrow-head protruding. The length of the shaft was slotted, so that a metal ring
for the playing rope could slide to the arrow-head when the
harpoon was in the gun, and to the back end of the shaft after
it had been fired. (See Fig. A, page 21.)

To the ring of each harpoon I fixed a coil of rope, and lashed
the harpoons to boat hooks to drive them into the fish. But it
was getting late in the season, and it was some time before I saw
another shark. Again it was near a lighthouse: Point of Sleat,
the most southerly point of Skye. Sharks are often found near
lighthouses, probably because these promontories produce cur-
rents which concentrate the plankton.

Besides Foxy, I had with me John Winter, the international
sailing-dinghy champion, who was spending a leave at Morar.
It was a bright but rather blustery afternoon; a choppy dark
blue sea was beginning to break white. Winter and I were sitting talking on the foredeck when there came a great yell from
Foxy at the tiller.

"Major, Major, sharks!"

He was pointing inshore to a little bay; a reef practically
closed it from the south, and the water broke viciously over

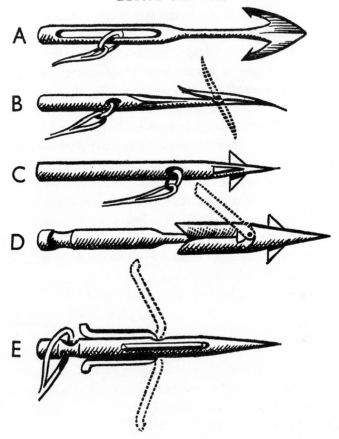

HARPOON HEADS

A: Old whaling harpoon used for early experiments in 1945

B: "T-type" hand harpoon, 1945

C: The "*idée fixe*," a barbless gun-harpoon with the ring attached far
forward, designed to lever the shaft around at right angles to its
course of entry, 1945

D: Two semi-tubular barbs, 1945–46

E: The final design, four barbs of nickel-chrome steel, total weight
ten pounds, 1947–48

other black teeth of rock in the bay itself. But were they all rocks? Suddenly one moved with a flash of light on a smooth wet surface; and with a leap of the heart I saw it turn into the broad dark triangle of a shark's dorsal fin. Then another, and another; there were half a dozen sharks in the bay.

For a few minutes everything was confusion: Foxy getting entangled with the ropes he was trying to prepare; I struggling with the engine, which had jammed in gear; Winter trying to help both of us and at the same time calling out a running commentary on the sharks. At last I got the gear lever into neutral, and we lay hove to and rolling uncomfortably while things were made ready according to our lights. We made the end of the rope fast to a cleat amidships, which, had we actually become firmly attached to a shark, would most certainly have capsized us.

We turned the *Gannet* and headed into the bay. The fins were not always visible; there was a big surge of water coming in past the reef, which washed over them from time to time, and sometimes they submerged to reappear on a different course. The first to come within range of the boat hook was quite unexpected; a fin surfaced almost alongside and on a parallel course, and it needed only a push on the tiller to bring it within a yard of where Foxy stood. He, being very much the strongest of us, had been chosen to push the harpoon home.

There was no question this time of seeing the fish below the surface—the water was dark, opaque, and moving; only the fin stood high out of it, a little ragged and feathery at the tip. Foxy drove the boat hook down with all his force into the water a few inches to the near side of it. I could see the boat hook shudder with the impact upon the solid mass below the surface, and saw Foxy pushing on the shaft for a final thrust.

Then came the fountain of water shooting up from the sea, and the shark's tail, obscured by spray, lashed down upon the water with several tremendous slaps.

Through all this Foxy was shouting, "Got him this time. Right in the b—— this time!" and he was dancing to keep his feet clear of the rope as it whipped out at tremendous speed from the coil in the hold. It was a full coil, eighty fathoms, and we were in only eight or nine fathoms of water. I expected to see the rope change direction for the open sea and began to turn the boat to lessen the wrench when the rope's end was reached. But the rope did not change direction, and suddenly it stopped running out and went slack. Tentatively I began to haul in; a fathom came in without resistance—

"Is he still there?"

"I'm afraid not. I think—"

As I spoke the rope was whisked from my hands as though attached to an express train, and the palms of my hands were skinned. This time about four more fathoms went out, and again it went slack. I began to haul in, more cautiously this time and ready to drop the rope at the first sign of life at the other end of it. Three fathoms, four, six—then I felt the slight drag of the harpoon's weight and knew the shark was lost. In silence we lifted the harpoon in. There was no sign of the boat hook to which it had been lashed; later we found small fragments of it floating in the bay. The harpoon itself was unrecognizable. It looked like a corkscrew which had been bent double and then crushed in a vice. It was coated with a dark viscous slime that gave off a bitter and as yet unfamiliar smell. There were small fragments of white flesh at the bottom of the ring-slot, showing that the harpoon had penetrated about a foot into the fish.

We took a sounding; the depth was exactly the length of rope that the shark had taken out. It was clear that he had gone straight to the bottom and rolled on the harpoon. At first, perhaps, this had driven it deeper into his back, but there was nothing to hold it there, and his one short rush through the water had pulled it free.

Foxy's disappointment took the form of anger. "Ach to hell! The harpoon was no good. It would have been better putting salt on his tail. And I was in the bastard, fair in him. I tell you, Major, there's not a f——g one in Scotland could have put it in further."

All the way home Winter and I discussed what a shark harpoon should be like, scratched diagrams on the paint of the foredeck, covered envelopes with scribbles and measurements.

A firm determination to catch a shark was growing in me; it seemed a challenge. And then, quite suddenly—without, I think, any conscious build-up—I thought that here was the industry for Soay, the occupation I required, new and utterly absorbing.

I had my first harpoon made in Mallaig a week later. The essential of a harpoon with holding power seemed to me to lie in movable barbs: something that would enter the shark in the form, as it were, of a furled umbrella whose spokes would open inside the fish and make withdrawal impossible. In the case of a hand harpoon, the spokes or barbs must fit very close to the shaft, since the force with which it could be thrust in would be limited, and any unnecessary protuberance would lessen its chance of deep penetration.

The possible variations upon the "umbrella" are almost unlimited, and the first hand harpoon I designed was T-shaped when open inside the fish. The horizontal top of the T hinged back to form a straight line with the upright, making a single fairly narrow rod. One arm of the horizontal top of the T was sharpened to a point to be driven into the shark, the other flattened and slightly "scooped" to give additional holding power. The other end of the harpoon was round, to fit it into the end of a twenty-foot length of iron piping. The weight of the piping would give extra power to the thrust, and the whole pipe would—I thought—be left in the hands of the harpooner after the harpoon itself had been driven into the shark. (See Fig. B, page 21.)

I did not have a chance to try that harpoon until the following year; it was now late September, and I did not see another shark. A month later our orders came to close establishment.

Before then I had begun to make intensive inquiries into the commercial possibilities of sharks, and when in November I found myself a civilian I had finally made up my mind to experiment in commercial basking shark fishing. I had gone further than that: I had taken the first false step and bought a worthless and entirely unsuitable boat.

I had made up my mind that we should need at least one sizable craft, so as to be better able to deal with large sharks, to extend our range, and to carry to Soay materials for building a small factory. I was in a desperate hurry to get the whole venture started the following year; I was trying to do a great many things at once, and as a result I made some serious blunders and put the project under a handicap from the outset.

That I bought a largish boat without seeing it sounds imbecile, but I had no expert knowledge and did not feel that my ignorant personal inspection could serve any good purpose. I sent an expert to survey an advertised boat and accepted his assurance that she was a bargain at a thousand pounds. She would have been expensive at as many shillings.

The *Dove* was an ex-sailing drift-net boat of the Stornoway fishing fleet; at forty-five years old she was still younger than many of her sister ships. She was a seventy-foot "zulu," lugsail rigged, with two Kelvin paraffin engines, a sixty and a thirty horsepower. For a year it was as if these two vied with each other as makers of trouble and delay, and there seemed a tacit understanding between them that in no circumstances would they work simultaneously.

When I bought the *Dove* she had already started the winter fishing from Stornoway, and I naïvely left her to carry on under new ownership until the plans for the factory were complete and I had work for her to do. In a short time she had accumulated a heavy loss; then, early in January, she collided outside Stornoway harbour with a boat of her own type called the *Lews Castle*. After more than a year's litigation the circumstances of the accident remained obscure; the only indisputable facts were that the *Lews Castle* was a total loss, sinking with all gear in a little under a quarter of an hour, while the *Dove* had only slight damage about her bows. It was a fortunate accident for the *Lews Castle*, older and more heavily insured than the *Dove*.

The details of marine law are intricate, and to the usual complication of legal phraseology is added a babel of spiky nautical terms, many of them archaic and otherwise in disuse; the eye rattles and bumps over whole pages that contain no recognizable word or phrase. From this confusion emerged an uncomfortable point of law; if the insurers of the *Lews Castle* could prove my skipper to be incompetent, I could be sued for a sum much larger than that covered by my insurance policy. It was with that cloud upon the horizon that I began the new year.

Meanwhile my inquiries had revealed steadily widening possibilities. In the autumn I had spoken of my intention to John Lorne-Campbell of Canna, and he was able to add a good deal to my knowledge. Before the war he had himself been enough interested in the sharks to find out the average oil yield from a single fish and to obtain a quotation from Glasgow oil buyers. He also told me that Anthony Watkins, brother of the explorer Gino Watkins who died in Greenland, had caught sharks in Loch Fyne during the three years before the war and was planning to combine shark fishing with herring fishing after his discharge.

The oil buyers with whom John Campbell put me in touch quoted me fifty pounds a ton for the oil extracted and barrelled. It was a rising market—in 1946 we sold for eighty pounds a ton, and in 1947 for a hundred and ten pounds. We could expect eight hundredweight of oil from an average fish.

As a result of this approach to the oil buyers I received a letter from Gordon Davidson, a senior partner in the Glasgow firm of J. N. Davidson, which handles everything even remotely connected with fish. He afterwards became a director of Island of Soay Shark Fisheries, Ltd., formed in 1947; until then, while I worked alone, he was the mainspring of the marketing side of the business.

In this first letter he told me that he considered the shark to have many commercial possibilities besides its liver oil, and that he would be interested to see them investigated. He told me that he expected the flesh to be marketable either salted, fresh, or as fish meal, that manure could be made from the refuse, that glue could probably be extracted from the membranes, that the skin should have a high market value, and that there must be many more possibilities at present entirely unexplored. He was enthusiastic and encouraging and offered his help in designing a small factory at Soay.

With him and the local contractor I planned the layout of a factory in Soay west harbour, to include at first only oil-extraction and fish-meal plants, and a small laboratory where a chemist or biologist could do experimental work. The building of the factory began early in the New Year of 1945. It was expected to be completed by June, and we hoped to catch a few sharks during the latter part of the summer (photographs 49 and 50).

The question of the catching equipment seemed to raise much greater problems. I had begun by writing to an arms expert and collector; he replied by sending me the name and address of manufacturers who, he thought, might be able to produce a harpoon gun suitable for catching sharks. After some correspondence they sent on approval a weapon about the size of a shotgun and firing (from the shoulder) a tiny harpoon about a foot long. I saw at once that it was intended for much smaller fish and was entirely useless for our purpose. The harpoon, however, incorporated a personal idea of the maker's, which in the light of later events I would describe as an *idée fixe* whose final elimination cost me untold time and money. Briefly, the harpoon was a perfectly straight rod without barb, the line being attached to it more than halfway down the shaft. It was intended that the whole harpoon should bury itself within the target, and that the strain upon the line should then lever it round until it was at right angles to the course on which it entered. (See Fig. C, page 21.)

The makers of this gun undertook to build something heavier for me before the summer, but the pressure of government work in their factory remained too great, and soon after the

New Year they subcontracted the building of the heavy harpoon gun to the expert whom I had first approached. This was to be built in his private workshop, using a twenty-millimetre Oerlikon barrel as a basis, and was necessarily experimental. The contracting firm was to make the harpoons for it, as well as a few hand harpoons to my own design.

We now had both a factory and a gun under construction, and two boats which we believed to be serviceable.

By this time I was installed in a tiny office in Mallaig. My days were spent in dealing with a mail that had grown to an average of nearly forty letters a day: permit forms, Ministry applications, correspondence dealing with the factory equipment, the catching equipment, the establishment of markets, the *Dove's* accident, and a hundred other matters. I had no secretary and no assistant; it seemed as though I must be swept away by that flood of paper. The humble little pier, for example, which we were to build at Soay harbour—a mere jetty of a few square feet—needed the approval of the County Council, H. M. Customs and Excise, the Admiralty, the Board of Trade, and the Ministry of War Transport. Each of these authorities required plans and applications in triplicate, and this was but a single example of what had become a daily routine. The water supply for the factory required the endorsement of a Ministry of Health analyst, and the assurance that it had already been the water supply of several crofts for more than a hundred years did nothing to alter the necessity. After a time I began to realize that these officials were as busy as I was myself. At first tentatively, then with a growing assurance, I began to ignore some of their demands. To myself I made the water supply a test case. The sample which I collected for dispatch to the Ministry of Health was so green and fungoid in appearance that I thought there was a real risk of its being turned down, and it was clearly simpler not to send it. The days passed, I ignored the repeated clamour for a sample, the Ministry letters referring to it became fewer and more widely spread, like the last drops of a summer shower. Eventually the subject was dropped; three years later that sample of water still stood in a whisky bottle—and dark enough to be whisky—on a shelf in the Mallaig office.

I soon found out, too, that the Scottish Home Department was willing to help me cut much of the red tape that threatened to strangle the project in its infancy. I first discovered this in connection with the telephone, whose installation in the Mallaig office had been quite firmly refused to me. The Fisheries Secretary made the necessary recommendation, and the telephone was installed in five days. It was a doubtful economy, as the telephone bill incurred in bullying other government departments soon approached ten pounds a week.

The Secretary of State for Scotland continued to give me really valuable help and encouragement in every possible way short of actual financial assistance. The department was naturally interested in the project; it held the possibility of a new industry in one of Scotland's problem areas; it promised the production of oil and foodstuffs at a time when both were desperately short, and the reduction of a pest by which thousands of pounds' worth of herring nets were destroyed every year.

With a price already on the head of every shag, cormorant, and seal, it seemed to me that the Herring Industry Board should have offered a small subsidy on the killing of each shark. They refused—I suspect because it must have been plain to them that no larger number of sharks would be killed as a result of such a subsidy. No one would go to the lengths of killing a basking shark and producing evidence of having done so merely for the five pounds for which I was asking.

There were a few times during that winter of early prepara-- tion when pieces of the jigsaw seemed to fall into place in a neat and orderly way. A biochemist to work in the Soay labo-- ratory appeared as though conjured up. I had been spending a week-end with Frank Fraser Darling (then director of the West Highland Survey) at Strontian. During my visit an en- tirely coincidental letter to him arrived from a certain Gilbert Hartley, who had read in Frank's *Island Years* of the wasted potentialities of the basking shark and the absence of scientific knowledge concerning it. Hartley was a marine biologist who wanted to do original work; his letter asked Darling if he knew of anyone who might provide the material for research on the basking shark. I wrote to Hartley at once and told him of our plans to begin catching sharks at the end of the summer. We arranged that he should come up to Soay when we began the fishing, so as to make certain of material in fresh condition, and he prepared for me a list of the minimum equipment for the laboratory.

But such coincidences did not often come our way; as a rule every day was a losing struggle with paper and time, and when at last the *Dove* arrived from Stornoway in February, it became clear that we were still at the very beginning of our troubles. From the moment I set eyes on her I knew, and at the same time tried to conceal from myself, that I had made a really gigantic blunder. She was in roughly the condition one might expect of Noah's ark were it thrown up now by some sub- terranean upheaval, nor would the engines have made one mar- vel at Noah's mechanical genius. With her arrival I engaged the very first employee of the shark fishery. Tex Geddes (photograph 16) had served with me in Special Forces; he had spent most of his life in Newfoundland, and as a boy had been with the Newfoundland fishing fleet. He was in his late twenties at the end of the war, and it was difficult to fit into his years the variety of experience with which he was credited—lumber-jack, rum-runner, boxer, knife-thrower, Seaforth Highlander, are only a few samples. He could handle a boat well and had a keenness for adventure which appealed to me; on the debit side were a rather violent temper and a periodic liking for drink.

It was some years before I succeeded in disentangling Tex's true history from the mass of assiduously cultivated rumour that surrounded it. His parents both came from Peterhead, on the east coast of Scotland. His mother died in giving him birth, so his earliest recollections were of his father and grandfather. The latter was a shipwright and also owned schooners trading to South America; in fact, he seems to have been a man of diverse activity, for he was a fisherman too, and Tex remembers hearing of his clinker-built *Zulu*, which he converted to carvel-build between fishings. Soon after the First World War he sailed in one of his schooners to South America and returned lamed by slashes acquired in a knife fight. That was his last appearance in Peterhead; he stayed only to refit his vessel and went back to South America, where he was knifed again. This time it killed him.

Tex's father was a seaman and a timber worker. He was fishing from Port Gordon when one of the great herring rows took place, ending by the police being thrown into the har-bour, and as a result he and a number of his fellows left the country. He went to Newfoundland, taking with him Tex, then two years old. He found work as a lumberman at Three

Rivers, and five years later he was killed there, blowing up a log jam in a big river drive. Tex was left an orphan at the age of seven and was brought up by his father's foreman, a Frenchman whom Tex knew as Peter.

Peter sent him to school, but when he was twelve he was expelled as unmanageable. He was afraid to go home to Peter, so he made for the woods and joined up with a lumber camp. He got a job as a "monkey," or "topper," one of the boys employed at a pound a day to climb with irons to the tops of the great trees to lop them off.

"If you didn't keep on sawing till the very last minute," said Tex, "the top would break and the branches would chew you up, or a spike of the main trunk go right through you. I saw boys killed that way; that's why we got that pay, and it was huge money in those days."

This phase was followed after a year or two by his first sea experience, which, in the light of what it led to, must remain still partially veiled. The boat of whose crew he was a member was at the time in question in the Straits of Belle Isle, between Quebec and Newfoundland, and she could not be said to be fishing. At Belle Isle were metal-ore mines, but the mines were not paying, and there was a profitable alternative in rum-running to the mainland. There were many methods of smuggling; one of the least ingenious being, perhaps, the commercial traveller carrying sample wedding cakes filled with concentrated rum essence. In due course the large numbers of wedding cakes excited suspicion, and the gaff was blown.

Tex, being one of a crew engaged in rum-running, got the danger signal to disappear, and a few weeks later he found himself back in Scotland. So far he had specialized in highly paid professions, and he was a wealthy and lawless youth with the world his oyster. He was sitting in a Glasgow pub, pondering the next step in his career, when he met a soldier. The soldier talked to him of life and adventure in the Far East, and Tex's imagination kindled. That, he thought, was the life for him. The next day he joined the Seaforth Highlanders.

"I wasn't in the Army five minutes till I was in jail for in-subordination, and when I came out I decided to clear out of it just as soon as I could. The colonel sent for me and gave me a pep talk; he must have been a bit of a psychologist, that man, because he chose the right line of approach straight off, and that wasn't easy to find with the frame of mind I was in. But he said I wanted to quit because I wasn't man enough to stick it, and that got me feeling the way I had to show him it wasn't true and that I could stick more than the next man. So I stayed on, and it had made me ambitious too, so I got a stripe after ten days. I used to have a pretty good time on the whole; I was always getting excused duty for athletics or shooting or fencing or boxing, once they found out I could do those things, though the stripes on my arm were always coming unstuck as fast as I got them stuck on—well, you know me. Then after the war started I got my leg bust up in Commando training and found myself working in the same show as you, and here we are."

Tex summed up the *Dove*: "There's a year's work there. And she's as full of rats as a town is of people—black rats, and carrying the plague, I shouldn't wonder. And when you start scraping the filth in the galley there's no wood under it, only more filth. And the Stornoway crew brought her down on one engine—the other's all mucked up. You've been had for a sucker this time."

We caught sixty rats in the first two days. They were the first black rats I had ever seen; they seemed to me far less repulsive animals than the brown; they were neat and tidy, with rather mole-like fur and very long tails, lacking the scaly and diseased look of a city gutter rat. I drowned our catch with some reluctance.

Catching the rats meant taking up a good deal of boarding, and every piece of wood so revealed proved to be rotten. There was very little in the whole ship that did not need renewing; only her massive timbers seemed to be sound. She spent three costly months in harbour before she was fit for sea. She remained in Mallaig, while boatbuilders and marine engineers revealed more and more of her senile decay, and the bills mounted daily.

Through that early spring I worked steadily in my tiny office, gradually assembled equipment and gear, and came to know more of Mallaig and its people than of any other community. It is a strange town, a boom town, a Klondike, a Dodge City; it is new and growing, but its newness and growth seem not those of this century. Sixty years ago the fishing port of the district was Tarbert, halfway up Loch Nevis, and with no road within thirty miles of it. It was a thriving community, with a church, long before Mallaig had one. Now in Tarbert there is only one inhabited dwelling, and Inverie, its onetime rival, is a small crofting community dependent upon Mallaig. Mallaig was a group of a few crofts, unknown and rarely visited, approached by forty miles of dust road, hardly more than a track, from Fort William. Then in 1901 the railway came to Mallaig, and everything was changed. Richer

than any gold mine, the sea was in front and the rail behind, a
rail that led to Billingsgate, and to the industrial towns of the
south. And the coming of the railway meant that Mallaig became the main port for the Hebrides. But Mallaig harbour
(photographs 12 and 13) has remained unchanged since the
early years of the railway, and there has been no enlargement
to cope with the steadily increasing traffic. The local boats
were twenty-two feet long in those days; now they are forty-
eight feet and there are many more of them.

The ground, steep and rocky almost to the sea, was an utterly
unsuitable site for a town, and the railway company owned
the only flat ground. They had staked their claim and were
expanding rapidly—a railway pier beyond the station and a
fish pier—and behind the ground rose steeply to rock and
heather. So houses began to spring up in a crazy disorder and
without a central plan. Some balanced precariously on pinnacles of rock; some wallowed in soft peat, into which they
threatened to sink. Small contractors came, and became rich
men in a few years; the ring-net herring fleets came to Mallaig
for the summer fishing from Ballantrae, Oban, Tarbert (Loch
Fyne), and Campbeltown; and the east-coast fleets came from
Fraserburgh, Peterhead, and Lossiemouth. A Glasgow firm
built a kippering factory, another an ice factory. Between
the railway and the sea grew "Chinatown," Mallaig's slum—
mostly of wooden huts and inhabited by the fish girls. Every
inch of ground near the waterfront was now taken, and this
had the curious effect of producing trade monopolies. A boatbuilder, a marine engineer, a carpenter, once established, was
secure from all competition. The fishing fleets must come to
Mallaig, the boats must be serviced—and serviced in a hurry,
for in the middle of a good fishing every day in harbour may

lose several hundred pounds. When the necessary repairs to some boat's engine should cost as little as twenty-five pounds, it might well be worth two hundred pounds to the boat's owner to get the work done at once and go back to sea.

Against this background fortunes are made or lost with extraordinary rapidity. A man may have saved and borrowed for years for the price of a modern ring-net boat, between four thousand and five thousand pounds at the time I lived in Mallaig. The age of the Kelvin paraffin engine was on its way out; every fisherman wanted Diesel power. But these new engines in the old hulls would have been new wine in old bottles, and the boats were built from scratch, rather larger than before, on the east coast. The Mansons, the greatest and luckiest of Mallaig fishing families, brought the first new ring-netter to Mallaig after the war; when, as old Manson put it, the old one was "growing far too wee to cross the Minch." Such a boat may earn her whole value in a few weeks' or months' fishing, or the pocket whose lining has already been explored for the last of those pounds may remain empty week after week while the gales blow and there are no herring.

Perhaps the worst of all is when the money is there to be lifted from the sea and the boat must lie in harbour waiting her turn in the repair queue, while her crew watches the fish buyers bid on the pier for the huge catches of other boats. In these circumstances a skipper is in danger of losing his crew. A ring-netter's crew works on a share basis, and in a big fishing a member of it may earn between fifty and a hundred pounds a week for himself. The number of shares into which the boat's takings are divided varies; as a rule a skipper-owner receives about half of the total. The boat, the gear, and the skipper have a share each; besides the skipper there may be five of a crew receiving a share each, though more often one of these will be a boy, with only a half-share. For good ring-net crews, as with certain of the Mallaig trades, the demand is greater than the supply. Among those who often change boats a frequent trouble is drink; they may be good enough workers otherwise—indeed, some of them are the best of all—but unreliable on this account. The euphemisms, and the precise degree of unreliability that they imply, are many. "He takes one now and again"; "He likes a drink"; "He takes a good dram"; "He's all right when he's off it"; "He's aye fou." It is to this last category that a skipper may have to turn in the end, if his crew have become impatient with too much waiting in harbour. To the "aye fou's" the more days in harbour the better.

The actual consumption of alcohol in Mallaig is probably a good deal less per head than in any industrial town, but because the people are at sea for the greater part of the week, often under conditions that a factory worker can barely imagine, they tend, as do most seamen, to make up for lost time while there is money in their pockets at week-ends.

The people have, in the main, a great friendliness and a natural generosity that is often unexpected; one and all, too, seem to share a common motto: "I'll not see you stuck." I was always on the verge of getting "stuck," and I heard those words, and saw them proved, many times.

To the tourist, Mallaig may be its poster self—the gateway to the Hebrides; to me and to many, it is a town of a different sort of romance: of herring scales and a million gulls, of energy and squalor and opportunity, of feud and fortune; the "end of steel"—the railhead—beyond which all is gamble.

It was late in April before the *Dove* was ready for her trial

trip. The ring-netters were already started on the spring herring fishing, and it was difficult to collect a crew. I had a temporary skipper, Foxy, Tex, and two boys. One of these was
a deckhand, seventeen, and as strong as a man; the other, fourteen and new to the sea, was ship's cook. He could be more
correctly described as ship's tin-opener.

I do not remember why we sailed at dusk, but I remember
the evening, clear and still, and how soon after the last of the
sun's light had gone the sky was velvet black and brilliant with
stars. We sailed north, up past Isle Ornsay and Sandaig Lighthouses and on into the narrows of Skye, the hills huge on either
side of us and the quick south-running tide chattering about
the bows. We were at sea at last, and whole loads of care
slipped away.

We put into Kyle in the middle of the night. We sat in the
cabin with the steady hiss of the hanging Tilley lamp above
us and drank black tea that tasted of paraffin, ate fried mackerel
that tasted of paraffin, and when we rolled our blankets round
us they, too, smelled of paraffin. The cabin, with bunks on
each side of it, was aft, and separated from the engine-room
just forward of it only by a rickety sliding door. Beyond that
door the antiquated machinery groaned and hammered, so that
when the ship was under way it was always difficult to make
oneself heard, and from the engines and the cooking stove
came a dense, suffocating heat, laden always with paraffin.
When the engines were at rest there was a fictitious illusion of
comfort only because that awful din had stopped. The *Dove*
was no luxury yacht; she had been one of that grim black procession that sails in line ahead from Stornoway to the distant
fishing grounds, each skipper in turn stepping out from his
wheelhouse to spit as he passes the ring-netters from the south.

That night I found we had not cleared the rats from the ship; before going to sleep I laid the contents of my trouser pocket upon a convenient but dark ledge in my bunk, and my hand came away foul with rat dung.

I went on deck at the first light, a pale primrose dawn on which lay the giant black silhouette of an aircraft carrier at anchor a quarter of a mile to the north of us. We sailed north towards the Summer Islands; the sun came up in a clear sky, and by noon it was boiling hot, with a sea shimmer like July. Off the Summer Islands we met a party of surrendered German submarines being escorted in by destroyers, then farther north we met two great ocean-going U-boats coming in unescorted with their flags at half mast. Foxy hoped that they would surrender to the *Dove*, but, to his great disappointment, they passed one on each side of us without so much as a glance from the officer in the conning tower.

The *Dove* gave us no trouble on that trip; she too seemed to inhale the coming summer and the end of the war. We returned to Mallaig the next evening, and the same week we began to carry factory materials to Soay: bricks, wood, cement, gravel, and machine parts. A week later we landed an eight-ton boiler at the factory site, without pier or jetty to run alongside. It was my first object lesson in the advanced use of lever and pulley, and had the apparent impossibility of a conjuring trick. At this stage the factory site had become recognizable as such; blasting had cleared a "stance," and there was now a flat floor of concrete some fifty feet by thirty on which our past cargoes lay covered with tarpaulins. Our chief shortage was of wood; we had failed to get licences for anything like the required amount and decided to spend the next week salvaging. The western shores of all the Hebridean islands are piled high with drifted timber on every beach where it can lodge, and after five years of sea war some of the lonelier bays had begun to look like Canadian logging rivers. All this wood, though it would otherwise lie forever where it is, remains the property of the Crown, and the salvager must pay for its cubic bulk as assessed by a representative of His Majesty's Customs and Excise.

To Rhum we went the following week, equipped to raft the timber and tow it back to Soay in bulk. Rhum is a strange place, eerie and haunted if ever a Hebridean island was. It is all mountain—hills as dark and savage as the Cuillins themselves, and falling for the most part as steeply to the sea. The hills even carry the same group name—the Cuillin of Rhum and the Cuillin of Skye; but they seem to have a different soul, something older and more brooding, almost evil. Their names are mainly Norse, given them long ago by the raiding Scandinavian long ships—Askival, Ainshval, Orval, Parkival, and Hallival—and if there is a place where I could believe every Gaelic folk-tale and wild superstition it is in their shadow. I know a man who found himself in a high corrie of Askival with a dead stag after dusk. His coat was clutched and he felt himself being dragged uphill, while from right below his feet a voice screamed as if in an extremity of fear.

The hills fall in precipice and scree to red sea cliffs, split and columned as though by some terrible torsion. At the top of the cliffs are tongues of vivid grass, on which in summer the hinds and their calves are warm orange-brown dots. They feed to the very edges of the cliffs, and upon the green ledges and gullies that lead down among them, picking their way among the teeming puffin burrows. Below them the cliffs are white with bird guano and partly veiled by myriads of kittiwakes, endlessly wheeling, drifting and turning, like a snow scene in a glass paperweight. At the cliff foot there is a swell even on the calmest day, a long oily swell which flashes up the red cliffs with a sudden sword of foam. In the cliff line there is one broad and shelving bay, perhaps half a mile wide: Harris Bay, where the Atlantic flotsam lies thick enough to hide the shingle. Behind it Glen Harris is a wide and empty cup in the hills, and just above the tideline is the tomb of the late owner of the island, a palladian mausoleum of pink marble whose voice of anomaly is subdued to a bat's squeak by the vast hills and the moving sea.

It was bright sunshine when we came to Harris Bay, and the sea was as nearly calm as it ever is there. I had added another boat to the *Dove* and the *Gannet*, a very solid little fifteen-foot lifeboat with a seven-horsepower engine, to act as tender and general messenger. I do not remember her name, but I know that it never stuck to her, and during the years I owned her my crew never called her anything but the *Button*. We went ashore in her, leaving the *Dove* anchored well out in the bay. We picked our way through that fantastic litter on the tideline as one might explore the rubble of some recently ruined city. There were ships' rafts, tanks of high-octane fuel, bales of raw rubber, great hunks of tallow, R.A.F. rubber dinghies, lifebelts—and timber, timber everywhere, like a fallen forest. We worked all day, carrying beams and planks to the water's edge, lashing and nailing them into rafts to be towed behind the *Dove*. Once, while we were extricating a massive beam from a pile, a hail from the *Dove* made us turn—to see a black fin cruising between her and the shore. We watched it for a long time; it passed close enough to the *Dove* to cause the skipper, left aboard, to struggle to rig a hand harpoon to a rope. All that afternoon the fin was close by whenever we looked up, a stimulus to effort, a reminder of adventure ahead.

We made several of these salvage trips; by degrees the pier at Soay began to take shape, and the equipment for the factory was being assembled and transported. But it was difficult to justify the high running costs of the *Dove* on her carrying work only, most of which could at this stage have been done by a much smaller boat, and I decided that we must kill one shark as soon as possible, so that samples could be sent to the many firms who had asked for them.

The gunmaker reported that the gun and harpoons would be ready by the end of June or early July and that he proposed to bring them up himself for personal test. But no sooner had we agreed upon a date for the arrival of the gun than the *Dove* required beaching once more for one of her interminable repairs (she had to wait her turn)—and she was still in drydock when gunmaker and gun arrived in mid-July.

The factory also was to have been completed by this date. I had written to Hartley, the biologist, and arranged for him to arrive at Soay at the same time. But by the end of the first weeks in July the factory, far from being finished, was barely half completed, and much of the machinery had yet to arrive. It was clear that the factory could not possibly be finished before September at the earliest. I decided to wash out all idea of trading in 1945 and to devote the remainder of the summer to learning more about the catching of the sharks.

The gun itself was impressive but useless; just how useless it took us some time to discover. Though it showed plainly the limitations of the subcontractor's workshop, it showed, too, his undeniable engineering genius. The barrel was an Oerlikon, the breech fired a ten-bore brass blank cartridge, propelling from the barrel a tubular harpoon which fitted over it. The whole was mounted on a steel tripod with a circular base. The harpoon gunner's face was protected from blast by a thick sheet of steel between him and the gun, which had to be aligned by peering through a narrow slit like the port of a tank. It was two hundred pounds' worth of pretentious nonsense, though I did not recognize it as such at the time.

But it was at the sight of the harpoons that my heart sank. Every one was made in conformity with the gunmaker's *idée fixe*, barbless and to my mind innocuous. As with the prototype that I had seen the previous year, the line was attached more than halfway down the shaft, to turn the whole harpoon sideways in the shark after the strain was exerted. I had told him that if he wanted to try out this theory he must also bring some harpoons of my own design, of which I had sent drawings, but he had brought only fourteen of these enormities and no others. Of harpoons in which I had any faith we owned only the two hand harpoons made in Mallaig the previous autumn.

On the first day we began to mount the gun upon the newly made gun platform in the *Dove*'s bows. Difficulties began to crop up at once. Below the barrel of the gun was a wooden box into which the first fifty feet of playing rope could be coiled, to avoid drag upon the harpoon between gun and target. This box prevented a reasonable sideways traverse of the barrel between the safety railing of the gun platform. The railings had to be cut and refitted. Then we found that the backward slope of the platform from the bows prevented a depression of the gun barrel which would put a shark within range. No sooner was one difficulty overcome than another appeared, and it was more than a week before the *Dove* was ready to sail from Mallaig with her gun mounted.

We went out into the Sound of Sleat and began some target tests. A fish box was thrown overboard; we circled it and made a careful approach. This required a great deal of gesticulation, because during the later stages of the approach the target was hidden from the helmsman by the height of the *Dove*'s bows. The gunmaker was to fire the shot; I was to observe and report upon the result. I tried to visualize the floating box as the high dorsal fin of a shark.

The engines were running dead slow, and the range decreased infinitesimally. Seventy yards, fifty; it looked within range now, but was still beyond the effective range of any harpoon gun ever made. He pulled the trigger at about fifteen yards. The noise was much less than I had expected—not more than that of two barrels of a twelve-bore shotgun discharged together. The air was full of flying rope, through which I could make out the silver flash of the harpoon heading straight for the target. Then, six feet short of the fish box, it playfully changed direction and plunged vertically into the water.

In all fairness to the gunmaker, I must remember that he had constantly protested the experimental nature of the equipment, but somehow I had not doubted its capacity until I had seen those harpoons.

I was to fire the next shot, and he was to observe. We began to manœuvre again, and I realized the great problems that would be involved in dealing with even a slow-moving target. I crouched to the shoulder piece and put my eye to the rear-sight—a tiny hole in the large guard plate. The position was acutely uncomfortable, and with the rise and fall of the boat it was not easy to keep the target in the sights. I pulled the trigger at about ten yards. The harpoon struck the water a few feet to the rear side of the box—the correct place, for the body of the shark, well below the surface, is the target—and disappeared in a heavy boil of water. A wake like that of a torpedo showed between the point of impact and the fish box, then the harpoon appeared momentarily at the surface beyond it. We considered it a perfect shot and foolishly thought no more of the strange result of the previous one.

Sharks were said to be numerous at the other side of the Minch, and we decided to sail the following morning for South Uist, working north from there to the Harris coast. There seemed every chance of having a shark waiting for Hartley the biologist when he arrived at the end of the week.

Hope is long in dying; we fired fourteen shots at sharks and five at killer whales—one of these being the only fair chance I have ever had at a big bull killer—and not one single harpoon struck home. We started at Uishenish in South Uist and worked north the whole hundred miles to Stornoway. There were not many sharks; we saw two or three each day, and I think that most of them were small. It was blazing hot, the sea and sky were a dazzling bubble of light in which the long chain of islands trembled and distorted themselves to mirage shapes. With the appearance of each distant fin there was at first a leap of excitement, but soon its stirring became numbed by the certainty of anticlimax. By evening of the second day, when we anchored in Lochmaddy, I had only one thought—to have hand harpoons ready for immediate use. We had one on board, but it required alteration, so I hired a car in Lochmaddy and bumped and jolted across to the west side of North Uist where lived the nearest blacksmith.

It was my first experience of that amazing island, and greater familiarity has not changed my first impression—a jigsaw puzzle of which every other piece has been removed to reveal water beneath it. The mouth of Lochmaddy harbour is not much more than a quarter of a mile across, but to walk dryshod from one point to the other one must travel nearly two hundred miles. Tentacles of the sea, intricate and winding as a maze, stretch for miles inland; they are as the warp to the woof of the freshwater lochs which twine among them but never mingle; there is water on every side, and only the colour of the weed to label it as sea wrack or peat loch. It was as though one looked at some weird map that evening, for the colour had gone from the land, leaving it dark and formless; only the water with its million arms reflected a deep orange sky, and when I reached the top of the watershed the stack of St. Kilda forty miles away in the Atlantic was silhouetted against the same unreal colour.

The blacksmith had no tools for the work we required, and at midnight I got back to the *Dove* in a black depression.

We sailed for Mallaig the following morning, and somewhere off the fjords we fell in with a school of killer whales. The killer (photograph 76) is one of the sea's enormities. He is the wolf of the ocean, savage, calculating, and cunning; nothing that swims, not even the largest of the great whales, is safe from him. Compared to them, his size is insignificant; it is a big bull killer that measures thirty feet, and the cows are little more than half that length. Killers hunt in packs of as many as forty, though I have never seen more than nine together, nor more than one old bull in any group. The cows and young are not particularly impressive, though they are easy to distinguish from the other whales of their size by the clear white patch on the side of the head, showing at each blow. The dorsal fin of the cow is twelve to eighteen inches high, a black, curved-back hook, much like that of several other species of small whale, and conveying no impression of the high explosive that moves below. The young bull's fin is much the same, but rather straighter. *Orca gladiator* is the killer's Latin name, and in the adult bull the fin is a sword, straight and vertical, higher than a man, a blazon of ferocity. When the killer is cruising, the fin rises slowly from the water at each blow; a foot, two feet, five—as though it would never end. The fins have been said to reach nine feet, and I thought this first one that I saw was no less. There were seven whales, travelling roughly in line abreast, and from the middle of the line rose the great black sword that seemed to embody all that I had ever read of killer whales: the attacks upon ponies stranded on ice floes, the killing of the great baleen whales by tearing out their tongues, the thirteen porpoises and fourteen seals found in the stomach of one twenty-foot *Orca*. They are reputed to use this monstrous fin to smash the ice floes upon which the seals lie, and when the young walrus climbs to safety upon his mother's back the killer throws him off with the same savage thrust from below. Probably there is nothing in the sea that is unmolested by killers; scars upon the flanks and back of many of the smaller whales are almost characteristic, and I have seen basking sharks with the marks of fearful wounds that may also have been the work of a killer's teeth. There is perhaps only one animal in the sea as ferocious as *Orca gladiator*—the leopard seal, or sea leopard, of the Antarctic, which feeds upon other seals and will chase a man across the ice.

The killers swam due south, and for forty miles we followed them along the coastline. They swam slowly—at about six knots—and they blew about every three hundred yards. Time and again we estimated the spot at which they would surface, and time and again, while I was standing tensely at the gun, peering down into the water, the harsh blast of their breathing, like the first escape of steam from a train getting under way, would sound from a hundred yards to one side or the other. There was a light breeze blowing from the shore, and when they blew to windward of us the faint mist of their breath drifted to us on the air, a smell fetid and intensely carnivorous.

We had followed them for more than twenty-five miles when at last the old bull blew right under the *Dove*'s bows. I could have touched him with a boat hook from where I stood at the gun. At first he was a great black shadow coming up in the green sea; then, as the fin began to rise almost to my face, I saw his head come clear of the water, and almost dropped the gun. He had rolled a little to the side on his forward thrust, and his eye was looking straight at me—an animal's eye, sentient and terrifying. His mouth was half open, and beyond the eye glittered the teeth of his lower jaw. I recovered my self-possession in time to fire the gun as he was beginning to sound; where the harpoon went I never knew, and there was no reason for that unique chance to be successful after the repeated failures at sharks. During the next three years, when guns and harpoons were working satisfactorily, I followed killers again and again, but that first chance was never repeated.

Hartley and the gunmaker left before we had caught a shark. Our hopes were very low; we were no nearer to catching the specimen that was so urgently needed to establish markets, and the season was more than halfway through. We made two new hand harpoons in Mallaig and rigged the traces and ropes so that both could be driven in simultaneously by two harpooners. We heard reports of sharks from the fishermen who had been working the west shore of Rhum, and with this new equipment we set off in the *Gannet*.

Rhum is only two or three hours from Mallaig, and we regarded it as a day's expedition, taking with us neither food nor spare fuel. There were three of us on board: Tex, Bruce Watt—my new skipper—and myself. Bruce had joined us a week or so earlier, and remained my skipper until the middle of the 1947 season. He was a man of my own age, a former Merchant Navy Engineer Officer; a good seaman, solid, reliable, teetotal, and of a native common sense, an absence of impetuosity, that sometimes made him seem slow in comparison with more volatile characters.

I do not remember the early part of that day clearly, because it has become obscured by the happenings of the afternoon and the night. It was grey and rather cold, with a westerly breeze. We reached Harris Bay about midday and cruised up and down for an hour without seeing anything. We made sure that if this time we found a shark we should not lose it for lack of forethought. We went over the whole of the gear from the harpoon to the rope's end, checking for any possible fault. Each harpoon was inserted into the end of a fifteen-foot length of iron piping, whose weight would help us to drive the harpoons in deep. The piping, we thought, would be left in our hands, after perhaps the whole harpoon had been driven into the shark's body. The first twenty feet of the line was steel rope, which we afterwards came to call the trace, and this branched like a letter Y to a harpoon at the end of each its arms. We had realized that there might be great danger in bad timing, and that if one harpoon went in appreciably before the other there might be some very violent action. We agreed that the second harpooner—the one farthest from the boat's bows—should give the word, as he might not have a clear target as soon as the other. I was to take the bow harpoon, Tex the second. To the trace was attached eighty fathoms of rope, and after the first thirty fathoms we fastened a canvas net buoy—a pear-shaped balloon about twice the size of a football—on the end of a separate six-fathom rope. This, if a harpooned shark was swimming ahead, would allow us to judge his direction and movements. Near the other end of the rope we inserted two powerful coil springs to reduce the shock and make a broken rope less likely.

We were about a mile offshore when we saw the shark, his huge fin now standing high and clear of the water with a foot or two of back showing below it, now almost disappearing in the long Atlantic swell. Bruce brought us up to him very slowly, determined to give us the best possible chance. Tex and I stood side by side on the starboard bow. There was no deck rail on the *Gannet*, and the swell and the unbalancing weight of the iron piping made it very difficult to stand upright. I thought we should be too much off balance to get any real force into the thrust. During those minutes of approach the suspense accumulated unbearably: this was our first chance with equipment which we had ourselves designed and which we trusted. At the last moment Tex and I had the same thought— our eyes running over the arrangement of ropes and traces, each fearing that we were standing on the wrong side of some vital rope.

The tip of the tail fin, just awash and moving slowly over a wide arc, appeared level with the bows, passed below me, and slid astern; the high dorsal fin approached and was suddenly right beneath me. Peering down into the water, I could make out the great brown bulk a few feet below the surface, white patches glimmering on the back and sides. I thought Tex would never give the word to strike. Then his yell came as though he were shouting into my ear, "Let him have it!"

I drove the iron pipe down with all my strength, nearly carried overboard by the force of the lunge. There was a fractional resistance; then the harpoon passed deep into the shark's back and came to rest. Nothing happened; it was the anticlimax of bayoneting a sandbag. I leaned on the pipe and pushed as hard as I could; from the corner of my eye I could see Tex thrusting and shoving furiously. Then suddenly through the long shaft I held I felt a volcanic surge of strength as the tail of the shark swung towards the boat in an effort to crash-dive. Everything was hidden in a great shower of water and spray. As the spray cleared I saw that the rope was running out at tremendous speed. The canvas net buoy, with its own six fathoms of rope, went overboard and submerged in the same instant. As the first rush began to slow a little we slipped the rope in a half-turn on the drum of the winch, and the *Gannet* began to be towed slowly ahead in widening circles. We seemed to be firmly fastened to a shark at last.

Every now and again the buoy would appear on the surface for a few seconds. At first we used the tiller to follow it directly; then, as half an hour became an hour, and an hour lengthened to two, we realized that until we started to haul in the rope there was nothing useful that we could do. We waited for the shark to tire himself out—we might as well have waited for him to die of old age.

We steered an erratic course, but at the end of four hours we were not more than two miles from where we had started. The shark was swimming deeper now, and we had not seen the buoy for over an hour. It was about five in the afternoon when we decided to try to haul the fish up. We all got together on the rope, and Bruce organized our effort to get the greatest possible use from the rise and fall of the boat on the swell. His "Heave!" came each time the *Gannet*'s bows dipped into a trough, so that we gained a few feet at each pull. At the end of an hour's pulling the shark had only six fathoms of rope left, and we could not gain another inch; it was like trying to pull a house. We were all tired; we had been using all our strength for an hour. We took two more turns of the rope round the winch and rested. The two coil springs that we had let into the rope to reduce shock were pulled out practically straight, and the boat began to shoot ahead in crazy jerks. The link between us and the shark was now so short that we were feeling each individual propulsive movement of his body. It was a deadlock: we had not the strength to pull him in, and he could not tear the harpoons from his back. The strain was terrific; something must give way, and it seemed that it must be the rope. We wondered, too, what would happen if the shark tried to dive now—whether he could take the *Gannet* under with him.

Suddenly it was all over, the rope hung limp in the water, and the *Gannet* lay hove to and wallowing. None of us said anything as we pulled in the rope. The last fathom was thick with the same acrid black slime that I had seen on the harpoon at Sleat Lighthouse. It seemed to be coming in too lightly to have two harpoons at the end of it. A moment later we were examining six inches of broken harpoon shaft—inch-and-a-half steel snapped off short at the body of the shark. The second harpoon had pulled out as soon as it took the single strain.

We did not know then that where there is one shark there are probably others, so we turned for home—northward, to pass between Rhum and Canna. It began to rain, and the hills of Rhum were blotted out in a cold grey mist.

We had not gone a mile before we saw another shark. He was perhaps a quarter of a mile to seaward of us, the fin rolling in the run of the increasing swell, and travelling slowly westward.

We had only one harpoon left; I fitted it to the iron pipe and disconnected the useless second trace, while Bruce turned the *Gannet's* head for the fin. There was very much more motion on the water now, and I could stand upright upon the foredeck only by using the iron pipe as a lever against the boat's side. The pipe was enormously heavy, and my arms were already tired when for the second time that day I found myself fairly placed for the harpoon thrust. It requires an entirely different grip on the piping to drive a harpoon vertically downward from that necessary for a thrust at, say, forty-five degrees, and we had run very much more closely over the shark than I had expected. I had been ready for a thrust outward from the boat, and when I found myself directly over the fish it was too late to change my grip. I seemed to strike the body too low down, and the thrust lacked power; I had no confidence in the result. Again the rope ran out quickly, the buoy submerged and never reappeared, and the shark began to tow us slowly southwestward. We made some tea on the primus stove and sat back to wait.

At the end of three hours the situation was unchanged. The light was going fast, and we were nearly stationary some three miles west of Rhum. There was a breeze coming up from the southwest, bringing ragged grey clouds against a primrose sky. The sea was of that blanched absence of colour that is seen only at dusk.

It seemed to us that we had lost the last shark because we had not allowed him to tire enough before trying to pull him in, and we were determined not to make the same mistake again. This time we decided to let him tow the *Gannet* all night.

Just before dark some ring-net boats passed to seaward of us, heading north for Canna harbour. One of them, a boat of Manson's, turned off her course, and a figure came out from the wheelhouse to hail us. The voice came faint across the water.

"You'd better get the hell out of here and make for Canna—there's a gale warning on the wireless."

But it would have taken an earthquake warning to make us lose that shark without a struggle. We made up our minds to try to hold on.

Saying, "Well, you're warned, anyway," the figure turned back into the wheelhouse, and the boat went on northward into the dusk.

Two lighthouses were visible: Sanday light on Canna, and Hyskeir, a lonely, wind-beaten rock ten miles to the southwest of it and the same distance northwest of us. These two lights flashed yellow in the thickening dusk; gradually Rhum was blotted out behind us, and they were the only visible things in inky darkness.

After an hour the breeze began to stiffen and it became very cold; then with the night and the breaking seas came the most beautiful of all the sea's jewels: the phosphorescence of *Noctiluca*. Each breaking wave glowed with pale opalescent fire, and when the water slapped against the boat's sides they were left sparkling with a thousand tiny lights.

I crawled up the foredeck to feel the position of the rope; it led ahead at an angle of forty-five degrees, and from it streamed a trail of phosphorus, which told me that our speed was increasing. We were heading west nor'west and making about five knots into a rising sea. Except for the sound of the breaking water, the night was very quiet; the *Gannet* had no rigging for the wind to play tunes upon. We sailed a dream sea in the dark and the eerie phosphorescence, towed by the wounded shark far below us in the dark water.

One of us at a time was to remain awake and check the bearing of the lighthouses by the boat's compass. My watch ended at midnight, when Hyskeir Light bore due north and our course was about westward. The wind was rising steadily; we were a long way from land and being towed farther seaward, with a small fuel supply and no food. I was too tired to care when I rolled myself in my duffel coat and went to sleep on the floor of the hold, leaving the outcome in Bruce's more capable hands. The last thing I heard before I slept was Tex's voice saying, "If we have to do this every time we catch a shark I'll be needing double pay."

Through my sleep I heard voices once or twice—when I became conscious enough to understand, I realized that Hyskeir Light was bearing northeast and that Sanday Light was obscured. I roused myself, stupid with sleep and cold, to find that it was nearly two o'clock and that we were in a really heavy sea, the breaking phosphorescence stretching around on every side to the limit of vision. There was a distant undercurrent of sound, deeper and heavier than the nearby breakers, which at first I could not place. Then through it came an unmistakable call, thin and buffeted by the wind but sweetly familiar, the calling of curlews—curlews that meant rock and reef.

We trusted to Bruce, and Bruce gave the inevitable verdict that we were as unwilling to accept as he to give. We must get free of the shark somehow and at once.

Again I crawled up the foredeck and felt the rope; it stretched out at an acute angle, and thirty yards ahead was a little boil of phosphorescence in the water. We were going fast and nearly due west; the shark must have been swimming almost at the surface.

We started the engine and went hard astern, trying to pull the harpoon out. The rope's half-turn on the winch began to slip yard by yard; we made the half-turn a double turn and tried again. It was impossible to tell whether we were making or losing way, but nothing gave. After five minutes it was clear that we could not pull the harpoon out—my bungling thrust had taken firm hold of a shark at last, and nothing would free us from him but to cut the rope. Bruce chopped through it with an axe, seven and a half hours after I had planted the harpoon.

Dawn came as we passed between Rhum and Canna, a bleak dawn with a heavy sea and lashing rain. The journey home took five hours; we were soaked and shivering, and I felt seasick for the first time in my life.

III

THE FIRST KILL

We had lost both of our hand harpoons, and it seemed to us that we could not haul up a hand-harpooned shark without a motor winch, though a gun might drive the harpoon far enough into the fish to touch some vital part, or at least weaken him. The winch had been on order for a long time, and the gun-maker was constructing a more sensible type of gun harpoon, but meanwhile we had no equipment to use. We spent ten days in Mallaig, while the *Dove* went on carrying factory materials, and we had two more hand harpoons made locally. At the end of that week I got a telegram from John Campbell of Canna, saying, *Huge shark off Compass Hill*. Compass Hill is the highest north-facing cliff of Canna, and is so called because the metal ore it contains draws a ship's compass several points. It is a stupendous precipice, six hundred feet high and overhanging in places, covered everywhere with seabird colonies. From the summit one can look down almost vertically to the sea, and I knew that John must have seen not only the fin but the whole body of the shark, like a submarine below the surface.

We sailed for Canna at once; there was some talk of a drifting mine in the neighbourhood, and as we put out from Mallaig harbour an incoming ring-netter hailed us, "Best find the mine and harpoon that for us!"

We saw the shark almost as soon as we had rounded Compass

Hill. The water was a mass of young puffins and guillemots, some scurrying in front of the fin as it furrowed the calm water. The fish seemed to be swimming in a fairly close circle, and sometimes he submerged so that there was only a ripple on the surface above the fin tip. We made two or three approaches, but each time he submerged completely when almost within range. The tiller of the *Gannet* was out of reach of the engine, so that if anything more complicated was required than an approach at a constant low speed there had to be one man at the tiller and another at the engine to obey his instructions. As the shark repeatedly submerged we overran him more than once, so I left Tex at the harpoon and went back to the tiller myself. Nothing I could do brought the shark within range of the harpoon. Sometimes he rode high on the surface, sometimes he would submerge altogether, always to reappear swimming round the circumference of that strange, tight circle.

At last the moment came when I had lost him altogether. I did not know whether he was ahead or astern of us, and I peered over the side to see if I could make out his shadow somewhere beneath the surface. As I looked, the *Gannet*'s side was almost brushing a large whitish object a couple of feet down. At first I took it to be some unfamiliar portion of the shark, then I saw weed clinging to a nozzle-like protuberance. My reactions must have been desperately slow—my eye had taken in a second protuberance and the giant football below it, now almost touching our stern, before I understood that I was looking at the mine. "Best find the mine and harpoon that for us!" —and out of all the miles of water we had found it, after all. Probably the long-delayed evasive action I took was too late to affect matters one way or another; we escaped, as we had run into danger, by hazard. We left the shark still cruising slowly round and round the mine, and all the way until he was out of sight we looked back over our shoulders, wondering whether he would go that inch too close that we ourselves had so nearly been.

We put into Canna harbour and telegraphed the position of the mine to Mallaig. I wasted several hours there, because I have never mastered a temptation to stay forever on Canna each time I go ashore. It is unlike any other island, and it is entirely beautiful. The hill that is brought up short by the cliff fall of Compass Hill is of green turf eaten short by a million rabbits. This expanse of green, when the eye has become accustomed only to red and grey rock and dark heather, is like an oasis in a desert, and round the small mansion house are elms as leafy as a deep English summer. The path from the pier, where the rocks are painted with white initials and dates and boats' numbers, as in England boys carve their initials upon trees, runs along the sides of a shallow bay, where eider ducks and their broods are as confiding and unconcerned as mallard on the Serpentine. At the other side of the bay is Sanday Island, whose lighthouse we had watched in the dark as the shark towed us out into the Minch from Rhum. Sanday, joined to Canna only by a bridge, is green too, and edged with low cliffs alive with gulls and guillemots. Everything on Canna looks neat, tidy, and appropriate to its surroundings; the mansion house is unassuming and architecturally satisfactory, the use of the land is efficient, and there is none of the dereliction that one must associate with so many of the Hebrides. On Rhum there is luxury, the huge and anomalous Scottish baronial Kinloch Castle, of dark red stone, sombre and appalling in its surroundings. It is said that when Kinloch was built, Sir George Bullough received two specimens of stone for his approval; both were the red Torridonian sandstone, but one came from Rhum and the other from the Isle of Arran, one hundred and fifty miles to the south. He chose the Arran stone. The interior of Kinloch is stately and deserted for the greater part of the year; Canna is habitable and inhabited, warm and living; its owner a scholar of all that is Gaelic in tradition, an explorer of every way in which his and like communities may be improved.

Bruce had stayed with the *Gannet,* and Tex and I, on different errands, had become separated. As I returned down the path I saw Tex at the pier, waving his arms and bellowing something incomprehensible. Following the line of his pointing arm, I saw a big shark's fin cruising very close to the rocks right inside the harbour. One had the impression that the shark did not want to remain at the surface, and that only the very shallow water of the ebb tide was periodically forcing him high enough for the fin to show.

I joined Tex, panting and blowing, and we shinned down the uprights of the pier to drop into the *Gannet's* hold. Bruce was already methodically busy, coiling down the rope and fitting the harpoons into their pipes. We were under way in less than five minutes.

The shark kept obstinately to the line of rocks; sometimes there was barely draught for the *Gannet's* keel. The wind ruffled the water's surface to royal blue, so that we could not see below it or follow the shark's movements. He behaved uncharacteristically: sometimes travelling a good deal faster than we had seen any other shark do at the surface, sometimes nearly stationary, but always changing course. At the end of twenty minutes we had been almost within range a dozen times, but at the last moment he had always either sheered off or submerged. The time came, as it had come with the shark under

Compass Hill in the morning, when we had nothing to follow, no idea where he would surface next. The *Gannet* had a very little forward way on her, almost hove to, when the shark surfaced on the same course, heading for the shore, right under her bows. The dorsal fin was two or three yards ahead and a foot or two to starboard of us. I could see nothing below the surface, but Tex, who had the forward harpoon, was looking down upon the narrow afterpart of the body where it thinned out to the tail. The delay had made him impatient, and he was not going to wait for a better chance.

He raised the iron piping over his head and drove vertically downward. As he did so, I tried to detach my own harpoon from its pipe shaft, thinking that the useless pipe would carry Tex overboard in the shark's first dash. I was bending over it when the whole boat seemed to be struck by a high-explosive shell. From the corner of my eye I was aware of the shark's tail somewhere high in the air and apparently about to slam down right on top of me. I ducked instinctively, and I was on all fours when two objects hit me almost simultaneously. The first was a harpoon pipe, whose end struck me a tremendous blow in the groin. Then Tex, whose body felt like a ton of rocks, fell backwards on top of me, bounced off, and tumbled back in the hold upon the coil of rope, which was streaking out at high speed. I realized dimly that Tex was in very great danger and that if any part of him got tangled in the rope he would have broken bones before he was dragged overboard. I fell back into the hold myself and was trying as I did so to lug Tex clear of the rope coil. He seemed unconscious and had a lot of blood coming from his head. Bruce had jumped forward from the tiller with the same idea, but as he landed in the hold his foot caught in a snarl of rope, and his problem was added to ours.

The *Gannet*'s bows were jerked violently round into the bay, and for a second or two we seemed to be travelling at enormous speed with no one at the engine or the tiller. Then the harpoon pulled out, and the *Gannet* gradually lost way, while Bruce and I struggled with the situation in the hold.

Tex was semiconscious and bleeding from a long open gash in his head; Bruce had a wrenched ankle, and I was feeling dazed and sick from the blow I had taken in the groin. It was not until some time later that we managed to reconstruct what had happened.

We were by this time quite familiar with the sideways and upward lash of a shark's tail after the harpoon had gone home, but until now the harpoon had always been very much farther forward, and not in the part of the shark that was actually lashing. Tex's harpoon had gone in only a few feet forward of the tail fin, where the body is narrow, hard, and very muscular. The first lash of the tail had been away from the boat and had carried the long iron piping with it. Tex was still trying to recover his balance when the tail came back, much higher out of the water, and carrying the pipe with it like a tilting lance. He had ducked just in time to avoid being impaled, but the end of the pipe had caught him a glancing blow on the head before hitting me.

We took Tex up to Canna House, and a guest staying there, a trained nurse, examined his cut. It was long and gaping and obviously required stitches. Tex was given the better part of a tumbler of whisky, and in the warm kitchen, among the Siamese cats, she stitched it neatly and efficiently.

A fortnight later, in August 1945, we caught our first shark. We had other failures in the meantime; not all as dramatic as

these, but the excitement and the bite of disappointment remained as keen.

Our first shark was a worthy climax; no fiction-writer could
have invented a longer-held tension, improved upon that
eleventh-hour near-disaster, or arranged for a larger audience
to watch it.

At that time I was staying with relatives at Morar, four miles
from Mallaig, and used to motor in every day after breakfast.
They were a forbearing family; I had come to stay for a week
after my discharge from Special Forces, and was still there
nearly a year later. In the end that original week's visit lengthened to an intermittent stay of between two and three
years.

Probably it is impossible to describe Morar Lodge as it was
then to anyone who did not know it; its passing, or rather return, to more conventional occupants a few years later removed
a richness from the face of the West Highlands. In fiction,
perhaps, old Mrs. Knox's house as described in *The Experiences
of an Irish R.M.* approached it most nearly; its atmosphere of
comfort, kindness, mingled squalor and riches, but, above all,
its animals. The house and its environs were inhabited, by invitation, by an infinitely greater number of animals than of
humans, and against their amiable but ruthless depredations had
accumulated an elaboration of uncouth barricades and defences
that seemed to dominate the main elevation of the house, and
crept like the spread of green-fly on a rosebush into the very
living rooms themselves. These were occupied by a numerous,
indeterminate, and largely floating population of dogs, to which
was added at this time my own somewhat bulky springer
spaniel, and the noise of their disagreements, attempted amours,
and harsh protests as they were stepped upon by some unac-

climatized guest was one of the more characteristic sounds of
the house. At bedtime each armchair and sofa was stacked high
with books and other angular objects to pin the dog population
to the floor during the dark hours, giving a nightly appearance
of the early stages of house-moving. Two pale grey cats, who
all night long would pursue each other through the shrubbery
with harsh unvarying cries, resulting in the female's almost
miraculously perpetual state of pregnancy, completed the official indoor population; but for a considerable period of my
stay a hen also lived in the drawing room, a scrawny black
pullet named Angusina who had some miscellaneous deformity
which at the moment eludes me, but which had qualified her
for the privileged position of trust that she now held.

Life in the rhododendron jungle that surrounded the house
was even more intense and varied, but was dominated, as the
dinosaurs dominated a stage of prehistory, by a vast black sow
called Minnie, whose lumbering but querulous form was seldom
beyond eyeshot or earshot; and it was, I think, against her exceptional strength and cunning in particular that many of the
entanglements, trip wires, and booby traps had been conceived.
They were in vain, these elaborate precautions; Minnie always
won out in the end, and often a meal would be interrupted by
a splintering crash followed by the delighted squeals that announced a penetration of the outer defences. They were abandoned at last, and her siesta ground became the veranda, where
her vast sleeping carcass was occasionally used as a convenient
seat by the younger members of the human family, and through
the french windows into the drawing room she would lollop
with bass grunts that turned to outraged and purely feminine
shrieks as she was ejected.

Whereas there was definitely traceable farming activity at

Morar Lodge, the pursuit of which occupied, indeed, much of the family's waking hours, it was for their charm or pathos that the livestock were mainly selected, and many odd specimens of sheep and cattle of egregious breeds gave the place something of the air of an agricultural zoo. Two animals of mine were later added to the collection: a Shetland ewe that had fallen into Mallaig harbour during transport of the flock to Soay and was christened Gavotte in a play upon my name, and a vicious great black-backed gull which I had taken as a young one from a rock in the Outer Hebrides, and which it had proved impracticable to keep on the boats. This bird, too, was a cripple, which automatically ensured its welcome at Morar Lodge. Only one obvious animal was missing from that house, but there was evidence of its existence in the past, for on a shelf in the bathroom there stood for a long time a bottle labelled in faded ink "Lotion for donkey's eyes—I *think*."

Every morning, then, I motored into Mallaig, and on calm days it had become a habit to stop at the top of the hill above the harbour and search the sea with field glasses. West, one looked down over fourteen miles of sea to Eigg and Rhum; when it was calm the sea would look flat and white, and every black dot upon it was suspect. It was hot that summer, and the atmospheric shimmer of the air would play tricks with one's eyes, distorting a floating fish box, a shag, or a cormorant, to the rounded triangle of a shark's dorsal fin. I remember many loudly acclaimed sharks that took wing and flapped heavily away across the sea.

On this morning I searched the nearer water first and lingered for some time over a motionless object perhaps a mile out before I identified it as a tin can. I raised the glasses higher, and into their field came a great concourse of resting shearwaters spread over the water like a carpet hundreds of yards square. They breed on Eigg, where the clifftop is honeycombed with their burrows, and these gigantic flocks rest motionless upon the water or skim past the boat at tremendous speed, an endless train of long narrow wings, keen and graceful as scimitars.

From the centre of the flock a patch of birds began to rise, running for a few steps upon the surface with wings held stiffly outstretched. This spread like a ripple from the centre outward, until the whole flock was on the wing, wheeling to reunite; and where the movement had started, a black object began to rise above the surface. It rose quickly, and in a few seconds it was unmistakable, glistening wet with quick flashes of light as the sun caught it. I watched while the tail fin appeared, moving from side to side with that strange ponderous leisure, and then I became aware that there were other black objects away beyond it. Turning the glasses on to them, I saw that the sea was dotted with fins for perhaps a mile beyond the one that had disturbed the shearwaters. I could count eighteen, and the farthest was very tiny, so that there were probably more beyond the range of the field glasses.

I got the car started and tore down into Mallaig, where I found that Bruce had already heard from the ring-net boats of a big shoal of sharks lying about six miles out and two miles south of Point of Sleat.

There was a lot of preparation to be done, as we had just moved the Oerlikon gun from the *Dove* to the *Gannet*, partly because the *Dove* was always either out of action or engaged in carrying factory materials, and partly because we hoped that the low bows of the *Gannet* might help to overcome the deflection of the harpoon which had caused our persistent failures. The gun platform of the *Dove* was ten feet above the sea, while the *Gannet's* was only three, allowing a shot at point-blank range. But the recoil of the gun firing a heavy harpoon would have split the *Gannet's* bows, and a great deal of reinforcement had been necessary below deck. This work was barely finished, and it was midday before we were ready to sail with the gun securely mounted near the starboard gunwale, and two double-barb harpoons that had just arrived from Birmingham. (See Fig. D, page 21.)

Besides Bruce, Tex, and a deckhand called John Cameron, we had with us the son of the house where I was staying, Jackie Shaw Stewart, and an Eton friend of his, who had a camera along.

The sky had become overcast by the time we sailed, a thin layer of cloud through which the sun diffused over a hushed white sky and sea, so calm that even the floatpods of drifting weed showed hundreds of yards away. There were nothing like the number of sharks at the surface that there had been in the morning. By standing up in the *Gannet's* bows I could make out the fins at about two miles—there seemed to be only three sharks, and none of them steady at the surface, though the three were never all submerged at the same time.

We decided to take the first shot that offered and headed straight for them; when we were still a mile away I saw a great grey shadow as big as the boat pass diagonally below us, and knew that we were on the fringe of the submerged shoal, but no more came to the surface.

We were hardly more than a hundred yards from the fins when for the first time all went down together. I was standing at the gun, trying to accommodate my shoulder to its unrelenting awkwardness, and taking practice sights along the barrel. We had removed the iron protection plate, but even without it the gun was as clumsy to handle as the fifteen-foot iron pipes on the hand harpoons had been. I heard the engine slip into neutral, and the *Gannet* stole very gently forward towards the rippled surface where the sharks had gone down.

Then, and up to the very last shark I killed years later, this waiting for a shark to resurface, straining one's eyes for the faintest ripple or gliding bulk below the water, set my heart hammering savagely against my ribs, as though it were a sort of overture, a roll of drums leading up to the climax—the gun's roar and the flying rope and the tail towering out of the water in a drench of white spray. This was the first time that it really happened.

The gun was mounted where we had become accustomed to stand with hand harpoons—well forward on the extreme edge of the starboard bow, so that one must approach the fish from astern and to port of him. At first thought it would seem more sensible for the gun to be on the extreme point of the boat's nose, giving a much wider field of fire, but to use this field of fire the gunner would have to step off the boat and into the sea to keep behind the gun when it turned. But when a shark does not swim on a steady course it is often impossible to make certain of a stern approach—one must take any shot when it comes within range, and that is what happened on this first occasion.

A fin reappeared fifty yards away on the same course, going slowly and straight away from us. The *Gannet* jerked forward as she went into gear and headed for the shark at half throttle; then I heard Bruce's voice to the man at the engine, "Dead slow," then, "Take her out," and we were drifting up to the shark on a perfect approach.

But at about ten yards the fish turned abruptly left, at right angles to his former course, so that our bows would have passed behind his tail, or at best rammed it. I yelled "Hard aport" to Bruce, but did not feel certain that the *Gannet* had enough way on her to answer the tiller. She seemed to come round very slowly, but the shark was moving slowly too, and his whole length was suddenly there, right across the *Gannet*'s bows, so that she would have rammed him amidships. I had slewed the gun round until it was pointing as much forward as its traverse allowed, and I pulled the trigger cord as soon as the dorsal fin came into the gun's field of vision. The Etonian succeeded in taking a photograph (11) a fraction of a second after the impact; it shows the very tip of the tail fin beginning its first swing towards the boat's side as the shark tries to dive.

The fish had been swimming very high; there were only a few inches of water over his back when I fired, and I felt quite certain that the harpoon was in him. The tail behaved as usual, hiding everything with a storm of spray; then, when it had subsided, I saw the shark a fathom or two down in clear water, swimming fast on an opposite course. I could see the end of the harpoon shaft sticking a foot or so out of his side—below the point I had aimed for—and a dark plume of blood trailing from it in the water, like smoke from a chimney. Tex saw it too, and gave his war cry for the first time, a war cry that I came to associate with every kill, and which in a later season I remember hearing across half a mile of sea, following the boom of his gun in the summer dusk: "He feels it! He feels it!"

The shark took fifty fathoms of rope in a rush before he slowed up enough for us to be able to take a turn on the drum of the little hand winch. We let him tow us sluggishly for two hours before we began to haul up.

For nearly another two hours the five of us hauled on that rope with all our strength, dragging it in almost inch by inch. Everything worked perfectly. When we began the tug-of-war the rope was leading down from the bow fair-lead at about seventy degrees, and for the first few minutes the shark tried quick changes of direction, the rope leading sometimes ahead, sometimes to port or starboard, then down under the boat. But after ten minutes the rope was vertical, as rigid as a telegraph pole, and he was three hundred feet below us in the green dusk of the sea, being dragged inexorably upward.

We had pieces of coloured cloth tied into the rope at ten, twenty, and thirty fathoms; when, after an hour and a half, the ten-fathom mark came up over the fair-lead and came edging down the dripping foredeck to the winch, I left the hold and went up to the *Gannet*'s bows. I lay flat on my face on the deck and strained my eyes to follow the rope down into the dim water. I could see perhaps twenty feet before it became lost in darkness; the three feet of it between the surface and the *Gannet*'s fair-lead felt as hard as wood, and if one pulled sideways upon it it would vibrate fractionally, but would not give half an inch. It was some minutes before I could see anything but the tensed rope leading down into obscurity; then, at the extreme limit of vision, I saw something that looked like a gigantic punkah swinging rhythmically to and fro.

I had already seen several sharks at close quarters; I had seen those giant tails sweeping clear of the water to slam down upon the sea or the boat; there was no logical reason for this tail to come as a surprise, but it did. Foot by foot it came higher into the clearer water and defined itself, six foot wide at least and swinging over an arc of several yards as the shark tried to swim vertically downward. Every now and again he would foul the rope as it swung past, holding the tail itself vertical for a moment, then he would break free with a shuddering wrench into his pattern of impotent effort.

I could see part of the body beyond the tail now; the body of a dragon, six feet through and showing a glimmering white belly as he twisted and lunged. At the far end of the belly there seemed to be two gigantic flippers—I was unprepared for the size of these pectoral fins, which had been minimized in the drawings I had seen.

As soon as his tail came clear of the surface the power of that punkah action became apparent; at each lunge it exploded a fountain of water from the sea. Several times it struck the *Gannet*'s stem, leaving gobs of black slime as it struggled free. We were busy with ropes now, and after several near misses succeeded in dropping a noose over the long upper half of the tail fin as it jammed momentarily against the bows. The next lunge carried the tail below the surface, and for a moment it looked as though the rope would be flung free, but as the tail rose again towards the boat we saw the other half of it slip through, and the whole fin was in the noose. We almost knocked each other overboard in our hurry to pull it tight, but we saw it close firmly on the narrow isthmus of body below the fin, and the shark was ours.

He behaved then as I do not remember any other shark behaving afterwards. The fight seemed momentarily to go out of him; he stopped trying to bore downward, and the whole length of him came up close under the surface alongside the *Gannet* like a great drowned elephant, rolling belly upwards before he righted himself. As he did so I saw a giant parasite detach itself from his back and wriggle quickly away into the darkness—an eel-like creature that seemed six feet long. Someone made a grab for it with the boat hook, but he was a second too late, and this monster specimen of *Petromyzon marinus*, the sea lamprey found on all basking sharks, but whose length is not known to exceed a yard, went unrecorded. We all agreed upon its length, nor, in the many that we saw later, did we find ourselves apt to overestimate their length at first sight.

The shark rolled and twisted as he lay alongside, and on one of these rolls the harpoon came uppermost. For a moment I think we all forgot that we had him securely by the tail—we only saw that the harpoon was practically out of him, turned sideways and holding by one barb just beneath the skin. I know I shouted and grabbed the rope to try to pull the barb in deeper before I remembered that the harpoon phase was over now. Our luck was holding, as it was to hold for the next twenty-four hours, no matter by how narrow a margin.

It was late afternoon before we had made the shark's tail fast to the stern of the *Gannet*. He was still alive, and with the boat hove to he still tried convulsively to bore downward. When we put the engine ahead his nose broke the surface twenty-five feet astern of the boat; we opened the throttle wide and began to move forward at a rate of perhaps half a knot, with a tremendous commotion of water astern. It was like trying to tow a house. We did not know then that we were trying to tow him in an almost impossible position, in which his distended gills were held open by the backward rush of water and formed a brake as effective as a large sea anchor. Later we learned to tow sharks tied fore and aft alongside the boat, nose foremost and with the jaws roped closed to give the minimum water resistance.

There was no other boat in sight, and our powers of invention temporarily failed. We had caught a shark and we were going to get him home; we just kept plodding away at less than a mile an hour over that oily white calm. Most of the shark's tail was inboard, and we fingered it curiously, examining the strange black slime and the great keel ridge of muscle that began at each side of its root and ran back to power the thin afterpart of the body.

After an hour's towing Mallaig seemed little nearer, and Sleat Point little farther astern of us. Five miles away we could see the white smoke of the evening train coming up to Mallaig; it ballooned out and hung motionless in the air as the engine passed through the short tunnel. Some small boats were beginning to put out for the evening mackerel fishing at Point of Sleat, and as the first of these passed half a mile to northward of us it turned and made south, a man standing up in the bows. With the field glasses I made out that it was Ian Macintyre, the marine engineer who had made most of our hand harpoons.

Within hailing distance his voice came from between cupped hands, "So you got one at last!"

"Yes, but not with your trash, Ian."

"Just for that I think I'll away and fish mackerel and leave you to it. Is he a big one?"

"Too big for us—it's all wake and no way. Are you on?"

He was on, and with his boat tied alongside the *Gannet* and both our engines full ahead we began to move at three or four knots. Until now we had believed the fallacy that this would kill the shark, that the back pressure of water through his gills would make him unable to breathe. It was a surprise to see that after several miles he was still very much alive.

It was near dusk when we reached Mallaig. It was the tourist season; Mallaig was performing its brief seasonal function of Gateway to the Hebrides, and the train had disgorged its cargo of holiday-makers, would-be mountaineers in huge climbing boots and swathes of rope, brightly tartaned Highlanders from Glasgow and the industrial cities, earnest hikers with gigantic rucksacks and skinny legs, and sad-looking elderly couples who seem to visit the Hebrides annually to lament the climate. Word had reached Mallaig that the *Gannet* was bringing in a shark, and the attention our project had received from the daily press had thronged the piers. As we passed the big stone pier where the island steamers berth, and headed on for the inside of the fish pier where the herring catches are landed and bid for, I remember that parts of the crowd began to run back to intercept us before we reached our berth beside the *Dove*. There were something like fifteen hundred people crowded on that short pier by the time we churned laboriously round the end of it.

With some difficulty we transferred the shark's rope from the *Gannet* to one of the uprights of the pier. First we made the rope fast to it, then took the knot from the *Gannet*'s hand winch. This almost cost Bruce his right arm, as the shark took up that extra six feet of line suddenly allowed to him. The rope slammed taut with a noise like the plucked strings of a double bass, catching the boat's gunwale a hundredth of a second after Bruce had snatched his arm away.

Tied there, the shark was evidently very much alive; again with slow rhythmic lunges he tried to bore down to the bottom. His tail was about a foot below water now, and from its hidden sweeps great ripples spread outward over the still harbour and slapped small disintegrated waves among the supports of the pier. From above we could see perhaps the first ten feet of him; beyond that there were distant glimmers of white where his skin had been torn in the long struggle.

We had intended to lift him on to the decks of the *Dove* with her steam capstan. I think we had very little idea of the weight with which we were dealing, which was certainly several tons. It took about an hour to get up steam on the *Dove*'s boiler. The rope was transferred again, this time to the *Dove*'s capstan, and the shark had something like three or four fathoms of rope between him and the boat. He used it at once, turning outward to the deep water of the harbour, and making the *Dove* strain at her mooring ropes. We started the vast and antiquated capstan, and he was dragged back foot by foot until his tail was once more below the *Dove*'s stem. After a great deal of difficulty we managed to pass a rope round the forepart of his body, attached this, too, to the winch, and heaved him up until he was lying horizontally at the surface alongside the *Dove*. In this position we meant to drag him up the boat's side until he would roll over the gunwale onto the deck. Time and again we raised him until most of his body was clear of the water, but each time the winch failed as it began to take the full strain unhelped by the water's support, the rope drum beginning to whir and slip as the limit of the steam's power was reached. There was a great sag in his body between the fore and after ropes that were lifting him; his head and tail would come up almost to the *Dove*'s gunwale, but there were tons of unlifted weight where his belly still sagged down into the water.

It was dark when we gave up the attempt. The disappointed crowds had already begun to disperse, but they reassembled when they learned that the skipper of a boom ship, lying at the big pier, had agreed to try to lift the shark. Two of these ships, which are equipped with huge cranes, were in Mallaig to lift the submarine boom (to prevent the passage of enemy submarines through the narrows of Skye) at Kylerea; and their massive derricks stood out against the night sky like the silhouette of a London dock. It was difficult to manœuvre the *Dove* alongside them, because with the drag of the shark we could not get her to answer the wheel in that confined space. It was a long time before we got her satisfactorily placed; the crowds grew denser, so that, from the *Dove*'s deck, the whole pier seemed serrated by a forest of heads.

At last we were ready to transfer the shark's rope to the giant crane above us. The second boom ship turned her searchlights upon the swirl in the black water at the *Dove*'s bows, where the rope led rigidly to the still-struggling tail. The stage was set.

Inch by inch the crane began to winch in. Even before the shark's tail broke the surface of the water the sense of strain was terrific. It gleamed and came clear, nearly seven feet wide, black and slithery, all movement stopped by that vertical lift from the water, but deeper and heavier ripples began to surge outwards as twenty feet below the surface the body of the shark still lunged fiercely from side to side.

The narrow neck just below the tail seemed infinitely prolonged; then, very slowly, the girth of the body began to rise. Size always appears greater in the vertical than the horizontal, and by the time fifteen feet of the shark were clear of the water and the girth was still increasing, he appeared literally monstrous, a creature of saga or fantasy, a dragon being hauled from its lair. The darkness, the shifting yellow reflections of the harbour lights, and the white glare of the searchlights combined to give a stage effect of mystery and magnification. There was an excited gabble from the packed crowds on the pier, gasps and exclamations, and a group of women near the edge panicked and forced their way back into the press behind them.

"Oh, wha' a crayture!"

"Ye wouldna' believe it!"

"It canna be a fish!"

The cogs ground on, the ropes creaked and juddered; each sound was one of infinite tension and effort, like sobbing breaths from lungs strained beyond endurance, and the elephantine black silhouette grew to a towering monument.

Then, with twenty feet of him standing clear of the water, there was a slight snapping sound, as a man makes when he steps upon a rotten stick. The crane stopped at a quick order, and for a second there was utter silence—followed by a tremendous crack and a sickening, tearing sound as the great carcass plunged back into the water. For a moment the severed tail hung suspended in midair; then that, too, fell with a mighty smack into the oily black water of the harbour.

After these six years I can still hear the noise from the watching crowds, feel again the almost unbearable disappointment of that moment, that last unbelievable frustration of Tantalus.

I did not think the shark was dead; even tailless he would probably wriggle or drift with the tide into deeper water outside the harbour. I felt quite certain that we should not see him again, and not even the tail remained to prove that we had at last caught a shark and brought him to harbour.

I slept aboard the *Dove* and was out at five-thirty in the morning. For nearly an hour we cruised about round the place which the boom ships had left during the night, but we could see nothing in the now limpid water. We were tying the *Gannet* up again when an outgoing lobster boat hailed us.

"Major! He's here—I can see him!"

The man was bending over the side of his boat, peering down

into the water about a hundred yards out from the end of the stone pier. I felt a tremendous leap of the heart, but I was not feeling strong enough to face a second disappointment, and I tried to be sceptical.

"Are you sure?"

"Aye—I can see the ugly head of him. Come out here and look for yourselves."

It was the shark right enough, lying in about four fathoms of clear water, his mouth half open and glinting pallidly. I had a polaroid filter for my camera lens, to cut out reflection upon the water's surface, and by screwing this into my eye as a monocle I could see him plainly. I didn't doubt for a second that we could recover him; we had a shark, after all.

Bruce and Shand, the owner of the lobster boat, took charge, lowering an ordinary line and fish hook to grip inside the open jaw. They were fast into him after not much more than ten minutes, and the great carcass, lightened by the formation of gases in the belly, came looming up in the water until it was once more alongside the *Gannet*. We passed a rope through the gills and out at the mouth, and a quarter of an hour later the *Gannet* and the dead shark were berthed by the *Dove*. It was only seven o'clock in the morning.

We were not going to try to lift him again. I went and called on Henderson the boatbuilder and got his permission to beach the shark on the boatyard's slip. When I got back to the *Dove*, Bruce and Shand had disappeared. Tex put his head up from the fo'c'sle.

"He wasn't content—they're away to look for the tail this time, so the shark'll be all complete when Mallaig wakes up. Come below for a cup of tea—they'll be hours yet."

But it was only twenty minutes before Shand's boat was

alongside us again, with the huge tail shining like patent leather across the bows, and our dragon was complete when Mallaig woke (photograph 12).

With the shark drawn up on Henderson's slipway we began our first, though superficial, inspection of the carcass, and sent a telegram to Hartley, the biologist. This was our first opportunity to examine a dead shark, and we began by taking measurements. The fish, a female, was twenty-five feet measured in a straight line over-all, eighteen feet in circumference, with a tail just over seven feet across. The head, from the tip of the nose to the foremost gill slit, was four and a half feet; the height of the dorsal fin was just under three. The jaws contained row upon row of tiny teeth, as small and as needle-pointed as a kitten's; and at the back of the mouth, where the gills opened, were the black broom-like gill rakers, which sift the plankton from the water as the shark swims with his mouth open, breathing and feeding by the same action (photograph 61).

The skin was as painful to handle as a hedgehog's, studded with almost invisible spines set in clusters, with the clear runnels between them that make a close-up photograph of a shark's skin reminiscent of an aerial view of a built-up area. These spines had a continuous direction, so that to pass one's hand down the length of the body was to feel no more than coarse emery paper; but a reverse movement, against the grain, would leave the hand raw and bleeding. Despite this heavy armour the skin was extensively scarred by parasites, both by copepods (photographs 70 and 71; they are giant editions of the "sea lice" found upon fresh-run salmon) and by lampreys, of which this particular shark had carried so large a specimen.

We began by trying to skin the carcass. A South American

manual, titled *Guide to Shark Fishing in the Caribbean*, had been my only available instructor, and when I reached the words "now turn the shark over" I realized that we were not going to get very much help from that quarter.

The skin itself was irregularly covered with the black mucous slime that I had several times seen and smelled on harpoons; immediately below the skin we found a thick white blubbery layer of connective tissue, and we made the mistake of trying to separate the skin from it, so that the first samples we sent away proved too thin for tanning. Below this white layer was the flesh, not much more than a foot thick on the flanks, for the whole body seemed little more than a case for the gigantic liver. The flesh alternated red and white, much as pork does, the red in the shark being muscular tissue; the liver, yellowish and slippery, weighed no less than twenty-two hundredweight.

By degrees a few hundred pounds of flesh were removed from the flanks; many of Mallaig's inhabitants took home a shark steak for experiment, and it was served that week in both hotels without protest from consumers. The shark being an elasmobranch, a boneless fish having only a cartilaginous spinal column and no ribs, the flesh was easily accessible once we had removed the skin, and some of the populace brought their own knives and helped themselves.

We did no more than uncover the vertebræ then, those great hunks of cartilage that afterwards littered the hillside behind the factory at Soay (photograph 65). They are amphiselous; that is, hour-glass shaped, with a hollow at each end, so that when put together there remains a cavity the size of a croquet ball between them.

We had gone back to sea to hunt for more sharks by the time

Hartley arrived. He performed protein tests on the flesh, vitamin assays of the liver oil and of the stomach content (which he found to be mainly *cannulus* and *temora*), and sent samples of the skin for tanning tests. There was still no equipment available for him to carry out any advanced work, but he did some simple dissections, and I remember that he sent me a description of the minute brain. Hartley never had the chance to do the detailed work of which he had dreamed, for he was recalled to the Admiralty the following spring, and it was not until 1947 that Dr. Harrison Matthews and Dr. H. W. Parker added that new chapter to the book of marine biology.

Ten days later I took the *Gannet* down the coast to the Treshnish Islands, to spend a week-end with Niall Rankin, who the following year became a subscriber to my experimental project. Twenty miles south of Mallaig we began to see fins (photograph 72) scattered over a wide area to the southward, and from there on to the Sound of Mull we were among more sharks than we had so far seen. There were many small fish, varying between ten and fifteen feet, but there were adults too, and the whole shoal seemed definitely to be travelling southward; for the next day, while we were on the Treshnish Islands, they had caught up with us, and there was none to be seen over the course we had followed the previous day from Ardnamurchan Point.

Frank Fraser Darling has written too exhaustively of Treshnish for me to add anything worth saying. The islands seem an ultimate concentration of seabird life; a teeming, myriad mass in perpetual activity, intent only upon the reproduction of their species. Here nature has run riot; not only the numbers but the variety of breeding species are astonishing, and on those often weird geological formations an ornithologist might spend a lifetime without reaching the end of exploration. Of the sounds, I remember best the crying of innumerable kittiwakes from the Harp Rock of Lunga, blending with the surge of the sea between it and the main cliff to make a diapason of sound like the peal of a great cathedral organ. It was in my ears all through the hot still afternoon of that idyllic day as we lay on the clifftop. We looked down upon the sharks cruising below us in the jewel-clear water; we watched the racing, gliding fulmars as they skimmed the rock wall; fished outraged puffins from their burrows; and in the evening, while Niall's children dived for coins thrown to the bottom of a sandy bay, the Atlantic seals that breed on Lunga came to stare inquisitively from a respectful distance.

We saw few sharks on the homeward journey and feared that a general southward migration had taken place and that there would be no more in the Hebrides that summer, but when we went to sea again the following week there were sharks near to Soay itself. We killed two more during the next week, and in those early days that represented success. The very small fish remained after the adults had gone, and we did not kill the last until mid-October.

IV

PREPARATION
Winter 1945–46

Our position at the end of the summer of 1945 was that we had caught a few specimen sharks and had discovered that practically every portion of the fish had commercial possibilities. We thought, erroneously, that we had overcome the catching difficulties. We had not touched the gigantic problem of transporting the carcass from killing ground to factory, the necessary equipment for which now made a formidable list. Yet at the very heart of our policy was a schism that must ultimately be held responsible for the failure of the venture. From the time that the project had first been conceived, my instinct had been to confine ourselves to the marketing of the liver oil, the value of which had been high in peacetime and had now practically doubled. I felt instinctively that the handling of these gigantic carcasses, their separation into components and the final reduction of the remnants—the head alone weighing a ton —to fish manure, would present insuperable problems. My advisers, however, accustomed to think in terms of handlable fish, and lacking the firsthand experience necessary to visualize the difficulty of moving or transporting even a small portion of a creature whose weight is measured in tons, were insistent that success could lie only in using every part of the fish. Nothing must be wasted, no possibility unexplored. I see it now as I saw it at first: an ivory-hunter in the deep Congo jungle, standing by the mountainous carcass from which he has cut out the tusks and pondering how he may capitalize the tons of flesh, the hide, the bones—all the apparent and gigantic waste. But so insistent were my advisers, and so apparently experienced in the mass handling of all that comes out of the sea, that I was won over completely to their point of view. The factory, not the ships, was to be the nerve centre—a nerve centre doomed from its inception to starvation from blocked arteries. I know now that the shark's liver is the elephant's ivory, and I felt then that nothing but a movable factory on the whaling-ship plan could ever make profitable the working of the carcass.

But by the end of the summer of 1945 the choice between these two widely divergent policies had been unwisely made, and we intended either to market or to explore no less than ten different products during the 1946 season: liver oil, liver residue, glue from membranes, frozen flesh, salted flesh, fish meal, dried fins, bone manure, plankton stomach contents, and glandular products.

It was clear that most of this processing must take place at sea if the factory was not to become choked, and my programme for 1946 therefore included the buying of a Tank Landing Craft Mark IV, for conversion to a small floating factory which could act either as parent or subsidiary to the shore factory. All this required more money; there was very little left, and the *Dove* also must be replaced by something more suitable and serviceable.

At this time the programme for 1946 represented an expenditure of a little over twelve thousand pounds. I had been lulled into a state of euphoria upon this question by apparently firsthand information from my intermediary that the necessary funds would be obtainable through the Scottish Development Council, whom I had approached earlier with the fullest details of the project. I was consistently encouraged in this belief until the autumn of 1945, when, feeling that six months was far too short a time for preparation, I tried to bring matters to a head. The president then told me that, whereas he was extremely interested in the project and anxious to help in any way possible, his Council was in possession of no funds whatsoever. He put me into touch with the Industrial and Commercial Finance Corporation, whose terms proved unattractive. The Secretary of State for Scotland and the Fishery Division of the Department of Agriculture, with both of whom I was in constant touch and who remained sympathetic and helpful in the cutting of red tape, advised me that under the existing organization there were no public funds that could be touched for the purpose. It was clear that the programme would require drastic modification.

I approached the heads of certain great concerns who might have had an interest in seeing the industry develop. Their attitude was in each case the same, expressed with the greatest clarity by the kindest and most human of them in the words, "My dear boy, if we were going in for a new industry like this, we should write off fifty thousand pounds and five years to experiment—you are expecting to make a profit on twelve thousand pounds and one year's experiment." This was wisdom, though I did not recognize it—in fact, it took three years and the partial misapplication of twenty thousand pounds to bring us tantalizingly within sight of success.

In November I drafted a revised scheme, based upon the bare minimum necessary for continuation, and circularized this draft to such of my friends as I thought might be interested. Nine of them responded with loans for continued experiment. Without their help at that critical moment this book could never have been written, nor the unique scientific work later carried out by Dr. Matthews and Dr. Parker achieved.

The modifications of our programme, such as cutting out the floating factory, reduced our capital requirements to a possible working figure of about seven thousand five hundred pounds.

Had our ideas remained unchanged from the spring of 1945, the factory would have been virtually finished by October. But the extra products which we now intended to market meant additions to the factory which were not, in fact, completed for another year.

Before Christmas I was fortunate enough to sell the *Dove* (which on a transport journey to Soay had narrowly escaped total wreckage when one of her engines had perished noisily with a connecting rod through the crankcase) to a man who had stepped straight from a Wild West film. He was the typical Hollywood "Western" character, with the whole background actually and factually behind him—gold rush, South American revolution—acting as buying agent for a combine who aimed at starting an Arctic fishing fleet, and who needed temporary stock pending the building of their new boats. He oozed goodwill and astronomical figures. I pocketed his cheque and said good-bye without sentiment to the *Dove*, thankful that she had found no resting place with me.

She got no farther than Loch Fyne, via the Crinan Canal, and in the spring was still lying in Ardrishaig with engine trouble. Later in the year I was told that she had struck a mine and sunk off Kintyre.

In November I had a meeting with the gunmaker and drew up a constructional programme with him for delivery by March 1. The programme included harpoons made this time specifically and undeviatingly to my own drawings, both for the Oerlikon gun and for a muzzle-loading whaling gun which I had bought and which was later to become our standard equipment. He had little doubt that he would be able to carry out the work to time. This relieved my mind of all major problems except the boats.

It was clear, after much discussion and detailed comparison, that the main catching craft should be an H.D.M.L. (Harbour Defence Motor Launch). These are much the same in appearance as the more familiar M.L.'s and M.T.B.'s, but have a round bilge construction and three-hundred-horsepower Diesel engines in place of the three-thousand-horsepower petrol engines driving the "hard-chine," or "stepped" hulls of the faster craft. We required the low flared foredeck common to both types, and the running costs of the H.D.M.L. were comparatively low. The main obstacle to acquiring an H.D.M.L. in the available time was that the craft were to be offered by auction by Small Craft Disposals under Admiralty Contracts Board. This meant that the ship for auction went to the highest "blind" offer, and that it could be lost for a matter of literally five shillings. A man who offered, say, four thousand pounds five shillings would secure the boat in preference to one who offered four thousand pounds, and in fact these tactics of offering a round sum capped with a few shillings or pounds were being rather freely employed at that time. After a long delay the Scottish Home Department came to my assistance and arranged for me to buy one by private treaty with the Admiralty. The delay, however, cost months of preparation, and the craft was not finally released until April 1946.

I remember that winter as one of endless frustration and delays, of business mails averaging forty letters a day, to be answered without a secretary, of the necessity for perpetual traveling. Even at this stage I felt myself in the position of a general trying to wage a war with a platoon and no staff. During all this time I was trying to investigate possibilities for keeping the factory working at something profitable during the off-season, together with other lines of development of the island which might hope to carry the Shark Fishery's experimental years. I investigated very thoroughly the possibilities of seaweed drying, of peat drying, of a lobster pond—in fact, of practically everything to which the position and character of the island lent themselves, but each in turn had ultimately to be rejected as unprofitable or requiring larger capital.

The whole island is made of an extremely fine building stone, varying from pink granite to hard purplish-red sandstone; besides, at the west end of the island, a paving-stone quarry on the seacliff, from which several streets in Liverpool were paved towards the end of the last century. At first sight stone-quarrying seemed a possible use for the boats during the winter months. Samples of the stone were sent to, and highly approved by, several large building firms, but this also had at length to be rejected as impracticable without great expenditure on quarrying machinery.

The New Year had passed without any certainty of obtaining the main catching craft we required. In January I assembled all the ropes and minor gear necessary for a season's work, and went to Birmingham for a firsthand report on progress from the gunmaker. There had, needless to say, been a great many difficulties. The purchase of a two-pounder gun had taken four months' argument with the War Office and the Ministry of Supply, and its conversion would not in any case be completed in time for the coming season. The supply date for the rest of the material was put back from March 1 to April 1. Privately I thought that this meant May; and, with no certain prospect of a boat, I began to wonder whether we should not make 1947, instead of 1946, our first working season.

But that winter had not yet fired its last round; it was, so to speak, still loaded.

In February I was informed by telegram that the factory had been struck by a cyclone. That night I went north from London, where I had been inspecting craft in the dock areas, and arrived at Soay late the following afternoon. It was as if I had stepped from one bombed dockland to another: the familiar rubble of scattered roofing, a hut that had been carried bodily across the harbour and deposited on the opposite side, the old crunch of corrugated iron and broken glass under foot. It had been with these as my surroundings that I had drawn the ring round Soay on the map in 1940.

The factory could scarcely have been caught at a more vulnerable stage of construction; and the cyclone, which in nearby localities had reached a hundred and twenty miles an hour, had handled much of it like a card castle. The spot estimate for repairs left me silent; moreover, we now had no boat to act as carrier.

The early months of that year were a nightmare, a dream in which one runs but does not move. Factory, boats, catching equipment—the completion of each seemed to retreat before me down the calendar. The *Gannet* was awaiting her turn for an engine overhaul in Mallaig, the new H.D.M.L. had not yet been finally released by the Admiralty and was still lying at a Clydeside dock. The factory seemed to progress at tortoise speed, labour was becoming difficult, and a note of caution had crept into the gunmaker's letters from Birmingham.

Our plans were very complete—all equipment and replacements were tabulated. On the catching side were the new H.D.M.L., renamed the *Sea Leopard*, to carry the breech-loading Oerlikon gun, and the *Gannet*, mounting a muzzle-loading whaling gun. The harpoon heads for each gun were to be the same, though for the Oerlikon the harpoon shaft was a tube fitting over the barrel, while the *Gannet*'s gun was to fire a short heavy harpoon on the end of an expendable wooden stick that fitted inside the barrel. The whaling gun was being "reproofed" for a determined safe charge of black powder, the Oerlikon was being repaired, and twenty harpoons were being made for each.

The minor parts of the catching equipment were the same for each boat—eighteen-foot steel rope traces to link the harpoons to the main playing rope, bulldog grips to fasten them, and heavy steel hawser slings to lasso and hold the shark's tail when it first appeared above the surface. We believed that the breaking strain of ordinary sisal rope would be too low for use as the main playing line, and we were equipping with nothing but costly yacht manila, on special permit.

The theoretical handling of a shark from the moment he was secured seemed, for the most part, simple. First he would be towed to the harbour. If it was low tide, the *Button* would put out from the factory to meet the *Sea Leopard*, so that the large boat would not have to cross the Soay harbour bar. The shark would be towed to the factory slipway—a steep railway leading down from the concrete cutting-up "stance" into the sea. The carcass would be floated on to a bogie-truck running on these rails, and hauled up the incline by a big steam winch. We anticipated a certain amount of difficulty in manœuvring the shark squarely onto the concrete. Once onto it, the first operation would be the skinning, for which I had ordered twelve pairs of armoured gloves to protect the workers' hands, as the mass of tiny spines would wear through the thickest leather gloves in a very few minutes.

Next the liver would be removed, cut up, and put into the barrels of the oil-extraction plant, to each of which led a steam pipe from the boiler. Then the fins and tail would be removed and placed in tanks for the extraction of glue liquor. The ver-tebræ would be set aside to dry for later shipment in bulk for manure. The flesh would be cut up and put into the icehouse, of which the concrete cutting-up stance was the roof. All the suitable residue would then go through a plant for conversion to fish meal. This plant, which, like most of the factory com-ponents, never fulfilled its function adequately, consisted of a mincer, a press, and an eighty-foot tunnel filled with trays mov-ing on rails, through which a fan blasted hot air from the boiler furnace.

Here was the ivory hunter commercializing the carcass in the jungle. I was a convert for the moment, and, like most con-verts, I was beyond reason. We had no separate carrying ship, and if any of these components were to break down, the catch-ers must leave their work and sail to the mainland for spare parts and replacements.

The *Sea Leopard* arrived from the Clyde via the Crinan Canal on April 20. I went on board her in Mallaig harbour with very different feelings from those with which I had greeted the *Dove* a year before. She had cost nearly four thousand pounds, and she seemed to be worth every penny of it. Lying among the fishing boats, she was like a greyhound among bulldogs, seventy feet long, sleek and graceful, and with Admiralty written in every line of her. The engine-room was amidships, below bridge and wheelhouse; it was twenty feet long, with a high deckhead, and the twin hundred-and-sixty-horsepower Gleniffer-Diesel engines gleamed with copper, chromium, and fresh paint. The crew's quarters were for'ard, and the afterpart of the ship contained the officers' wardroom, minute but with all the comfort and fine fittings of an expensive yacht. I went to live aboard her at once, and for two years I regarded that cabin, ten feet by ten, as both my office and my home.

It was another ten days before all the gun equipment had arrived from Birmingham and the bare essentials of the factory were ready for use. We repainted the *Sea Leopard* from stem to stern inside and out, and the *Gannet* began her engine overhaul.

We had got a crew together before the *Sea Leopard* arrived. Bruce was skipper, and had found for mate his brother-in-law, Dan MacGillivray. Dan (photograph 15) was a Skye man, and of the finest type the islands produce. He was in his late forties, a big, strong man with a smooth face, blue eyes, and hair turning prematurely silver. He had first gone to sea in a sailing schooner when he was seventeen, and had been at sea all his life but for five improbable years as boundary rider on an Australian sheep ranch. The rest of his time he had spent for the most part in big cargo steamers, and there seemed to be few corners of the world with which he had not at least a nodding acquaintance. He was always good company. He had kept the soft island speech; his voice was gentle, slow, and dignified, and his manners at all times perfect. Dan was a really efficient seaman, quick in decision and imperturbable, one of those men whose very presence inspires confidence. He would have had his Master's Ticket years before had it not been for a technically disqualifying degree of colour blindness.

The engineer was a temporary and stayed with us not much more than a month—time enough for him to run one engine dry of oil and cause costly damage. I suspected him of systematic thieving from my drink store, and was glad of the opportunity to dismiss him. Ship's cooks were ephemeral that season, and few lasted more than a fortnight.

Tex and a seventeen-year-old Soay boy, Neil Cameron (photograph 18), were to be regarded as the normal basis of the *Gannet*'s fishing crew whenever she was cast off from the *Sea Leopard*.

One morning Bruce popped his head into my cabin at dawn and said, "Come up on deck, Major, and see a great sight. The opposition's here."

"What opposition?"

"Watkins of Carradale. The whole fleet's in here to start the shark-fishing season. They came in during the night. Some nerve, to choose Mallaig."

I pulled on my trousers and went up the companionway. It was a full spring tide, and the *Sea Leopard*'s decks were well above the level of the pier. Berthed at the opposite side were three strange ring-net boats—the *Paragon*, the *Perseverance*, and the *Dusky Maid*—and a steam drifter—the *Gloaming*—carrying a big clumsy derrick amidships. Each of the ring-netters mounted a canvas-shrouded gun in her bows.

My first feeling was one of intense anger that Watkins had

forsaken Carradale and Loch Fyne, far to the southward, for what I had begun to regard as my own preserves. I knew enough by that time to be sure that the sharks that visited the Hebrides had certain favoured bays, and that if Watkins and I had equally good judgment and information service, our catchers would be in direct competition on the same fishing grounds. I looked up to the *Sea Leopard*'s bows to make sure that the worthless secret of the Oerlikon gun was as well guarded as his.

There was days' more work to be done on the *Gannet*'s engine, and the gun's full equipment had not yet arrived. The ring-netters were already reporting sharks in Loch Bracadale and Moonen Bay.

"He'll be at sea before we will."

"Aye, and he'll likely make straight for Moonen."

"I wish we could get a look at those guns."

"He'll keep them covered while we're around. They're converted two-pounders, by the shape of them."

Trouble started very soon. Tex, installed as skipper of the *Gannet*, was helping a marine engineer with her overhaul that afternoon when Watkins himself spoke from the pier. Tex came to me in a rage.

"He's got wooden harpoon sticks, and he wanted them bound with metal at the bottom, the same as ours, so the wood won't get blown to bits. He knows there's only one man in Mallaig could do it, and he was on the *Gannet*'s engines. Watkins said money was no object, and the b—— just dropped his tools and away back to his workshop. That's business."

"Did Watkins say anything else?"

"He asked in that sneering voice of his if we thought we'd catch a shark in that silly little boat. I told him that if I ran across him on the fishing grounds I'd let him have a harpoon through the boat's side."

Tex did not like Watkins, who later became my good friend.

Poor little *Gannet*—she had well cleared her name of that insult when, in 1949, battered and scarred by victorious struggles with nearly two hundred sharks, she returned to the lobster fishing for which she had been made. She was built by Henderson in Mallaig, and in fair tribute I doubt whether any other boat of her size could have survived those years.

Two days later I met Watkins myself. He came aboard the *Sea Leopard*, and eyed with surprise the comfort of my cabin and the office equipment of filing cabinets and typewriter. There was a carpet on the floor, a bookcase, a sofa, and a bunk; the paint was fresh and clean, and I was as pleased with it all as a self-made millionaire who realizes his dreams of luxury and magnificence.

The conversation circled as warily as two sniffing terriers, hackles up and a muted rumble in the throat. I said I thought it was a pity that he had chosen to base himself on Mallaig too.

"Well," he replied, "if there aren't enough sharks in the sea for both of us, we might as well both give up. It's the last part of the season that's best in Loch Fyne, and I'll be going back there in June or July."

Neither of us could extract much useful information from the other; each guarded the secrets of his difficulties and doubts. Remembering that Watkins was said to have struggled for a whole day the year before to lift a shark aboard the *Gloaming* with her derrick, I asked him how long the operation took.

"Oh, we reckon to have a shark aboard the *Gloaming* half an hour after harpooning, and the liver into the steam barrels in another half-hour. I could never waste time towing back to a shore factory—one's got to be able to deal with everything at sea."

This was uncomfortably near my original conviction. "Then what will you do with the carcass after the liver's out?"

"Dump it straight overboard."

I said I thought that a number of rotting carcasses would clear the rest of the sharks out of the area.

"It's possible, but not likely. If they do move on I can follow them." The missing words "and you can't" seemed as clear as if they had been spoken.

"It'll foul the water for herring—the herring men won't like it."

He brushed this aside. "Oh, we can dump a bit away from the herring grounds, in deeper water. I don't think they'll make a fuss."

I was full of resentment, and I thought, "They will, if I can do anything to encourage it."

He seemed to sense this and added, "There's no need for a spirit of cut-throat competition; the sea's big, and there's plenty of room for both of us. And if we do happen to be working the same area, I can sell you my carcasses cheap instead of dumping them."

Watkins' equipment was finished several days before all of ours had arrived from the south, and his boats sailed from Mallaig at six one evening. For the next few days we heard reports that his fleet lay every night in Loch Bracadale, but no one was able to tell me anything of his success or failure. We followed him, with all our equipment apparently to specification, on May 7.

Our hackles did not go down that season. Neither trusted the other an inch, and each crew vied with the other in the magnificence of their lies, forgotten failures, and multiplied successes, though Watkins and I became more frank with each other. When the crews met in Mallaig throughout the summer, they would ask casually where the other was sailing for the next day, and each would be immediately sure that there could be no sharks there. One Sunday late in May I met Watkins' skipper in Mallaig, and he asked where I was going on the morrow.

"Moonen Bay and the Skye shore," I replied, though we were sailing at midnight for Barra. "They're thick there."

"Aye, I've heard that. That's where we're going ourselves."

Very early the next morning we were stealing through a cold grey sea mist off the Barra coast when I made out the indistinct silhouette of the *Perseverance*'s bows and gun, running on a parallel course two hundred yards away.

V

MOONEN BAY
May 6–20, 1946

The 1946 season, which was to have been our first as a working fishery, became a year of trial and error, a gradual achievement of efficient technique by rejection and replacement of equipment. It was a season of fruitful experiment, though at the time I regarded it as a working failure rather than a necessary period of learning both for the catchers and the factory.

On May 17 I wrote in my diary:

Lord —— was right. Five years and £50,000 to experiment. I can afford neither. We have been at work for ten days, the first ten days of what was to have been our first trading season, and every day has revealed more of our ignorance and the inadequacy of our equipment. We should be at school, if there were a school to teach this new trade, not trying to earn money. Every day, almost every hour, teaches us a new lesson, but at a cost we cannot pay. I do not think our capital can carry us beyond this season. We must capitalize in experience every failure and disappointment—nothing now can prevent this summer being full of both.

We had sailed from Mallaig to Soay on the evening of May 6. We checked that the essential parts of the factory were ready for use, and a little before dawn, towing the *Gannet* behind us, we crossed the Soay harbour bar on a full tide and headed up the coast for Moonen Bay. As we crossed the mouth of

Loch Bracadale the grey sea mist was beginning to lift on the dawn breeze, and the fantastic three-hundred-foot rock spires of Macleod's Maidens showed partially unveiled right ahead of us. The mist furled up quickly, and when a little farther north we passed the single rock An Dhusgeir the early sun was covering the whole sea with light. We came up into Moonen Bay, the giant cliffs of the south headland towering above us, and a pair of golden eagles wheeling above them against a pale blue sky.

We ran on to a shark almost before we knew it, the fin shining high out of the water a stone's throw ahead. The gun was loaded and a harpoon already on the barrel. I reached it in time to have quite an easy shot, and missed—the harpoon passing over the shark's back with the same playful change of direction that I had seen a year before. A few minutes later I had a second shot, with exactly the same result.

We hove to and held a consultation. It was difficult to concentrate; we were in the middle of a big shoal, and they were all round us. Some, close inshore under the cliffs, were "breaching"—shooting clear out of the water, turning half over on their sides, and falling back on to the surface with a tremendous smash. It was like the report of a gun, and left the surface dotted with seething white patches. I wondered what speed the shark must reach below water to carry several tons clear of the sea. There were never more than one or two fish in sight at the same time, but it was obvious that the bay was full of them.

We put Bruce, Tex, and Neil Cameron aboard the *Gannet* and cast her off to try another shark with the whaling gun. From the *Sea Leopard* I watched them close alongside a big fish, and saw the shark go down with a great flurry, but they did not fire. I supposed them to have run too close to the shark for the depression of the gun, for the *Gannet*'s gunwale prevented the muzzle from going below forty degrees—a range of about seven feet. After a few minutes of, apparently, working on the gun they turned back to us. They had not been able to get the whaling gun to fire at all—the caps blew but not the main charge of powder. I wrestled with it for half an hour, drew the whole charge and reloaded, but for all the result I could get the black powder might have been coal dust.

There were still two sharks showing, so we rigged the harpoons onto the iron pipes, and the *Gannet* set off as a hand-harpooning boat again. I stayed on board the *Sea Leopard* and watched them with a growing despair. The harpoons were too bulky to be driven far in by hand; they had been designed to be propelled at very short range by a heavy charge of powder, and probably not even Foxy could have pushed them far into a shark.

During the next five hours the *Gannet* harpooned eight sharks but never managed to keep one for more than half an hour. Again and again I watched Bruce—who, though small and compact, was enormously strong—struggling to push the harpoon in deeper in the first moments after the shark had been struck. On one occasion he seemed to forget all sense of self-preservation, and I saw him still holding the pipe and thrusting fiercely while the tail seemed through my field glasses to be right over his head, bouncing him up and down on the *Gannet*'s foredeck like a marionette with the harpoon pipe for puppet string. After three hours I decided to take the *Sea Leopard* northward up the coast, so that I could at least find out the extent of this shoal and add to the slender data on the fish we were hunting.

I rounded the Neist Lighthouse point and turned north up

the coast of Skye. The wind was freshening, and round the point there was a very short, almost pure white sea, on which the *Sea Leopard* bucked and jolted sickeningly. The lighthouse men, whom I did not yet know, were watching both boats through telescopes, and I felt ashamed of their having seen so many failures.

I waited some time under the immense nine-hundred-foot cliffs of Poolteil without seeing a shark. There was a big whale cruising round the entrance of the bay, his glistening back giving the appearance of a great elliptical wheel revolving below the surface, the tiny recurved dorsal fin far back upon the visible circumference.

After half an hour I turned south again and headed for Moonen, and at two miles I could make out with the field glasses that the *Gannet* had a shark on in the choppy water off the lighthouse point. She was being towed slowly, and it looked as though a harpoon had really taken hold. I circled her and lay hove to a hundred yards off while they prepared to transfer the shark to the *Sea Leopard*, but in the middle of these preparations the rope went slack, and they hauled in a harpoon whose barbs had bent backward like a reversed umbrella.

We had barely got Bruce on board and the *Gannet* in tow when a freak gale blew up out of a clear sky. We headed into Moonen Bay and anchored under the cliffs. The force of the wind was terrific; it formed pockets and shrieked out at us from the cliff wall, turned and came howling back from the sea; it was ahead, astern, everywhere. The day was still bright and sunny, and the wind whipped the sea into a thousand spray whirls, each with a brilliant rainbow upon it. There was no time for big waves to form; the whole surface was a flying mass of thin crystal spray dashed in all directions by those hurricane gusts. One gust carried away the *Sea Leopard*'s galley chimney with a tremendous clatter, another lifted her dinghy from the deck and whirled it overboard.

We lay riding out the gale for the rest of the day, examining each of our failures in minutest detail. The first and main cause was of course the whaling gun's failure to fire at all, but Bruce had actually pushed the harpoons far enough in by hand for the barbs to engage, and in both cases they had bent backward as though made of putty. The weakness was at the curve, where the barb hinged into the harpoon shaft and the steel was thinnest. Bruce had harpooned one big male shark a few feet forward of the tail; the fish had paid no attention at all, apparently not even feeling that foot of steel in his back. He remained at the surface as though nothing had happened, then swam very slowly away about a fathom down in clear water. Only when a snarl in the rope caught the fair-lead and jerked on the harpoon did he feel the check and start running; then the barbs bent back easily and the harpoon pulled out.

That was point number one; the steel used by the gunmaker was too soft, and it would be a long time before new barbs could be made. None of us could find an explanation for the failure of the whaling gun. We decided to test the Oerlikon at targets again, and abandon it altogether if the harpoon deflection seemed consistent.

When the wind began to drop in the evening we sailed south into Loch Bracadale and lay the night at Port-na-long. We found Watkins' fleet anchored at the other side of the bay, with no sign of activity from the *Gloaming*'s boilers, and the *Perseverance* not among the catchers.

Bruce's gloom lifted for a moment, and he chuckled. "That'll be why they weren't in Moonen today. They'll be having some sort of trouble, and the *Perseverance* 'll be away to Mallaig to put it right."

It was a fine calm dawn the next morning, but we decided that we could not carry out tests with the Oerlikon gun under the inquisitive eyes of the opposition ships, so we sailed at first light for Soay and anchored in the east harbour. There we fired twenty shots with the Oerlikon at floating targets. It was clear to begin with that the water was deflecting the harpoons almost on impact, and after a dozen shots the tubular harpoons began to bulge under the pressure of the explosions, so that they stuck halfway up the barrel. It was one lesson learned; we never used that gun again.

We sailed at once for Mallaig, and all afternoon the telephone lines to Birmingham sizzled under my anger. I told the gun-maker of the total failure of all the equipment he had sent, useless guns and useless harpoons; that I had a full factory staff and a full crew to pay, overhead of a hundred and sixty pounds a week, and no apparent means of catching a shark. I arranged for him to buy another whaling gun to replace the Oerlikon on the *Sea Leopard*, and to make some harpoons with nickel-chrome steel barbs that would not bend. He could not promise these before the end of the season.

In a pretty despairing frame of mind I walked down the pier to the *Gannet* and went over the whaling gun with minute care. The system was that of an ordinary muzzle-loading gun on a very big scale—the powder charge being poured down the barrel from a measure. After that the wads are rammed on top of it, two hard felt discs of exactly the right diameter, pushed home with a ramrod. A wooden stick of the same length as the barrel slides down inside until its metal-bound end rests upon the wads. The top end of the stick, just showing at the muzzle, has a socket into which the harpoon itself fits. The charge of black powder is exploded by two caps struck by a big hammer, the caps fitting onto nozzles, which have connecting channels to the powder chambers.

This system sounds elementary, but there are many possible reasons for the charge failing to explode. The caps themselves may not fire, if the hammer-spring is too weak, or if some minute obstruction in the hinge prevents its striking with the spring's full force. The caps may be damp—it is extraordinarily difficult to keep things dry in a small boat at sea—or they may be duds, of which one may expect one or two in every box.

If the caps explode and the main charge does not, the connecting channel may be blocked, or the main charge may be damp with spray that has seeped down the barrel, or the grains of powder may be too coarse to be fired by the caps' explosion. To overcome this last difficulty it is usual to pour in a little fine-grained powder before the main charge.

Tex and I went over that gun millimetre by millimetre, as though we were looking for a mouse's fingerprints. We withdrew the wads and charge with a claw-like instrument made specially for the purpose, and cleaned out the chamber with swab after swab until the last came out as clean as it had gone in. We probed the connecting channels with fine wire, and blew down the barrel until we both had the wide black rings round our mouths that later became almost a hallmark of our trade. We tested the hammer-spring and lubricated its action; we dismantled the trigger mechanism and checked it for any possible fault; we fired cap after cap to make certain that we had not been sent a faulty lot. At the end of two hours there was nothing more left to examine, and we decided to fire a test shot.

"Let's wake Mallaig up," said Tex. "If we're not firing a harpoon we can put in a hell of a great charge of powder without any danger."

We loaded with as much care as we had cleaned the gun, and I think we put in something like twenty drams of powder. With the 1946 harpoons, which weighed about eight pounds, the gun was "proofed" for seven drams, with a recommendation that four or five would probably be enough.

"Ready? Let go!"

There was a roar like a cannon, and all Mallaig's gulls rose in a clamorous white canopy above the harbour. A big puff of grey smoke drifted away across the water, and there was a cheer from the decks of the *Sea Leopard* lying not far off. Startled heads popped from the hatches of the ring-net boats, some grinning and some churlish.

The relief was enormous; the whaling gun was not, after all, quite useless, and we felt that if it would fire even once in three tries we could catch enough sharks to keep the factory supplied.

"Let's take her outside the harbour and try again, this time with a harpoon stick."

We started the *Gannet*'s engine and took her half a mile out to sea. We reloaded with eight drams of powder, slid a harpoon stick into the barrel, and turned the gun seaward, pointing upward at an angle of thirty degrees. I jerked the trigger cord, and the little boat shuddered under the recoil as again the gun fired perfectly. The harpoon stick was invisible at first; then we saw it perhaps two hundred yards away and a hundred feet in the air, sailing outward and upward in a giant parabola. At about a quarter of a mile its trajectory seemed to flatten out about three hundred feet up; it sailed on, a tiny matchstick against the pale evening sky, and it was almost lost to sight when it began to slide down in a long arc to the sea.

Neither of us had been prepared for this, and we talked excitedly.

"How far was that?"

"Half a mile at least—you couldn't see it when it hit the water."

"More like a mile, I'd say, if you compare it with any bit of boat's rigging—after all, it's a yard long and seven inches round."

When I went to sleep in my cabin on the *Sea Leopard* that night I felt that the previous day was removed from the calendar. Success would begin tomorrow.

We sailed for Soay that night and lay at the factory pier during the short dark hours. At the very first light we crossed the harbour bar and set north for Moonen, with the *Gannet* in tow. Tex stayed aboard her, refusing to have breakfast until he had fired innumerable practice charges from the gun, which for some personal reason of his own he had now named "Sugan." Our progress up past Loch Brittle and Loch Bracadale in the dawn was like a royal naval procession as "Sugan" boomed again and again in our wake. Tex was satisfied at last, and we hove to a mile south of the Maidens to take him on board. He had had two misfires that he couldn't explain, but each time the gun went off with the same caps and charge on a second trial.

We were all keenly excited; we sat in the fo'c'sle, eating a second and a third breakfast, telling each other that there would be no more time to eat that day. The wireless threw the first sand upon our rekindled spirits. The voice came into the fo'c'sle on a sudden hush.

"Iceland, Faeroes, Shetland, Hebrides: moderate to fresh northwest wind, backing west, strong to gale later. Visibility good."

Tex said, "There'll be shelter in Moonen as long as there's north in the wind."

"Moonen'll be hopeless as soon as it starts to back into the west. We'd better make the most of our time and get going now."

We put Tex and Neil Cameron abroad the *Gannet* and sailed north towards the Maidens. The wind was just beginning to freshen, and tentacles of white mist about the steeple summits were writhing as they began to lift clear. A great dark bird was circling round the pinnacles, as big as an eagle but with an unfamiliar flight; I knew that it was no bird I had seen before. As I watched, it turned and flew up Loch Bracadale, gliding down in a long plane to alight on the water—a great skua.

We were a mile off the Maidens when we saw the first sharks. They were scattered over a wide arc to the north of us, seven of them steady at the surface, and others appearing with a flash of fin as they rose and submerged.

We took the *Gannet* to within a few hundred yards of the nearest fin, and Tex cast off the towing rope directly our propellers had stopped. We had constantly to bear in mind the danger of towing ropes or shark ropes fouling our screws. The *Gannet* swept on past us under her initial impetus, and in another second she was in gear and away at five knots.

We kept abreast and a little to seaward of her and watched as she made her first approach. The shark's course was erratic, and the *Gannet* failed time and again to follow it. We could hear Tex yelling a steady and stentorian stream of blasphemy to poor Neil at the tiller, and after twenty minutes without getting a possible shot Tex came back to us to ask for another man. It had irked me not to be at the gun myself, but the *Gannet* was Tex's charge, and it was no fault of his that my own gun on the *Sea Leopard* was useless. Here was my chance, and I went aboard to steer the *Gannet* myself with Bruce to work the engine.

The shark behaved less capriciously with me than it had when Neil was trying to follow it, and at the end of five minutes' manœuvring we were running down on him from astern, a trifle too fast, but with the certainty of a fair shot at point-blank range. The gun was at its maximum depression, and by chance the boat rolled a little on a wave at that moment, so that a slight extra push on the tiller brought the harpoon head within a yard of the shark's back. "Sugan" boomed, and the boat shuddered down her whole length as the harpoon went squarely home; even in the jumble of foam I could see the yard-long harpoon stick jutting from the shark's side. The tail was somewhere under the *Gannet*—the shark could not raise it to dive, and the tiller was jerked out of my hand as the rudder caught blow after blow from the tail. The harpoon stick jammed against the boat's side and snapped off short, then the rest of it became levered from the harpoon, and for a fraction of a second we had a clear view of the steel wire trace leading straight into the shark's side. The whole harpoon was inside him.

"He feels it!" yelled Tex. "He feels it!"

The shark got clear of the boat with a wrench and a long forward run that took seventy fathoms before we could check him with a half-turn on the hand winch. I had visions of those soft barbs gradually bending backward, and we handled him with infinite caution, letting him tow the *Gannet* for an hour, while the *Sea Leopard* kept close by, waiting to take over and haul him up.

While we were making the transfer I saw boats coming up from the south. There was no need for the field glasses—a drifter and three ring-netters heading up to Moonen could only mean Watkins.

A mile and a half to southward of us the *Gloaming* and the *Dusky Maid* turned inshore and lay hove-to a little to the north of the Maidens. The other two catchers headed straight on up to us at full speed, with quite a respectable bow wave.

We took the shark rope onto the *Sea Leopard*, and the transfer was complete when Watkins' boats were still half a mile south of us. I stayed on board myself and told Bruce to get away north into the bay and try to get another shark as quickly as he could before Watkins' catchers overhauled him.

But the *Perseverance* and the *Paragon* had the heels of the *Gannet* by several knots. I watched Bruce setting for a fin which was showing close in under the cliffs, but he was still more than a quarter of a mile from it when they passed him one on either side. For a moment, remembering Tex's temper, I thought there was going to be some ugly drama, but the *Gannet* altered course and steered out to sea again as soon as they were past. I watched them curiously; through the field glasses I was getting a good look at the guns and harpoons at last. They were, as Bruce had thought, converted two-pounders, and the harpoon heads showing at their muzzles looked monstrously clumsy.

The two boats kept abreast as though running a race until perhaps a hundred yards from the fish; then I saw signals exchanged between them, and the *Paragon* began to lose way and sheer off. The *Perseverance* seemed to run up on the shark at a tremendous speed, and the gunner had to alter his stance completely to get an alignment at all. There was a puff of very white smoke, several high spurts of spray, followed after a few seconds by the report of the gun, rolling in a long echo round the black cliffs.

There was a lot of activity on her deck, and two men ran to the starboard side and peered into the sea. There seemed to be some sort of altercation between them, and then I saw that the harpoon gunner was hauling in a slack rope. The harpoon came up on the end of it, and they all examined it critically.

I turned the field glasses onto the *Gannet*, now half a mile to the north of them, and saw Tex doing a sort of war dance on the deck and thumping Bruce on the back. Such a public failure by the *Perseverance*, while we had a shark visibly attached to the *Sea Leopard*, was the next best thing to shooting another himself.

We had to haul up our shark under the massed eyes of all Watkins' crew, and we decided to play for safety rather than show. We brought him up very slowly, and it was an hour before his tail broke the surface under the *Sea Leopard*'s bows. The *Gannet* was out of sight somewhere to the north of us, and the opposition catchers had followed her. We lassoed the shark's tail without very much difficulty, and then tried—for the first time under working conditions—to get a second steel hawser round the gills so that he could be made fast fore and aft alongside. It is a job that requires endless patience, and after forty minutes we were all out of temper. The promised westerly wind began to blow up then, and it was only when, as a result of it, the *Gannet* came back to us, that we were able to get the hawser into position by the combined efforts of both boats.

Bruce and Tex had not seen another shark, and the *Perseverance* and *Paragon* had gone on north up the Skye coast.

I shot the shark roughly between the eyes, where I knew the minute brain to be, with an eight-bore shotgun, and we set off for Soay, very cautiously, in case some unforeseen accident should rob us of this first success of the season. Even with the *Sea Leopard* the drag seemed very heavy, and after a mile we stopped to close the gaping jaws with another steel rope. That was another lesson we learned that day—to tow a shark nose foremost alongside the boat, secured by steel ropes round his tail, his gills, and his jaws. Small Admiralty craft like the *Sea Leopard* are of light construction, two layers of very thin mahogany placed diagonally one over the other, and we did not know how much strain they would stand. We were unwilling to risk more than five knots that day, so it took us six hours to get back to Soay, and it was dead low tide when we anchored outside the harbour bar at about eight in the evening. Not even a rowing-boat would get over the bar now; the level of water in the harbour was several feet higher than the outside sea, and a little river a few yards wide ran down over the exposed shingle and boulders.

We lay just outside the harbour, getting what shelter we could from a rising wind, and began experiments to inflate the dead shark with compressed air so that he would float easily onto the bogie-truck the next day. Big Diesel engines are started by compressed air, so we were able to lead a long rubber tube from the air compressor in the engine-room. To the end of the tube we fastened an instrument we had made in Mallaig, a hollow rod six feet long, sharpened at the tip and with a number of perforations for a foot above the point. We drove this into the side of the carcass, as low down as we could reach, and then turned on the compressed air. For a long time it seemed like trying to make a sieve hold water. The air came out at his gills, his vent, the harpoon hole, and the small wounds left by parasites; and as we tried more and more positions for the nozzle we left an even greater number of small escape holes. But gradually the air began to collect in the body cavity, and at last the carcass rolled over belly-upward, as we had expected, and floated with a few inches of the white underside clear of the water over the whole length.

We saw then that the fish was a female, and in the four years we hunted sharks we landed seven females for every one male. The male's external sexual organs are very apparent; two "claspers," each a yard long and about eight inches thick, and in clear water it was often possible to see them even before the shot was fired (photographs 10 and 60).

It was still slack tide, and we could not cross the bar to reach the factory, so we tied the shark to the shore and took advantage of the opportunity to paint on a smooth wall of rock a scale of depths in big white letters, so that when we approached the factory in future we should always be able to see at a glance the true depth of water over the bar. We went to bed feeling that we had done a good day's work.

The next morning I sent off the *Sea Leopard* and the *Gannet* at dawn and went ashore on Soay myself. I wanted to learn at first hand all the problems with which we had to deal at the factory and on the catching boats.

I watched from the shore forty feet above, while the factory foreman and a boy set out in the *Button* to bring the shark in.

It seemed a very incompetent piece of work. The boat was towing a carcass twice as big as herself, and they got into every possible kind of difficulty. The shark fouled the shore, the propeller, the bar; the boat wouldn't steer and went round in circles. There was a wonderful flow of entirely unacrimonious bad language—they had to shout to each other above the noise of the *Button*'s engine, but to us on shore the engine was practically inaudible and their voices stentorian. The boy was only fifteen, but he could have given a bargee points and left him flattened. All the monosyllables were used in turn, as nouns, adjectives, and adverbs in every conceivable permutation. It was nearly an hour before they had manœuvred the shark to the end of the slipway and secured him there to wait for the tide.

It was obvious to me for the first time that the rails did not stretch far enough into the sea to float a shark at anything but high spring tides. It had probably been plain to the factory staff for a long time, but no one had thought of mentioning it to me.

We lowered the bogie-truck down the rails and began to try to float the shark onto it at about noon. By two o'clock we were exhausted; by three we had the shark precariously balanced on the bogie and started the big steam winch to haul it up the rails. The man operating the winch could not see the shark and the bogie—a middleman had to stand at the edge of the concrete platform and relay signals. The bogie had not gone a yard up the rails before it was clear that the weight was lopsided and bound to overbalance, the carcass lying aslant across the truck and beginning to slide. The relay of the information took a second too long, and with a rumbling crash the bogie turned over onto its side, tipping its five-ton load into the shallow water. The shark lay between two rocks, in a horrible position for us to cut him up (photograph 51).

It was useless to wait for another tide and risk a repetition of that failure. We worked on the carcass all evening where it lay, with axes, saws, knives, and armoured gloves. The tide began to flow, and we were standing up to our waists in water when the *Gannet* came in about dusk, towing a very clean and beautifully marked fish of twenty-eight feet, well inflated and floating dead straight, belly upward.

We knocked off for half an hour while we listened to the story of Bruce's day. It was cold now that the sun had gone, and between water, blood, and liver oil we had not a dry inch among us.

Tex had got the shark early in the day and handed it over to the *Sea Leopard*; he had got another in the next half-hour, and had to wait to transfer it while the first was hauled up and secured for towing. The second shark was a big male and had fought savagely the whole way to the surface. When the *Sea Leopard* had winched him up to her bows the tail had kept on slashing to and fro so that there was never a clear moment to lasso it. They had tried for three-quarters of an hour, during which part of the *Gannet*'s gunwale had been torn off, before the steel trace broke and the shark went off with the whole harpoon inside him.

We kept on working till midnight on the first carcass. We got the liver into the barrels of the oil-extraction plant, the head into the experimental glue tanks, and a ton of flesh washed and iced in boxes. When at last I went on board the *Sea Leopard* I had had no food for more than thirty hours, and having struggled all day in that mountain of soft cold flesh and entrails, I felt that I never wanted to touch any again.

We were out at five-thirty in the morning to load while the tide was high. It was a Saturday; custom decreed that a Mallaig crew must be ashore in Mallaig by midday, and Soay decreed that no Soay man could sail before a minute after midnight on Sunday.

We sent the iced fish to sixteen firms who were going to try to market it. Samples for U.N.R.R.A. had to be sent to Philadelphia for test before any order could be confirmed.

It was a fretful week-end, with the knowledge that it was useless to go on catching sharks until the alterations to the slip-way were made. With the Mallaig contractor I planned its complete reconstruction, but he had not got the necessary wood, and telegrams to all the islands where it might be available produced negative replies. We had to start salvaging wood on Rhum again, while the sharks were there for the catching.

We called at Soay very early on Monday morning, with a miscellaneous cargo of small factory requirements, and dropped off the contractor, a joiner, and an engineer to try to get the fish-meal plant working. We could not send away any more iced flesh until the reports on the marketing of the first consignment were through.

Harris Bay was as full of timber as ever; the crew worked magnificently, and by three in the afternoon we had four bales floated out to the *Sea Leopard* to be taken aboard. There was a fresh breeze from the sea, and it was a hard job loading, the floating timber trying to break away from the boats the whole time. There were squalls of wind and rain as we came home, and we comforted ourselves by saying that it was no weather for catching sharks, anyway.

At the factory we found that the second shark had been a

repetition of the first; the bogie had derailed under the weight, and the carcass lay totally submerged. The morning's cargo had not been cleared off the pier, nor had the remains of the first fish been removed. The gulls had gathered in; they swarmed in a gabbling mass over the great heap of carrion, sat in gorged rows along the rooftop and the rocks, wheeled in kaleidoscopic patterns against the grey sky, and filled the whole harbour with sound.

It took all the week to rebuild the slip, and we had every kind of difficulty. There was disaffection among the factory staff, some of whom said they were employed only to cut up sharks; there were constant lists of new equipment to be fetched from Mallaig, fifteen miles away; there was a joiner who left on the steamer for more tools and did not return, and an engineer's mate who never turned up at all. An expert technician, sent out to produce an experimental sample of glue, spread poison round him like a upas tree. His job, he said in effect, was to advise, not to work; also he had a sore back, and wouldn't be a labourer for any man. The men we needed to rebuild the slip must be taken off to do the manual labour of his experiments. He was a nagger, a grumbler, and a hyper-trades-unionist, an arch enemy of development and experiment. I could barely keep my hands off his smug face as he prophesied our total failure.

I replied that it wasn't my crew's job to haul wood and build slips, nor mine, but no one made a fuss; all were, on the contrary, anxious to help; that I had synovitis of the right ankle, a duodenal ulcer, and an enlarged heart, and that he was likely to survive me.

I had a glimpse that week of the folly of building a factory upon a remote Hebridean island, though at that time I had not seen more than a very few of the problems involved. A year later I was writing:

No amount of equipment, no amount of capital expenditure, and no amount of good intentions will be of any avail in this business without a competent, experienced, and hard-working foreman-manager at the factory. This man would have to be on the spot during every working hour of the day. Paying island labour without direct and constant supervision is pouring money down the drain, and I know that outside people are only too easily infected with island fecklessness. The islanders of all the Hebrides have been going their own way for far too long to take easily to hard work and punctual hours, and have so far succeeded in Soay in taming to their own ways the various genuine hard workers who have come out to the factory. I consider this point to be of absolute and permanent importance. The foreman whom we eventually have, if we must remain shore-based instead of having a factory ship, must be capable of organizing labour which does not take kindly to organization, and must have an eye on every piece of work that is being done from morning till night.

The logic of selection was against my labour problems; there were hard workers and good men on Soay, but it followed that these were for the most part either already employed by Powrie at the salmon nets, or had made their own businesses in lobster fishing. With a few exceptions I tended to get the rejects, and the imported labour from Skye only swelled the numbers as dummy figures upon castle battlements did in the Middle Ages.

But the rebuilding of the slip was finished somehow that week, and when we sailed for Mallaig on Saturday morning there was at any rate nothing to stop us trying to catch sharks the next week. It was a strange spring; we woke that morning of May 18 to see the Cuillins covered by a fresh snowfall, and it began to snow again as we left the harbour, the flakes twisting slowly down into a desolation of grey sea.

It was like winter, too, when we left Mallaig for Moonen Bay before dawn on Monday morning. It blew hard from the north during the whole five hours' run, and there were heavy squalls of cold rain, so that more than once we wondered whether it was worth carrying on. But the sharks were there, and at the surface, a little north of An Dhusgeir, in a sea almost too big for us to follow them. We boarded the *Gannet* and set off, drenched through almost at once. The gun, which had been keeping dry in the fo'c'sle, took an interminable time to fit, and with the lurch and roll of the boat its eighty pounds of metal were the most unrelenting weight I have ever handled. Our hands were stiff and blue, the iron of the barrel was so cold to the touch that it seemed to sting, and once we almost lost the gun overboard. It was hopeless to try to keep the powder dry—baths of white spray came sluicing up over the bows and poured down over everything. It took half an hour to fit the gun to the steel plate on the *Gannet*'s deck, and the sea was rising the whole time, so that when at last we were ready we could see the sharks only when we heaved up on top of a wave. There were a lot of them, widely scattered, and behaving as we had never seen sharks do. Some seemed to be swimming at not less than six knots, the whole dorsal fins and a foot or two of back showing as they rode up on the waves, some with the whole upper part of the head clear of the water but no fin showing at all. For the first time I saw pairs swimming nose to tail and was able to identify the rear fish as a male.

It was difficult to follow anything in that sea; the waves were seven feet high in the runs of the swell, and more than once we

rammed a shark that we had been following, without any opportunity to fire the gun. The *Gannet* would climb up to the
crest of a wave that hid the target and come sliding down the
trough to bump a shark whose fin was no longer showing. Tex
had to hug the gun to stay on board.

At last we got a poor chance, and Tex, who knew as well as
I did that the powder was probably drenched by now, decided
to take it. It was a strange shot; nothing but the head of the
shark had been showing, and it was just beginning to be hidden
by an oncoming wave. The gun fired, the report sounding
muffled by the wind, and the *Gannet*'s bows lifted high on the
wave, so that we could see nothing. There was no splash from
the tail, and I was amazed to see the rope beginning to run from
the coil in the hold.

"He feels it! He feels it!"

And indeed he did more than feel it. The rope slowed up and
began to uncoil very sluggishly; Tex took the half-turn on the
winch, and on a sudden doubt began to haul in. There seemed
to be a dead weight on the other end, but one that he could
definitely lift a little with his full strength.

"I've killed the bastard! That's what I've done—he's dead!"

The *Sea Leopard*, whose crew had not heard the shot, had
been cruising round us at a distance, blowing her hooter to call
our attention to a shark astern of us. We beckoned and gesticu-
lated, and she came up to a cable's length from us and lay hove
to and rolling hideously. Watching her, I wondered what I
had left unsecured in my cabin.

It took an age to transfer the rope; we could not safely get
close enough to her to pass it by hand, and in the end we had to
throw the coil overboard with a net-buoy and wait at a respect-

ful distance for her to pick it up before we could cast off the shark's rope from the *Gannet*'s bows.

We waited, miserably wet and cold but triumphant, while the *Sea Leopard* winched in. The shark was practically dead. Tex's harpoon had penetrated between two of the vertebræ just behind the gills and entered the central nervous column, paralyzing the whole body. Had it not been for this the harpoon would never have held; the barbs had never had a chance to open, and the least struggle would have pulled it free.

The inertness of the shark's body made it even more difficult than usual to lasso the tail, and eventually it took the help of the *Gannet*, plunging perilously under the *Sea Leopard*'s leeside, to complete the job.

We towed the shark north into the shelter of Moonen Bay and tied the carcass to the lighthouse pier. There were no sharks showing in the comparatively calm water below the cliffs, so we carried on south to An Dhusgeir, where we had killed the first.

We had three more shots, but we had used our ration of luck for that day, and we did not get another fish. Tex and I made one clean miss each, and once the charge, fresh-loaded and dry, failed to explode. We went into Port-na-long for the night, and found Watkins' fleet, inexplicably lifeless, lying at the opposite side of the bay.

I heard later from Watkins that they had been having trouble with the lifting gear of the factory boat and were stuck in port until it could be repaired. He had news of sharks in the Clyde area and soon returned to his home fishing grounds.

The wind moderated during the night, and we lay late in Port-na-long next morning, waiting for the sea to go down.

We sailed out of Loch Bracadale and up to the Maidens at about eight—a bright gusty morning with a choppy sea of dark blue and silver. We had our troubles that day; we had unexplained misfires, at least one miss, and a harpoon whose barbs bent backward. The harpoons seemed to vary individually, some were strong and some were weak, and we were beginning to separate the sheep from the goats. But we killed three sharks before five o'clock in the afternoon, and the season was under way at last.

VI

LOCH SCAVAIG AND LOCH HOURN
May 20–June 2, 1946

We went on fishing Moonen Bay and the neighbouring coast for another fortnight, and we had killed twenty sharks before we shifted our fishing grounds. We came to know that stretch of coastline intimately, as every day we caught sharks in the few miles between Macleod's Maidens and Neist Lighthouse on the point which closes Moonen Bay to the north. We saw much else besides sharks: there were big and small whales, and the seals that at low tide would bask on An Dhusgeir, lying fat and sleepy in the sun while we passed within a hundred yards of them. There were the eagles who had their eyrie on the south cliff of Moonen, and when there were no sharks to be seen we would watch them wheeling in great arcs high above the precipice, or sweeping down to the eyrie, carrying food for the downy eaglets that we could occasionally make out through the field glasses. There were the fulmar colonies, where against the dark cliffs the birds would weave their intricate patterns of aerial ballet, skimming the rock wall with their wingtips, climbing, turning, and diving in endless symmetry. There were the cliffs themselves, huge and black; when the boat was close underneath them their headlands seemed to reel and swim against the driven clouds, as one has the illusion of movement in a stationary train when another moves out from the platform.

There was the sea itself. In the early morning it was sometimes bright and opaque like crumpled silver paper; sometimes colourless, and confused with big formless waves; sometimes bright blue, hard, and enamelled, without patina; sometimes pallid and translucent with dancing green lights showing in the banks of a long, unbreaking swell. I remember how when it was rough a big wave would smash right up over An Dhusgeir in a tumbling lather of foam, and as the wave receded rivers like pouring salt would stream from the rock's weed-covered shoulders. We had all kinds of weather during that fortnight, from sudden fierce squalls to days of mist and glass-calm when the surface was stippled with pinpricks of gentle rain.

The *Sea Leopard* became a background, a world, a life separated from any other that I had known. The cabin was my home, and I felt that I had never lived elsewhere. Though I could find my way blindfold over that ship now if she still existed, it is the sounds that I remember best of all. Just above my bunk was the ship's alarm, which we had agreed should be used only to signal sharks in sight or for extreme emergency, and it was only once used for the second reason in the *Sea Leopard*'s two years as a catcher. But almost every day it was sounded to signal that fins had been sighted from the bridge, and if I was asleep in my bunk it would scream, shrill and urgent, almost into my ear. When, later that season, we had a working gun on the *Sea Leopard*, it meant a race to reach it before a possible chance had been lost, and I would be out of my bunk and up the companionway before I was fully conscious, in any stage of undress, and once stark naked. We became really efficient in this speed of turn-out, and later I kept a submarine officer's quilted overalls beside my bunk, which I would pull on over my bare skin as I dashed for the companion-way. Even when all the crew had been asleep, we could have every man at his station and the gun fired within three minutes of the alarm's sounding. A harpoon and trace were kept permanently attached to three different coiled-down ropes, and as I ran up the deck a man would pass me a harpoon stick, a wad, and a measured powder charge through the window of the wheelhouse. These had to be stored in the warmth above the galley, so that the sticks should not warp or the powder become damp. We found the caps to be the most easily forgotten or mislaid, and I kept a box of them in each of the five pockets of the submarine suit.

I hear that alarm buzzer in my dreams sometimes now, and wake to find my legs twitching, like a dog who is chasing rabbits in his sleep.

Sounds that touch one's sleep are often the best remembered, imbedding themselves beneath the surface layers of consciousness and persisting when much that belongs only to the waking mind is forgotten. The night-long soft bump of a ship's fenders against the pier at which she is lying; the small caressing slap of wavelets against the boat's side a few inches away; the scuff of gulls' feet upon the deck above and their sad incessant crying; the raucous blare of the ship's hooter calling the crew aboard when we were ready to sail; the hum and vibration of the *Sea Leopard*'s engines starting up; Tex on the deck overhead cutting wads with a hammer; the rattle of the anchor chain—these and a hundred others seem not so much things remembered as part of a permanent existence to which I could return with no memory of intervening years.

The visual images remain clear but less precise in detail. There was, for example, some object that hung from the deckhead of my cabin; it would remain vertical when the boat rolled in a heavy sea, and by it I could judge the angle of the roll—because of the heavy armour on her superstructure it was sometimes as much as fifty degrees—but I cannot bring that hanging object into sharp enough focus to identify it. I see most of the cabin plainly: a sliding mahogany door at the forward end, a blue carpet, and under the side decks, where there was just headroom to sit down, a sofa and flap-sided table on the starboard side and a bunk on the port. At the stern end of the cabin was another door, leading through into a compartment with lavatory and wash basin on one side and a cool space for drink on the other. I find an inventory, made by Bruce at the end of the 1946 season, of the contents of the bookshelf—as ill assorted a list as one could imagine. Eliot's *East Coker* was, I remember, stained by the damp kiss of its green-covered neighbour, *Le Tannage des Peaux des Animaux Marins; Adamastor* rubbed shoulders with its avowed enemies, *The Condemned Playground* and *Enemies of Promise*, and next to them came Hogben's *Principles of Animal Biology*, Empson's *Seven Types of Ambiguity*, Huxley's *Evolution*, and *A History of the Whale Fisheries*. Technical works on ballistics and navigation alternated with tattered novels, of which Evelyn Waugh claimed seven out of twenty, and books whose foreign titles must have tried Bruce's patience to copy out.

The weeks became a routine, though a routine of uncertainty. We returned to Soay only when we had sharks to tow to the factory, and to Mallaig only on Saturday mornings to sail again at midnight on Sunday. These week-ends were for me the hardest work of all; the accumulated mail of the whole week would be awaiting me at the Mallaig office, a mail that was seldom less than a hundred business letters. Those of any urgency had to be answered before Sunday night, or wait for posting until we returned to Mallaig the next Saturday. Before midsummer the situation had become impossible, and I took a resident shorthand typist to live aboard the *Sea Leopard*. The alarm buzzer would shrill in the middle of a dictated sentence, and the papers and typewriter be sent flying as I raced for the companionway.

When I used to speak to others of this clerical aspect of the shark fishery, they would say, "But where does the paper work come in? What's it all about?"

It was a difficult question to answer in general terms, even at that time, still more difficult at this distance, so I have searched through the files for the mail of that third Saturday in May 1946. It has been a comparatively easy task, because, owing to the posting difficulties, we used to note the dates of receipt of each bulk mail.

There were a hundred and eighteen letters that morning. The largest category of them—forty-one—dealt with the products, established or possible, of the shark's carcass. There were letters from sixteen firms asking for quotations for flesh, iced, salted, and light-salted, with estimated bulk and supply dates. They requested approval for marketing under the name of "sail-fish." There was one from a great catering firm with whom we had been negotiating, saying that the amount of publicity which the project had received, together with the connotation of the word shark in the public mind, prevented them from confirming the huge order they had considered placing for flesh to be made into fishcakes. Three chemical firms wrote asking for vitamin assays of oil from various parts

of the body. Four tanning companies and one private individual
wrote for specimens of the skin, with conflicting instructions
as to how to prepare the sample. A Chinese wrote from Cairo
to inquire whether I was aware of the aphrodisiac value of the
sharks' fins, and offered a thousand pounds per ton for the
fibres in a dried state for export to the Far East. He, too, asked
for samples. A letter of more than two thousand words came
from the manager of a great firm, who said that whereas his
main interest lay in isinglass and the glue that might be obtainable from various parts of the fish, he would like to explore all
possibilities and redesign the factory if need be. He asked to
be allowed to visit Soay in the immediate future. A trout farmer
asked for samples of the plankton stomach contents, which
he thought might be used as fish food. An agent of an Asiatic
fishing company required specimens of teeth and bone, to be
made into souvenirs. Two oil buyers made competitive bids
for the liver oil from the whole season's catch. A long letter
from Davidson in Glasgow outlined an impossible programme
for dispatch of all the season's products, asking for immediate
comments so that his end could be organized accordingly.
Three more dealt with the possibilities of marketing medicinal
glandular products, one with fish manure, and the remaining
letters were vaguely enthusiastic, offering to buy almost anything.

But these forty-one that dealt with products were little more
than a third of the total mail. Of the remaining seventy-seven,
eleven were from government or official bodies. It is perhaps
difficult to remember now that there was a time of greater
rationing than the present day; practically everything that we
used required applications and permits—petrol, coal, oilskins,

and boots for the factory workers and the crew, Admiralty
permit for the special yacht manila ropes. The Inspector of
Factories must visit Soay, and transport must be arranged for
him; the Inverness County Council had not received up-to-date
copies of the ground plan; a boiler inspector must carry out a
separate inspection. I had sponsored appeals from the inhabitants of Soay for better communications, and there were letters
from three divisions of the Scottish Home Department pointing out the impossibility of our demands. Another was from
the Ministry of Agriculture and dealt with returns on the flock
of Shetland sheep I had imported into Soay. The last of this
batch was from the Ministry of Information, asking permission
to publish photographs in the Moscow paper *Britanski Soysnik*.

There were still sixty-six left in the pile. The top one was
from a crofter in the Orkneys to whom I had sent, in reply to
an urgent appeal, a small bottle of shark oil with which to dress
the fetlock of an ailing horse. He thanked me touchingly and
said that he was sending in return a small cheese under separate
cover. The next four were in response to inquiries that I had
made myself: an averaged-out meteorological report for the
months of June and July in the Hebrides over a thirteen-year
period; an analysis of the requirements of a firm of seaweed
buyers; the experience of someone who had tried to dry peat
commercially; and the possibilities of obtaining "Mulberry"
equipment (precast floating concrete piers used in the invasion
of the Continent) to afford greater facilities to the steamers
visiting Soay.

Sixty-one left. Twenty-two, mostly from obviously unsuitable people, seeking employment; fifteen from journalists,
press, and cinema companies, asking for cooperation in making

a feature. One from a crofter in Argyll who wanted to come and live on Soay. He started, somewhat disconcertingly, with the words "Dear Sir, Excuse me for interrupting you."

A memorandum from the contractor, confirming my suspicion that the factory icehouse was incapable of keeping ice, and suggesting that it should be converted to a salting tank. This was a serious blow.

Two letters asked for my autograph—a Rugby schoolboy and a Glasgow nurse, the latter suggesting that the hazards of shark fishing might call for a resident nurse on board. I visualized an intriguing hybrid between Florence Nightingale and Grace Darling.

One from an inhabitant of Soay—five hundred laborious words that must have taken an age to string and polish. It began: "As I am of the opinion that you are thinking that I have a grudge against you, I wish to state that such is not the case, rather the reverse, if you are out to improve conditions on this Forgotten Island, I shall be only too willing to give any support I can." It ended: "As I have told you already, you are only a stranger among the Soay people, but as time goes on you will learn the truth." He was right—as time went on I learned the truth.

One from a Skye factory worker: "I was most sorry to forsake your employment without telling you personally. I have the croft to look forward after. I was most pleasant in your service and hope to be with you in the next 1947 season."

The remainder were in answer to my printed circular, sent out during the winter to all likely points on the coast, asking for reports on the appearance of sharks. Three letters reported sharks from Barra, South Uist, and Lochmaddy. The last of the whole pile announced a small stranded whale on the north coast of Skye and offered to sell it to our factory. It turned out to be a very small basking shark and wasted a whole day of our time.

This was a fair sample mail for a week, though it contained fewer horrors and heartbreaks than many that I remember during that summer. From each batch of a hundred letters there were perhaps thirty that required immediate answer, and the fact that we were ashore only at week-ends made it impossible to deal with them by telephone.

I would sit typing in the Mallaig office all Saturday afternoon and Sunday, longing for my first hot bath for a week, and thinking with the Emperor Seth, "If I had one man of progress and culture whom I could trust." But no Basil Seal walked by my office window.

All this time we had seen few sharks close to Soay itself, and none in the Sound of Soay, which my earliest information had led me to believe was a favorite locality. On Friday, May 25, we lay late at the factory pier, because we had to discuss with the foreman the preparation of the week's products for carrying to Mallaig the following day. Instead of sailing for Moonen Bay before dawn, as had become our habit, we did not cross the harbour bar until nearly nine o'clock. It was a glorious morning, calm and sunny, with big white cumulus clouds high on a blue sky—the very first day of the intoxicating Hebridean summer. Tex and Neil were in the *Gannet*, towed astern of us; the rest of the crew had not yet breakfasted, so I took the *Sea Leopard*'s wheel from Bruce as soon as we were over the bar and turned north up the Sound of Soay without a glance at the sea astern of us. We had become accustomed to head straight for Moonen, and if I looked at anything that morning it was at the Soay shore, where the birch trees were clouded with the sweet intense green of bursting bud, and at the Cuillins, whose soaring summits were still laced with the drifts of the last spring snowfall. I had that strange too-fullness of the heart which the sensory sum of my surroundings would often bring, and Tex's shouting voice from the *Gannet* jolted me sharply into consciousness.

"Muldoan!" he was yelling from between cupped hands, "Muldoan!"

Tex had already adopted this fisherman's name for the sharks, though it was not until later that season that it became our common currency of warning, like the whaler's "Der er blàst!"

He was pointing back over the *Gannet*'s rudder, and there, a quarter of a mile astern of us, was not one fin, nor two, nor four, nor any number that was immediately recognizable, but a whole group in close formation. Every fish was showing his tail and dorsal fins high above the surface, and the pendulum swing of more than a dozen tails spread wide ripples over the calm blue water. Their progress was leisurely and infinitely impressive, leviathans strolling in the park on a spring morning.

For the man at the *Sea Leopard*'s wheel there were a number of things to be done at once when sharks were first sighted—sounding the ship's alarm, orders to the engine-room through the copper speaking tube, changing course, an immediate lookout for other fish, possibly nearer at hand. The *Sea Leopard*'s twin engines and propellers allowed her to turn on her axis like a polo pony, and the order "Stop starboard, full ahead port" brought her surging round to an opposite course with a cream of white foam under her bows, the *Gannet* following on the end of her towing rope like a cat swung by the tail. The alarm buzzer sounded thin and distant below decks, and by the time our new course was made good with "half ahead both" the crew were tumbling up on deck with their mouths full.

The sharks were making eastward into Loch Scavaig; we overhauled them quickly, and at two hundred yards we hove to and I went aboard the *Gannet* to steer for Tex. With all those fins showing—fourteen fish in that one group, and other parties showing far beyond them—the temptation was to "brown the covey," and it was difficult to remember that a fish must be singled out of the pack and approached with as much care as if he were alone—greater care, in fact, for the accidental bumping of one shark might make the whole shoal submerge.

It was the first time I had entered a tightly packed shoal, and it was the most extraordinary sensation. I chose a shark toward the rear of the party and tried to concentrate on him to the exclusion of the others. But when we were still ten yards from him, another, a little ahead and on our port side, changed direction to cross our bows, and I saw that if I held course we were bound to ram him before any came within the gun's arc of fire. I sheered off to starboard, to the accompaniment of a stream of invective from Tex, and the fish we had avoided submerged without much disturbance. I peered over the boat's side to see whether he had been alarmed. What I saw was comparable in its effect only to that first shark I had seen off Isle Ornsay Lighthouse two years before.

Down there in the clear water they were packed as tight as sardines, each barely allowing swimming room to the next, layer upon layer of them, huge grey shapes like a herd of submerged elephants, the farthest down dim and indistinct in the sea's dusk. A memory came back to me from childhood—Toomai and the elephants' dance, and the drawing of the great heaving mass of backs in the jungle clearing. My face must have showed my feelings; Neil, crouched at the engine and watching me for instructions, shouted, "What's up, Major? What do you see?" and his voice recalled me to the moment.

I looked up to see Tex's angry face turned back towards me. There were sharks all round him, and I was giving him just the sort of inefficient tiller work that used to make me mad when I was at the gun myself. I pulled myself together, chose another fin, and did my best to follow it. We were right in the middle of them now, and they were amazingly undisturbed. Close alongside where I was at the tiller, a huge bull fish swam lazily, almost brushing the boat's side; beyond him and below him were more and more—great yawning mouths and mammoth backs. I thought, "This is a shoal of fish—*fish*." The words were meaningless; they might equally well apply to mackerel or herring as to this herd of giants that seemed to belong to a different world and age.

Even if the boat had been unguided, Tex could not have avoided getting a shot sooner or later, and he got it in about thirty seconds. It was barely audible, for only the caps had gone off, but his voice was very audible for some minutes afterwards. We stopped the boat and forced fine powder down the nipples in front of the caps; while we were doing so the submerged rear half of the shoal went on passing below us in a seemingly endless procession.

The top layer was still at the surface a few hundred yards ahead of us when we were ready to go in again. This time I did not allow myself a glance down into the water as we came up astern of the fins. We made a normal approach, as if to a single shark. At the last moment I felt the boat bump on something solid below us; a second later "Sugan" had gone off with a roar and a lot of smoke, and only then did I look over the side. Neil had automatically taken the *Gannet* out of gear as soon as he heard the gun go off, so that the rope should not foul the propellers, but our forward way had brought the harpoon rope into my field of vision. I saw it leading down among the tightly packed sharks, running out steadily, then, as I watched, it changed direction, and in doing so it managed somehow to loop itself round the gills of another shark nearer to the surface. This fish dived too, his tail rising just to the waterline as he did so. At one moment the *Gannet* was floating high on a calm sea, at the next her bows were dipping almost to the gunwale under the pull of two big sharks sounding simultaneously. It might have been three or more, for all we could tell; it was difficult to see how any one fish in that pack could have a rope attached to him without gathering in his neighbours. I have not the slightest doubt that the *Gannet* would have gone under then if the rope had not cleared itself from the other fish. When it did so the boat bounded up again so freely that we all thought we had pulled out of the harpooned shark, but a second later there was the familiar steady strain, and a wood-hard rope leading vertically downwards from the boat's stem.

We were growing more confident now: we took a double turn on the winch almost as soon as the rope tightened; and handed the shark over to the *Sea Leopard* within ten minutes.

We set off in pursuit again. There were patches of sharks' fins showing all the way into Loch Scavaig (photograph 38); it was, as Dan said, a shark-fisher's dream. But as truly "Sugan" was a shark-fisher's nightmare. Again and again she misfired as we ran into the dense shoals, again and again she would fire perfectly if she was not aimed at a shark. It was mid-afternoon when the last fin disappeared below the surface, and we had killed four sharks, where with the technique evolved in later seasons we might well have had twenty.

Bruce had been experimenting with the first shark we handed over to the *Sea Leopard*. He had hauled the tail right inboard over the stern and towed him round and round at full speed to see if he could be killed outright by drowning, and the fish was seemingly lifeless by the time we had handed over our third shark. When the fishing was finished I had gone aboard the *Sea Leopard*, and Tex and Neil began to tow the catch singly over the harbour bar and into the factory; it was half-tide, and there was not enough water for the *Sea Leopard* to pass. They began with this apparently dead fish, and he showed no sign of activity when they secured him to the stern of the *Gannet*. Once inside the harbour they put the boat's nose into the shore at the first convenient rock close to the pier and pre-pared to tie the shark's rope to it. Neil jumped to the rock from the *Gannet*'s bows, and as soon as he was ashore Tex threw him the rope to which the shark's tail sling was attached. Neil was steadying himself to make the rope fast when he found himself holding with his bare hands to a rope at the other end of which was a very live shark weighing several tons and swim-ming firmly for the open sea. Tex saw what was happening and tried to get the rope back into the *Gannet*, but it was im-possible for one man to make it fast again without anyone at the engine controls. Neil got a turn of the rope round the rock, but he could not hold on, and for a time it seemed as though that first shark of the day, harpooned seven hours before, would swim away with the harpoon and the whole eighty fathoms of rope. At last Tex managed to bend a new rope on to the old, and while Neil slowed the passage of the last few fathoms, he secured this rope firmly to a rock. After that it was all the

Gannet could do to haul the shark back to shore again, and the factory workers told us afterwards that the fish was still alive when the tide left him high and dry the following morning.

But "alive" was a meaningless term where those carcasses were concerned. We found later that there was no way in which local muscular movement could be stopped quickly. If the brain was blown out with a shotgun it had no apparent effect; even the severing of the entire forepart of the head, from a point several inches behind the brain, sometimes produced no change for several hours. One Billingsgate firm to whom we sent samples of flesh wrote jocularly to say that they had asked for the sample to be fresh, not alive. The blocks of flesh, each no bigger than a large book, had been twitching in a disgusting way when the cases were opened in London, and had continued to do so for half a day afterwards.

We had a few more days' fishing at Moonen and the Dhusgeir before, in the last week of May, our temporary engineer allowed one of the *Sea Leopard*'s engines to run dry of oil, and we had to put back to Mallaig for repairs. We sailed again on June 1, a dirty dark day with a blustering northwest wind. There were a few sharks at the Dhusgeir, but they would not remain for long at the surface, and we never got a shot. The next day was a Sunday, and it was still blowing when we sailed from Mallaig at midnight. We had a visitor on board, one of the nine men who had subscribed to the season's experiment, and for the very first time that summer we saw no sharks at all. We made a long circuit—Dhusgeir, Canna, Rhum, Eigg—and had seen no fin in a hundred and twenty miles when we went into Canna harbour for the night. Next morning it was blowing a full southerly gale with lashing rain, and we did not sail until it began to moderate a little after noon. We returned to the Dhusgeir then; there was a heavy grey swell right up the Skye shore, and we saw nothing. It seemed that we were wasting time and fuel, and we went back to Mallaig in the evening.

We heard very soon after we berthed that the ring-net boats had seen sharks in Loch Hourn, a long and precipitous sea loch ten miles north of Mallaig. Loch Hourn—the word means "hell," and it is a grim-looking chasm at most times—was one of the few places that would be sheltered from that southerly gale, and to spend the next day there seemed preferable in any case to lying at Mallaig pier.

The weather was no better in the morning; there was a touch of west in the wind now, and speeding grey clouds above a leaden sea breaking white—as black a June morning as any of us had seen. Inside Loch Hourn it was dark but amazingly calm; all the noise and confusion were going on outside, and the loch was like an unused city alleyway at night, from which a man may watch the surge of crowds and traffic outside.

We cruised up and down Loch Hourn for the better part of the day without seeing a shark, and in the afternoon we landed on the bird rocks at the head of the loch. It was early evening when we decided to go back to Mallaig.

We towed the *Gannet* simply because we thought she would never make Mallaig against that head sea under her own steam, but as soon as we turned out of the shelter of Loch Hourn and into the Sound of Sleat it was obvious that we should have our work cut out. For an almost landlocked piece of water the savagery was amazing. It had been blowing a gale from the one open quarter for two days, and the tide was against the wind, so that the water was all white, troughs and crests alike. Tex and Neil were aboard the *Gannet*, towed by a four-inch-thick

rope which had been spliced into an eye at each end for quick-
ness of taking on and off when we were fishing. This towing
rope was a little short for a heavy sea, and the *Gannet* was in
difficulties from the start. The waves themselves were near
the limit of what she would stand—perhaps fifteen feet high,
and all breaking water.

But it was the towing rope that brought disaster. The *Sea
Leopard* would stagger up the face of a wave with the rope
slack, and as she lurched down the other side of it the rope
would slam taut with a wrench that seemed as if it must tear
the *Gannet* apart. The eye of the towing rope was fast to a
small hand winch in the *Gannet*'s stem—we never used this as
a winch, but it made a convenient bollard or cleat—and the
other end was on the bitts of the *Sea Leopard*'s square stern.

Bruce and Dan and I were on the bridge when I noticed Tex
gesticulating fiercely to us. I could see his mouth open and his
hands cupped, but no sound reached us above the roar of the
water and the wind shrieking through the *Sea Leopard*'s rigging. Tex, seeing the *Gannet*'s deck begin to lift and crack
under the force of those tremendous jerks, was yelling that he
was about to cast off. He crawled up the deck on his belly, and
from the *Sea Leopard* it looked touch and go whether he could
keep a grip. Those sudden violent tensions made it impossible
to lift the rope off by hand, and he was carrying between his
teeth one of the big skinning knives from the factory, to cut
through the rope in front of the winch.

Had he remained on his belly all might have been well, but
there was always some imp in Tex driving him to the spectacular and dramatic. The boat steadied for a moment in a trough,
and he swung his legs round till he sat astride the boat's nose
like a figurehead. In this position, with the winch behind his

buttocks, he took the knife from his teeth and began to cut. Neil was in the engine-room, following Tex's instructions to have the engine going and ready to make away for shelter. Dan was at the *Sea Leopard*'s stern, ready to haul up the cut rope and keep it free of the propellers.

At this moment the winch tore out of the *Gannet*'s deck. The *Sea Leopard* had reached the crest of a wave, while the *Gannet* wallowed on a slack rope in the trough; then the rope yanked taut again as the bigger boat slid down the wave's back. The *Gannet*'s deck gave way, and Tex was shot forward into the sea under her bows. From the *Sea Leopard* it looked as though he had gone completely. The *Gannet* was well down by the bows, and in the breaking water we could not see that one hand had never lost its grip of the stem post. His other hand came up, and he hauled himself vertically from the water to reboard—in this position he had his back to the *Sea Leopard* and his chest and belly pressed tight up the whole height of the *Gannet*'s stem, his head just level with her decks. It was an amazing recovery.

The *Gannet* was now on the crest of the same wave that had started the trouble, and she came charging down the slope towards our stern with Tex as a human battering ram on her bows. The effect was sickening; Dan was yelling to Tex to jump, but Tex could hear nothing above the noise of wind and water, and the *Gannet* was bearing down on us at terrifying speed. I think there were not more than ten feet between the two boats when Tex heard Dan's voice and looked round. His reaction was instantaneous; he kept his head and jumped at once, where many men would have clung on a second too long and been smashed. He disappeared in a turmoil of broken water, and the *Gannet*'s stem, to which he had been clinging, rammed the *Sea Leopard*'s stern squarely in the middle with a smash of splintering wood.

At that moment there was only one thing to be thankful for—the *Sea Leopard* had a watertight bulkhead between the stern locker and the after quarters, so that she herself was not disabled as a rescue boat.

Neil, who had been squatting at the *Gannet*'s engine at the moment of impact, hit his head a tremendous blow on the paraffin tank; he recovered himself to get a brief glimpse of Tex in the sea, and, thinking that the *Gannet* was wrecked, he began to strip off his oilskins in preparation for abandoning ship himself. Tex's head showed once or twice on the *Gannet*'s port quarter, and we were bawling at Neil, with his oilskin half over his head, to turn the boat and pick him up. It seemed minutes before he understood the real situation, but probably it was only seconds. He leaped back to the engine, only to find that the shock of collision had jammed the gear lever astern. He wrenched and kicked at it unavailingly, and then began to unship the *Gannet*'s mast to throw to Tex. But Tex was no longer in sight.

When Tex had jumped from the *Gannet* he had gone under with no fear of drowning but in terror of being cut in pieces by the *Sea Leopard*'s propellers. He let himself go down; it got dark very quickly, and he felt that he was in a great depth of water. Illogically his thought was for the shore nearly a mile away, not for the boats. He fought back for the surface, and his head hit something hard above him. He put his hands up and gripped the keel of a boat, felt his way along it, and recognized it as the *Gannet*. His legs were swung from under him by the wash of her propeller; he let go and came to the surface ten yards away. He had a blurred vision of Neil struggling with the gear lever before a big wave broke over him and pushed him under again. The next time he came up it seemed to him that he was in much the same position, and Neil was trying to unship the mast. He had a clear thought that if Neil were to stop the *Gannet*'s engine the boat would be lost, and he tried to shout this through the water that kept breaking over him. Then his big leather sea boots began to fill, and he went down again into the darkness, pressing and muffled. His oilskins, which had at first spread like a crinoline and given him buoyancy, were now waterlogged too, and he felt himself dragged down as by a great weight. He began to fight to get the boots off, but when he had kicked the second one free he was far down and in pitch darkness.

"Eventually," said Tex afterwards, "I did get them off, and I found I was in great order then altogether; I seemed to go shooting up like a damn rocket. There was a bit of my Balaclava that kept jamming up my mouth, but I got my teeth in it at last and ripped it away. I could see the *Sea Leopard* when I came up, but every damn one of you seemed to be looking the other way. She seemed a hell of a long way off, and I started to try to swim to her, but each wave began to break before I reached the top of it and tumbled me back down the slope. I got tired and turned my back on the sea and just waited for the *Sea Leopard* to spot me. I was still getting slapped under by the waves, and just when I saw that you had spotted me at last I took an extra heavy one on the head and I was right down under in the dark again. I was quite sure I was going to drown then—it wasn't frightening, and I could hear and see, only I was seeing big trees in a wind and hearing music and bells, bells forevermore."

While Tex was hearing his bells, Bruce was getting really

worried for the first time. He had kept a fair idea of where Tex was from momentary glimpses of head or arm, but Tex had been astern of the *Sea Leopard*, and she had to turn on an opposite course before we could do anything. By the time she was round, one engine full ahead and the other full astern, Tex had gone down for that last time and was listening to his bells, and it did not look as if he were going to come up again.

It seemed a very long time before he reappeared, and in that mad mass of breaking water it did not appear possible that we should reach him in time if he showed again. I felt, too, that he would come up under the boat's keel, and that we ourselves should be holding him under. But Bruce's judgment was perfect, and when at last the top of his head showed in the trough of a big wave, it was only a few yards from us on the port bow. A boat hook, a rope sling round his body, and he was hauled up on deck, not one minute too soon.

"You may think I was unconscious, Major, but I tell you I was madder than a wet hen. First I had it in my mind that it was all somebody's fault, and I wanted to find who it was and knock the guts out of him. Then I was tired out, had it, finished, and you and Dan were sitting on top of me pumping the water out of me like a fountain, when all I wanted was to be left alone and go to sleep. I could have killed the lot of you. And then someone was trying to make me drink whisky, and I didn't want the damn stuff. I knew it would make me sick, and it did."

We got Tex stripped and rubbed down and wrapped in blankets in the wheelhouse, and an hour later, when we were back in the shelter of Loch Hourn, the strains of his signature tune, played on the bagpipe chanter, were coming from the wheelhouse. Tex was indestructible.

VII

THE OUTER ISLANDS
June 1946

And I give you the sea and yet again the sea's
Tumultuous marble
With Thor's thunder or taking his ease akimbo
Lumbering torso, but fingertips a marvel
Of surgeon's accuracy.

It was June 10 before we were able to leave Mallaig again with
the repairs to both boats finished. We visited our old haunts of
Moonen Bay and An Dhusgeir, but the sharks had gone, and
the lighthouse crew told us that they had seen none for a week.
It was a fortnight since we had killed a fish, and between overhead and repairs we were some five hundred pounds poorer
than we should have been. It was fortunate that the film of
L. A. G. Strong's *The Brothers* was being made at Elgol, just
across Loch Scavaig, and I was able to make up a little lost way
by hiring out two small boats to the film company. I began to
understand why films made on location seem to require such
disproportionate capital, for I was gratuitously handed a considerable "advisory fee."

On June 12 I got a telegram from Uishenish Lighthouse on
South Uist: *Good number of sharks here. Davidson.* It was
the signal for us to shift our fishing grounds to the Outer Heb-

rides, and for the rest of that season we never again caught
sharks on the inner island shores. From then on, and for most
of the next season as well, we fished at the other side of the
Minch, and for the greater part of the time in three places
only—off Barra Sound, Uishenish Lighthouse, and Scalpay
Island in Harris. If there were sharks about at all, they were
almost always to be found in one of those three areas. Uishenish, and the bay of which the lighthouse rock forms the south
headland, locally called Shepherd's Bight, was the favourite of
them all, and we hunted sharks there days without number, so
that it is difficult for me now to separate one day from another.

The chief lighthouse-keeper, Davidson, became our friend
and ally; he kept us constantly supplied with information and
seemed to feel our failures and our successes as keenly as we did.

Uishenish has an appearance and a structure all its own. The
escarpment on which the lighthouse stands is of a dark rock
that looks strangely artificial, like the papier-mâché rock upon
which uncouth and faded sea fowl squat in the glass showcases
of museums and the halls of Victorian country houses. Every
ledge and projection is rounded and has the appearance of having been conscientiously dusted over with fine sand before
being painted with the appropriate blacks and greens, with here
and there a sparse tuft of self-consciously conventional herb-
age. In place of Moonen's eagles are pairs of peregrine falcons,
and instead of the fulmar colonies are caves full of rock doves
upon which the peregrines prey.

When we were short of food we would take the *Sea Leopard* as close in to the cave mouths as we dared and shoot at the
pigeons as they came catapulting out high overhead. I never
shot worse at anything in my life, and I remember long argu-
ments and paper calculations designed to prove that the cave

top from which the pigeons issued must really be out of range of the deck.

We reached Shepherd's Bight that first time in the middle of the afternoon, a warm day with a light variable wind, and there was not a shark in sight. We cruised round under the cliffs for half an hour, and went right up into the head of Loch Skipport, but not so much as a resting seabird broke the smooth surface of the water. We headed out of the Loch again, and as we turned south under the lighthouse headland I saw a figure waving its arms from the clifftop above us. We hove to and waited while Davidson made a wide detour, came scrambling down the steep grass slope to the north of the cliff, and hopped from rock to rock until he was at the water's edge.

We could not get the *Sea Leopard* quite close enough in to hear what he was saying, so we put off the *Gannet* to pick him up. He came aboard the *Sea Leopard* for the first of many times; I made the acquaintance of a friendly and delightful man, and in that and many other hours I began to learn about a lighthouse-keeper's life. It was usually a hereditary vocation, he said, a lighthouse-keeper's son often becoming a lighthouse-keeper himself. He told me of the naval standards of efficiency and cleanliness that were traditional; of single rock-island lighthouses where a man would do a two months' spell of duty followed by a month ashore; of mad lighthouse-keepers of fiction and of fact; of wrecks and disasters, and of much else that I have forgotten and wish that I could remember.

But then and at all times his first concern seemed to be for our success, and he gave a detailed report of the sharks he had watched during the past few days. They had appeared in the evening only, he said, an hour or two before dusk; first a single fin would show, then another, till within half an hour Loch

Skipport and the tide run off the lighthouse point would be full of them.

"I came down because I thought you were going to clear out when you didn't see any—just wait on and you'll see all you want. It was about eight when they came up last night, and I'm sure it'll be the same today."

It was, or very nearly. At seven-twenty the lookout on the *Sea Leopard*'s bridge spotted a fin rising half a mile to the north of us, and the ship's alarm burst into our conversation. We were lying in glass-calm water just inside Shepherd's Bight, and we made straight for that fin, but before we had covered half the distance I saw two more inshore, well up into the Bight. They began to come up all round us, and when we fired the first shot there were more than twenty in sight.

It was a slow and frustrating business; the *Sea Leopard* had no working gun, and once on the fishing grounds her only function was to take over and haul up with her big hand winch sharks that the *Gannet* had shot. According to our lights at that time we made a killing—we secured five sharks before they disappeared two hours later. "Sugan" performed all her tricks of misfire, two harpoons pulled out with their barbs bent backwards, and we lost a harpoon and shark with a broken trace. But we had three hundred pounds' worth of shark tied alongside the *Sea Leopard* when at last we went to anchor in the head of Loch Skipport.

The sunset was amazing, incredible; I am not sure whether it was beautiful or hideous, but it was outside any previous experience of mine. The whole dome of sky was a fierce blood-red from north to south and from east to west; across it lay a wild disorder of purple streamers bursting into flame-colour at their edges, and reflected in an almost unrippled sea. I have seen sunsets far north of the Arctic Circle which would last all night long, the sun circling the horizon in a kaleidoscope of fragmented jewel colours, but never before or since have I seen anything like the pure savagery of that evening sky at Uishen-ish.

Early the next morning we sailed for Soay, forty miles away, towing the five sharks to the factory. It was our first clear object lesson of the folly of a shore-based factory to which every kill, no matter how distant, must be towed. To make matters worse, we could not leave the *Gannet* to go on fishing in Loch Skipport, for neither boat was independent of the other. The *Sea Leopard* had no working gun, and the *Gannet* had no winch, and to kill a shark needed the cooperation of both. It was a Friday, and it would be Monday before we could be back on the fishing grounds.

We called at Soay in glorious weather the next day. The factory, which had been in a state of catalepsy for fifteen shark-less days, sprang into instant action, much as an old gentleman who has fallen asleep in his club armchair will pretend absorption in *The Times* leader from the very second his own snores awaken him. After we had got up steam on the factory boiler and hauled the first shark up to the concrete, I slipped away unobserved to walk over the hill. I was seeing too little of Soay, and there was much of that enchanted island that was to me still unexplored. I sat at the edge of a small hill loch; the foreground peat hags were full of waving white bog-cotton, and the loch itself was a sheet of flowering water lilies on a reflected blue sky. Behind rose the Cuillins, their jagged fierceness softened by the sun to pure beauty; soft cotton-wool clouds lay in the high corries, but the tops were bare and infinitely remote.

A single gannet was fishing in the Sound of Soay; he rose in a spiral, snow-white against the dark sea cliffs, and descended arrow-like, vertically, to strike a small splash from the surface of royal-blue glass.

I was absorbed in the future and the financial problems of my enterprise; I was so preoccupied that only gradually did I become aware of the immediate life about me. Everywhere were little dragonflies of a bright electric blue; they darted low over the surface of the water, soared and remained momentarily stationary, alighted gem-like and delicately poised upon the smooth jade-green of the water-lily leaves. One pair, joined in that brief embrace of the insect world which seems so pathetically improbable, alighted near me; there was a whirring rattle of wings, and they were swept away by a huge yellow-banded dragonfly. He circled me, carrying the struggling pair, and alighted upon a lily leaf close by. He did not finish his meal, but flew away, leaving them dead but still joined, a spot of colour suddenly robbed of meaning.

As, when I was a child at a preparatory school near Eastbourne, I used to lie on my back upon the Sussex Downs, so that I could see only the big white cloud galleons on a blue sky overhead, and with the bitterness of childish homesickness made believe that the chalk turf under me was the black peat of my own Galloway moorlands; so now, with an almost perverse desire for the full savour of the moment, I tried to make that Hebridean sky a backcloth to Blackwall in September 1940, and to imagine that just beyond the limit of vision at the corners of my eyes were the silver barrage balloons, that the sirens had just finished their warning, and that in a moment the guns would begin. So completely did I succeed that when I again turned my head and saw, instead of the dust and rubble of the docks, the hills and the heather and the sea, it was as though I saw Soay for the first time.

Every corner of the island was a fresh surprise to me then; each seemed more beautiful than the last, and there was much that I never had time to explore during my few years of ownership. When at last Soay was mine no longer, I came back one day to this same loch, and remembered my childish pride of possession. The Cuillins were in a different mood then; they looked black and terrible, a sea-girt Valhalla, and great grey curtains of rain swept them in towering procession. In our pretence these hills were the property of an individual human; if they could speak they could only be indifferent to this piece of urchin impudence, indifferent as they are to the ant-like figures who scramble over them for a moment of time. As an ephemeral insect is to us, so in a million times greater degree are we to the hills, and the realization brought the loss of my island into a fairer perspective to me, shamed into insignificance by all that endures and does not care for men.

We sailed from Mallaig at dawn on Monday morning, and because the sharks were only showing for so short a time in the evening at Uishenish, we decided to work up the North Uist coast during the daytime and return to Uishenish at night. By five o'clock we had seen nothing but one big shark jumping repeatedly close inshore at the Sound of Harris. We had waited for more than two hours for him to surface when Bruce saw fins a mile to the north of us. There was a fresh westerly breeze coming in through the open sound, and where the sharks were there was quite a respectable chop of water. The fins were often hidden in it, and the *Gannet* bucked and reared among the waves like a rodeo steer. The first time we got ourselves fairly placed for a shot, Tex peered down into the water and made a gesture of disdain.

"No good," he called. "It's a wee haggerty of a thing—about twelve feet long—not worth the powder."

There were about ten sharks altogether, as nearly as we could judge, and about half of them were "haggerties," but so little of the fins was showing that we could not tell the large from the small until we were right on top of them. We got two big fish in the first hour, then shot a "haggerty" by mistake, and finally, as the appearance of the fins became more and more irregular, another by intention, feeling that he was better than nothing. As a rule these small fish were much more alert and difficult to stalk than the adults, and later we learned, too, that their appearance on the surface was an ill omen, nearly always presaging the disappearance of the adults. This day, June 18, was no exception, and we had only one more day of plenty before another heartbreaking fortnight of inactivity.

We took our catch into Lochmaddy harbour, deciding to leave it tied to the pier next day and try the same spot again. I shaved and washed, put on my cleanest jersey, and went up to the hotel. It is a famous fishing hotel, and the evening conversation of the hotel guests—serious fishermen who have come hundreds of miles for their sport—is usually of their day's catches of loch trout and of sea trout. I must have achieved some semblance of respectability, for one conventionally tweeded and white-moustached figure asked me with genial condescension whether I had been fishing that day. I replied respectfully that I had.

"Any luck?" he asked.

"Yes," I said. "I got four, two large and two small."

Up to that moment I had somehow assumed that he knew our quarry; the coastal antics of the *Sea Leopard* seemed to have been widely observed in the Hebrides, and we would usually find when we berthed in some strange harbour that everybody there already knew the minutest details of our project. But his next question showed that he thought me a trout fisherman.

"What did your biggest weigh?"

A devil entered into me; I could not resist it. "He's not weighed yet," I said, "but I think he'd be about six thousand pounds."

The joke fell a little flat, for my questioner was too outraged to give me an opportunity to explain, taking refuge, I think, in "residents only" quarters. I referred to this incident in a broadcast six months later, and soon afterwards I received a letter from the man himself, pointing out stiffly and unnecessarily that he had not supposed me to have been fishing in the sea.

The log entry for the next day reads:

Wind light variable. Dull, heavy rain in p.m. Lochmaddy to Loch Shell. Fishing under Brollem Light-gun. No. sighted 30–40. Numerous attempted kills. Kills 2. Two misses and 3 harpoons pulled out. Fish wild and strong. Lay night at Lochmaddy.

I remember that day vividly, the rain pelting down into water as quiet as a mill pond and sharks everywhere. In some places where fog is especially common an automatic gun is substituted for a light, and even in the clearest summer weather the gun fires all through the twenty-four hours. That light-gun on the cliff banged away every few minutes, and "Sugan" answered from the water—it was like a battle in progress.

Some of the sharks were in the bays, right in under the rocks;

they were difficult to follow, and because there was not enough depth of water for them to dive when harpooned, they gave us every kind of fireworks. I remember one in particular, in a bight just south of the light-gun. He had his head diagonally in towards the rocks and not much more than ten yards off them. I was steering the *Gannet* for Tex; the fish was quiet and steady, and it was an easy approach from astern. When Tex fired—and, almost simultaneously, the light-gun answered— the shark was between us and the cliff. As the harpoon went home the fish seemed to lose his bearings and charged straight ahead towards the shore. Tex saw that the boat might be run slam into the rock by that first rush and began to pay out slack rope for all he was worth. The shark must have bumped his nose on the rock before he realized that he was not heading for the open sea; then he turned and came back, not half a fathom down, still between us and the cliff. I should like those who believe that the basking shark is invariably a slow mover to have seen that fish. As it may seem that a driven grouse is flying his fastest, until an eagle appears and he doubles his previous speed, so, I believe, a shark in deep water is rarely exerting himself as he does when he panics on finding that he has not enough depth to sound. That fish came streaking past us on an opposite course, almost too fast for the eye to follow. Tex was still heaving slack overboard, but he could not pay it out quickly enough. The shark reached the limit of the rope just as he was getting into deeper water, and for a moment it seemed that the *Gannet* must capsize. Her bows were being pulled downward and astern with tremendous force, and they dipped almost to the water; then she was yanked round, pivoting on her keel and with the port gunwale almost awash as she headed for the open sea. The shark had the whole length of the coil—

I think it was a short one that had already been broken—and it was more than an hour before we could recover enough rope to transfer him to the *Sea Leopard*.

The rain kept plugging down and soaked everything; it hammered on our oilskins in endless tattoo; it found its way into every corner of the *Gannet;* it seeped down the barrel of the gun so that the powder became damp and we had misfire after misfire, and after each one the light-gun on the shore would fire as though in derision.

This shoal of sharks behaved differently from the Uishenish fish, and by five in the afternoon there was not a fin showing. We headed back for Lochmaddy, with a big shark strung fore and aft on each side of the *Sea Leopard*, and spent the evening reshuffling our catch to be towed back to Soay. Altogether we had four large and two small fish to transport the fifty miles back to the factory. The *Sea Leopard* was more than seventy feet long, so we were able to tow two large fish, one behind the other, on each side, and after some hesitation we decided to lift the two "haggerties" aboard the *Gannet*. We slung them up from the water with the *Sea Leopard*'s hand derrick, and, "haggerties" though they were, they weighed not much less than a ton each and were difficult enough to handle. They were not worth the killing; each had barely a barrel of liver in him, we had as yet no established market for the flesh, and it was clearly a bad long-term policy to kill immature fish.

The rain had stopped, and a pale golden sunset was beginning when we had finished; the air was full of the desolate music that is Lochmaddy's own sound of summer, the calling of the red-throated divers as they fly inland from the sea. When the sun had almost set, laying a shivering pencil of light across the surface of the harbour, the water was yellow, with shifting purple shadows against the dark background of the land, and on its almost unruffled surface floated mosaic patterns of white gulls, crying continuously.

We carried our catch to Soay next day. The factory was making heavy weather of our last killing; there were still three inflated sharks in the now scum-covered harbour, the concrete was swimming in oil and blood and littered with gigantic piles of offal. At one corner someone had accidentally slit a shark's stomach, and about a ton of pink semi-liquid plankton was adding to the confusion. Rain during the past two days was given as the reason for lack of progress, a reason with which I grew very familiar during that and the following season.

The fragments of offal in the harbour had attracted quantities of scavenger fish, and I remember a huge conger eel, not less than six feet long, weaving his way lazily between the uprights of the pier. The gulls were in thousands, and among them was a rarity, a mature glaucous gull, asleep on the roof ridge of the storehouse. On the heather slope behind the factory building were scattered over a wide area the cartilaginous vertebræ, drying for future use as fish manure (photograph 65), and among them scuttled and bobbed innumerable pied wagtails, hunting for the fly-grubs that hatched in the crevices of the cartilage. Many of these must have come over from Skye, for there was not a fraction of that number resident on Soay.

At Soay we picked up a second visitor to the *Sea Leopard*, a friend whom I had not seen for some years, and who was on leave from the Far East. He must bitterly have regretted his visit, for it had precisely the effect that our last guest had had: we saw only one shark during the whole week. I was the worst possible host; I was by now really worried about finances and the factory's failures, and as the days went by I grew more and more morose and shorter in temper. After he had left I sent him some sort of apology, but I never saw or heard from him again, and the actuality of his leave must have been very different from his anticipation.

The one shark that we did see during his stay was a piece of pure comedy, had I been able to see it as such. It was off Eillean Glás Lighthouse in Scalpay. We had been cruising for five days without sighting a fin, and the *Gannet* was being towed with no crew aboard her.

A big shark surfaced not more than thirty yards away on the starboard bow and on the same course as ourselves. It was the first basking shark our guest had ever seen, and appropriately enough he saw it first. There was a tremendous bustle and confusion as the five days of frustration found outlet in action. The *Sea Leopard* hove to and began to haul in the *Gannet*, but before we were properly aboard her the shark had turned and was swimming straight for us. He came right up to the gun while we were still putting the caps onto the nipples, his huge gaping mouth not a yard from the harpoon head. He had passed under the boat by the time we were ready. Then he circled the *Gannet* again and swam straight up to the gun. We were prepared for him this time; it was a shot at point-blank range into the open mouth, the first we had ever had. The gun misfired. The caps blew, but not the charge, and the shark swam leisurely away. We fitted two more caps, and inside three minutes we had another perfect chance, with exactly the same result. The shark seemed to get bored and submerged gently. We could not see anything funny about it; we were all practically in tears of rage and frustration, and the *Gannet* echoed with every known and unknown obscenity in English and Gaelic. We decided to test the gun once more before withdrawing the charge and reloading. We took out the harpoon, put on fresh caps, and fired into the air. It went off with a roar that brought out the lighthouse crew with telescopes. The shark did not resurface, and after waiting two hours we abandoned him. What a memory of shark hunting our guest must have taken away with him!

These inexplicable misfires dogged us periodically for two whole seasons and were finally cured only by converting the actions of the guns to fire sizable blank cartridges in place of the caps. I felt, and still feel, that the gunmaker responsible should have found that solution earlier.

We were no more fortunate when our visitor had left. Only one ring-net boat reported seeing sharks, at Canna. The weather was impossible, a strong southerly wind blowing from a bleak sky, and we spent two days prowling round the Canna cliffs without seeing anything. A telegram to Davidson at Uishenish produced the reply: *No sharks since you were last here*, and when the wind began to shift a point or two into the west we set off for the Barra shore. When we had crossed the Minch the wind was backing into the south again and near gale force; there was nothing we could do but put into Castlebay harbour and wait. And wait we did, for three days of unbroken gale, reaching hurricane force in gusts.

Castlebay has always seemed to me a grim place, as stark and depressing as a northern mining village, and I had never been there long enough to acquire friends, as we had in other ports, who would perhaps have led me to see it with a different eye. When I summon a mental picture of Castlebay the colour is all grey—grey hills, grey houses and sea-worn pier, grey sea that laps the rock on which ruined Kismul Castle, from which the village takes its name, is built on a jutting rock-island in mid-harbour, a rock so small that at high tide the sea beats upon the very walls of the Castle.

On the second day I walked across the island to watch the seas coming in on the Atlantic side. In comparative shelter I climbed the eastern side of the low watershed, past straggling crofts and out into open country. Some of the crofts were the smallest and most primitive I had seen, dry-stone walls leaning dourly inwards where the heavy stones had begun to settle, and the grass springing green and luxuriant from the edges of the thatch. But I noticed that most of the tiny windows held flowers and a glimpse of spotless curtain. Besides these there were houses of the age of invention and culture, with roofs of the ubiquitous red corrugated iron. The low ground was marshy and yellow with flag iris; higher up was nothing but the sparse heather, through which the rock showed every few feet and had here and there claimed an acre or more for its own. The wind blew wet and gusty over everything, and gulls hung tensely upon it, poising and turning over the small cultivated patches.

When I reached the top of the watershed the wind hit me with bewildering force. It lifted the skirt of my mackintosh and slapped me viciously across the face with it, whirled me round, and, while I was trying to regain my balance, rushed me back a dozen steps the way I had come. Between the gusts it was blowing a full gale; during the gusts it was mad, irresistible. Even through the sound of it I could hear the steady boom and roar of the great Atlantic seas breaking a mile away. As I topped the ridge it was there before me, a wide bay of pure white sand with rock and reef at each side and high cliff headlands to the north and south. At the white sands the rollers came in massive and unhurrying, huge plumes streaming from their shoulders, and as I looked to the northern headland the whole three hundred feet of cliff was suddenly blotted out by a fountain of white water which shot up from its foot and seemed to subside as though on a slow-motion film. When I reached the edge of the white sand, a few hundred yards from the tide, the wind was whirling it up into a sandstorm, smoke-like spirals careering along the beach like ghosts. Every crevice of my clothing was instantly full of sand.

I reached the rocks at the side of the bay, bent double, and with eyes shut. Here the noise of the sea was stupefying. Over the reefs and isolated rocks a little to the north, the sea had lost all form and architecture; here was no articulated procession of rollers, but a tumbling, leaping, white confusion, out of which shot up every now and again a column like a single vigorous puff from a big steam engine. Farther off the rollers were in vast and orderly ranks, thirty feet high and lead-grey, with the white spume snarling back from them—the gradual, terrible piling up of force before each crest curled over and the whole ridge of water came roaring down in collapse. I turned to look at the big cliff to the north and watched as again and again it was hidden by a mighty white mushroom of close-packed spray.

I tried to take photographs, but I had to cling to the rocks with one hand to avoid being blown away. Spray drenched the lens and the reflex; the empty leather case of a telephoto lens disappeared at fifty miles an hour. There was, in any case, nothing to photograph; the waves were grey, and when they rose high above the sea line they were grey against a grey sky; no combination of lens and filter could reproduce what the eye saw.

Of all natural subjects, the sea is the most difficult to record photographically. When an apparently satisfactory result is achieved, it is a tiny fraction of the sight that produced the emotional reaction; it is as if one were to record one stone of a mosaic and by it hope to recall the whole intricate pattern, or by the writing of one note to convey a symphony. I have taken a very few photographs of waves which have in themselves some form and design, but in none can I recapture the least feeling of the sea's mood at the time, or of my response to it. And it is as difficult to describe as to record by any other means.

> And so each venture
> Is a new beginning, a raid on the inarticulate
> With shabby equipment always deteriorating
> In the general mess of imprecision of feeling,
> Undisciplined squads of emotion. And what there is to conquer
> By strength and submission has already been discovered
> Once or twice, or several times, by men whom one cannot hope
> To emulate. . . .

When first I read that I drew from it a great deal of comfort, until I reached the last lines of the same poem, so completely giving it the lie and replacing comfort with the undisciplined squads of emotion:

> Through the dark cold and the empty desolation,
> The wave cry, the wind cry, the vast waters
> Of the petrel and the porpoise.   In my end is my beginning.

Surprisingly great sea imagery occurs sometimes in works of a very much lighter character:

> Perched on my city office stool
> I watched with envy while a cool
> And lucky carter handled ice. . .
> And I was wandering in a trice

Far from the gray and grimy heat
Of that intolerable street
O'er sapphire berg and emerald floe,
Beneath the still, cold ruby glow
Of everlasting Polar night,
Bewildered by the green half-light,
Until I stumbled unawares
Upon a creek where big white bears
Plunged headlong down with flourished heels
And floundered after shining seals
Through shivering seas of blinding blue.

I was beginning to be afraid of the sea; that is to say, my landsman's fear of it was just beginning to be tinged with a seaman's fear, and with a faint, very incomplete concept of its almost illimitable power.

That evening, as we sat in the *Sea Leopard*'s fo'c'sle, I remember asking Dan, who had sailed all the oceans of the world, what was the biggest sea he had ever seen.

He thought for a moment, and smiled, as though pleased at some recollection; his eyes were remote. I knew his tremendously vivid visual memory, and that he was seeing some great sea of the past careering by on a mental cinema screen.

"Oh, well, well," he said at length; "oh, well, well, well."

This was a characteristic preface, especially when some experience or idea was too large for easy translation into words.

"I've seen waves so big that I wouldn't like to be looking at them," he went on; "I would just turn my back on them and pretend to myself that they weren't there. You'll find there's many a deep-sea man who's had the same experience—you just can't be standing there and watch those things coming up, getting bigger and bigger every moment, unless you've got a job to do. If you think of them the height of big trees, and you

right in underneath them, you'll maybe understand my meaning."

"When you say a big tree, Dan, what actual height do you
mean?"

He thought again for a long moment; then he said, "Well,
Major, this will give you some idea. It was in 1923. I was in a
ship of more than twelve thousand tons, a big cargo boat, and
we were crossing the Atlantic. There was a westerly gale; it
had been blowing for days and days, and we were ploughing
into a head sea like a moving mountain range. The danger in
a big head sea is when you're climbing up the face of it—if it
starts to break, to curl over, when the ship's nearly at the top
of it, she can be put right under by solid water. Well, I was
in the crow's nest of this ship at the time I remember, and that
would be more than fifty feet above sea level if it was calm.
Well, I'm telling you, Major, the top of that wave was higher
than I was in the crow's nest. It began to break a little before
it reached the ship, and the whole foredeck of the ship below
me just disappeared under the sea. I would be twenty-five or
thirty feet above the decks, but the crow's nest—like a big open
barrel—was filled right up with water. Not spray, you'll
understand, but pure green sea. Maybe that's just words to you,
Major, but I tell you men who haven't seen big ocean seas cannot understand the power of them."

They were not just words to me; at that moment I saw that
mighty cinematograph as clearly as he, and I found nothing
to say.

"I don't remember being frightened then," he went on, "but
it stands out in my mind that I was really frightened after that.
I would be about thirty-five years of age, and we were sailing
from Dunkirk to Boston with a cargo of French clay, soon

after I left the sheep ranch in Australia. She was a ship of about eight thousand tons, the *Arundel*, with a deep well-deck for'ard. I was on the middle watch—that is, midnight till four a.m. It was a westerly gale and a head sea; she was taking it green over her bows—and, Major, when you talk about seas it's hundreds and hundreds of tons those old ships used to take solid over the stem. We'd reduced speed till we were almost hove to, and she kept taking those mountains right over her till you'd wonder she didn't break into wee bits. It was only the hatch covers saved us going right under—they were breaking loose, and the mate had been at the tarpaulins, trying to secure them to hold down the hatches. We found him lying all smashed up, behind the spare anchor where it was lashed for'ard against the bulkhead. You'd say he hadn't a whole bone in his body—he'd just been hammered out by sea after sea coming over the stern. I'd had the wheel from twelve till two, then a spare hour, and then that last hour, three till four, as lookout. Of course the lookout would usually be in the stem, but when there was a sea like that—and I'm telling you we might thank God it wasn't often—the lookout would stop in the lee wing of the bridge. Well, I'll never forget that voyage, and I know I was frightened, really frightened, then. We'd sailed from Dunkirk on the first of December, and it was the twenty-fourth when we dropped anchor in Boston harbour, a westerly gale the whole way, and the ship's pumps working all the time. We averaged just five knots for the whole voyage—a man can row a dinghy at five knots—and I don't want to see another like it. No, Major. We lost that ship later, carrying grain from the Black Sea to Hamburg, lost her on a reef off Ceuta, but I don't think any of us was frightened in quite the same way, and I hope I'll never be again."

VIII

THE OUTER ISLANDS
July 1946

We sailed from Barra the next morning. The wind was still
nearly at gale force, carrying obliterating squalls of rain before
it. One cloudburst soon after we left the harbour was like a
tank of water emptied from low altitude; a solid mass, with no
feeling of individually distinguishable drops. The land looked
black and sodden, with a thousand waterfalls streaming from
it into a tumbling and confused sea. It seemed as though it
might be weeks before the Minch would be calm enough for
us to tow the *Gannet* home, so we took her gun aboard the
Sea Leopard and left her at anchor in Castlebay harbour.

When we reached Mallaig in the late afternoon we found
that the midday train had brought all that we had been waiting
for since the beginning of the season. As case after case was
opened, the *Gannet's* motor winch, the *Sea Leopard's* gun
mounting, and finally the gun itself, came successively to light.
Once on the fishing grounds each boat would now be an independent unit, each able to harpoon and winch up a shark un-
aided. But still it blew, and the *Gannet* was at the other side
of sixty miles of heaving grey sea.

We lay two days in Mallaig, fitting the new gun and mount
to the *Sea Leopard* by the same process of trial and error as we

had used with the *Dove* eighteen months before. The wind was moderate at last when we sailed for Uishenish on the afternoon of the third day, and when we reached Shepherd's Bight an hour or two before dark it was glass-calm, with only the long, slow undulations of a distant groundswell. It did not take Davidson, gesticulating from the clifftop, to show us the sharks; they were everywhere, all the way from the jabble of tide race off the lighthouse point right up into the head of Shepherd's Bight and north to the mouth of Loch Skipport.

The log for the day is reticent. It records three kills and "innumerable" shots. The truth was that none of us could hit a shark from the *Sea Leopard*'s bows. I had three easy shots in the first ten minutes, and each was a clean miss. The crew were incredulous; they remained polite, but with apparent effort, as bonus after bonus plunged free into the deep water. After the third shot I handed the gun over to Tex, acutely aware of Davidson's telescope trained on us from the lighthouse wall. But Tex could do no better, and he and I retired miserably to the bridge while Bruce planted himself stockily and with obvious confidence behind the gun. Bruce killed a monster with his first shot and was beginning to be a little smug about it when the fish winched up easily and without fight to the surface. It did not come up as usual, tail first, but rolling belly upwards, with the harpoon trace wrapped round the body, and as the bulk broke the surface we saw that Bruce's harpoon had missed the body altogether and passed through the left pectoral fin or flipper; rather near the tip. In other words, Bruce had missed his target by at least four feet. I am afraid that Tex and I were delighted, but the delight wore off when Bruce's next two shots were both clean misses. I do not remember how many shots we fired altogether, but we finished with three sharks, of which

Bruce, Tex, and I had killed one each before the last fin submerged at about eleven in the evening.

We lashed the three carcasses alongside and steamed all night for Soay. The light went gradually; at first the hills were sharp and black against an apple-green sky, then they blurred slowly as the sky darkened to a dull remote blue pricked by the hesitant light of the western constellations, and for a bare two hours it was night. It became hard and brilliant with intensely burning stars, and in the north the Aurora began to flicker, as bright as winter. The lashed carcasses plunged and rolled with the ship's movement, churning the water into a hissing foam above them that began to break into silver phosphorescence; all the dark brilliance that the night and the sea can bring. By two in the morning the eastern sky ahead had begun to pale, grey and translucent at first, becoming infused with a cold bitter red that silhouetted the mountains of the mainland and climbed the long steeps of the dawn with tenuous vermillion plumes. By the time we came into Soay harbour the sun was up over the hills, blinding and tremendous, but without warmth.

The factory was as yet deserted; we tied the dead sharks to the pier and sailed at once for Barra and the *Gannet*. That flaming dawn carried out its threat, and it began to blow again from the east, a strong biting wind as cold as winter, with squalls of icy rain.

We put into Lochboisdale to refuel; and there, in reluctant response to an urgent appeal, we took on board a woman passenger for Castlebay. She had missed the island steamer and had to be in Barra before night. Jockie Wiseman (photograph 22), the *Sea Leopard*'s engineer, would not come up on deck while she was aboard; he remained in the engine-room, muttering maledictions to himself, forecasting imminent reprisals for this flying in the face of the sea's gods, and having endless cups of tea carried down to him. Many fishermen are as full of superstition as a dictionary is of words, and there is a long list of animals and objects that may not be mentioned aboard a fishing vessel, much less actually seen. Thus salmon were to Jockie "cold iron," the words themselves spoken hurriedly and with bated breath, pigs were "those grunting things," and rabbits—the most dangerous of all—"the furry long-eared things." Once I shot some rabbits on Soay when we were short of food and came on board carrying a bunch of half a dozen swinging by the legs: there was nearly a mutiny. Some fishermen go even further, and will neither have eggs on board nor anyone who has eaten them and not yet completely cleared them from his system, but here Jockie had allowed practical issues to override his fear.

But the belief that a woman on board a fishing boat will bring bad luck is persistent, and many islanders will not put to sea if they even meet a woman when going down to their boats in the morning. Coincidence and natural causes seem to conspire to perpetuate these superstitions, and the many occasions when no disaster has followed their defiance are forgotten under the impact of their occasional and apparent confirmation. Early one morning a Soay man was walking across from the east bay, where his croft was, to his boat in the west harbour, when he met an old woman who had an evil reputation in some quarters. She was at some distance from the houses, coming over from the west side along the stony track where it passes above the lily loch. He passed her without speaking; then, feeling that he might goad her into some admission, he turned and called to her, "Why are you up so early to meet me this morning?"

She answered, scornfully, I imagine, "Be it according to your faith," and went on her way to her croft. He, too, walked on, pondering her words, "Be it according to your faith," and certainly his faith at that moment was in her power of misfortune rather than in any Almighty protection. When he reached the harbour his boat was not to be seen. He ran to the rocks opposite to where it had been moored, and there under the water he could see it—sunk to the bottom of the sea. He had had a lot of heavy stone ballast in the scuppers, and he had moored the boat in such a way that when the tide went back she was lifted by a rock below her keel and capsized by the weight of the stones—but he was not likely to remember his inefficiencies when he had so desirable a scapegoat as the witchwoman to bear them into legend.

To Jockie our passenger was a plain defiance of the powers of evil; she was a woman, and she was on board the *Sea Leopard*. What was more, she was probably full of eggs to the throat, and, for all one knew, her rather shapeless clothing might conceal a positive butcher's shop of rabbits and pork. So he stayed below and muttered, and we stayed on the bridge and watched for sharks.

We were about halfway between Lochboisdale and Castlebay when I saw a fin a mile ahead of us. Even at that distance it looked huge, and through the glasses I could see that despite its great thickness it had the "flop-eared" droop at the top which is characteristic of big sharks. As we drew up to him and I could at last see the whole bulk under water, I knew that he was the biggest shark I had ever seen; he was, in fact, the largest that I myself ever saw during the years we hunted them.

We had been trying to account for our inability to hit from the *Sea Leopard* a target some thirty feet by five at a range of fifteen or twenty feet, and had done our best to eliminate all the possible contributory causes. We had the harpoon head set in the gun so that the closed barbs were vertical rather than horizontal, which we thought might have caused water deflection on their flat surface, and we had tied the barbs against the shaft with string, so that they could not open until they were inside the fish and a strong pull exerted on them. This was our first shot with these modifications of technique. The gun itself was infinitely easier to handle than "Sugan." I had had the butt end made to my own design—a pair of motorcycle handlebars on which the trigger release was a Bowden clutch-grip. One could swing and align the heavy gun with ease and speed.

The fish was steady in the water and swimming very slowly straight away from us. He looked vast and unusually pale in colour. The fin was very much higher and thicker than any I had seen, and had a more pronounced droop at the top.

I was able to fire into him at almost point-blank range, the gun at maximum depression, and the gigantic expanse of his flank practically stationary below me. I had loaded with a slightly increased charge of powder, and I could feel the decks below me shudder with the recoil as the harpoon went squarely home. The shark reacted very quickly, tipping to dive almost in the same instant as the harpoon struck, and the tail rising level with the *Sea Leopard*'s decks in a tremendous flourish. The tail was on a par with the rest of him; it seemed half as big again as any that I had seen. An average tail is about seven feet across; this looked to me like ten at least, and I bounded back from the gun as the flat of the tail slammed wetly on to the boat's side a foot below the gunwale. Then the shark was down under the water and the rope streaking out from the fair-lead at tremendous speed.

I stared incredulously, watching a thin trickle of smoke rising from the rope where it passed over the metal—the first time I had ever seen a rope running out fast enough to be practically catching fire. I was aware of Dan behind me, trying hopelessly to slow the rope enough to catch a half-turn on the winch, but the speed was too great for him to do anything. It was a matter of seconds before the heavy thump of the rope snapping off short at the iron ring to which it was tied—a three-inch yacht manila rope with a breaking strain of about seven tons, the heaviest we had ever used. It had been just too short for the depth of water we were in—another ten fathoms of rope and the shark would have reached the bottom without coming to its end.

I looked back, to see the face of the woman gazing calmly down from the bridge without interest or excitement, the expression of one replete with eggs and rabbits.

But that disappointment was a definite step towards the development of our final technique. The idea that it suggested was, in fact, based upon a misconception, but its application had very far-reaching consequences. It seemed to us that if the rope, instead of being attached to the deck, had been fastened to a large buoy, such as a fifty-gallon paraffin drum, it would sooner or later have returned to the surface when the shark left the sea's bottom, and there would be a harpooned shark attached to it. The idea had further obvious advantages. When the catchers found a large shoal of sharks that were at the surface for perhaps not more than an hour or two, they would not have to waste the time involved in winching up and securing each shark as he was harpooned. They would only have to throw the rope and barrel overboard and reload and shoot another shark, taking the fullest advantage of the short time during which the fish were showing. When there were no more fins in sight the barrels could be hauled up singly and at leisure. (Photographs 28 through 33.)

This last was the real value of the idea, for we discovered almost at once that the steel barrels would collapse if they were dragged far below the surface, stove in by the pressure and weight of water. But as a means of remaining mobile and aggressive towards other sharks immediately after one or more had been harpooned, it was the most important development in technique so far, though it was not for another year that we were able from the *Sea Leopard*'s bridge to count a dozen barrels within a mile's radius, each with a large shark attached to it.

We reached Castlebay soon after midday, put our passenger ashore, and refitted the *Gannet*'s gun. We made up four ropes with a harpoon at one end and a forty-gallon metal paraffin drum at the other, gave one to Tex for experiment from the *Gannet*, and kept the other three aboard the *Sea Leopard*. We had meant to head north again for Uishenish. There was a strong wind blowing in from the Atlantic, and the Minch itself was rough, so we kept close inshore under the lee of the islands. We had got no farther than Barra Sound when we saw fins outside us.

The *Gannet* was the first to get a shot. It looked a fair shot at point-blank range, though the boat was plunging a good deal in the choppy water. Tex had an extra man aboard to heave the barrel overboard at the right moment, when the shark had taken out the greater part of the rope coiled down in the hold.

Tex had for some time shared my own suspicion that the gunmaker had been overcautious in "proofing" the guns for so small a charge of powder. To him discretion had never been the better part of valour, and while I had been stepping up the charges in my gun by half-drams at a time, he had been feeding "Sugan" some really purgative doses. We were perfectly right in thinking that the guns would stand more than double the charge for which they were then proofed, but unfortunately the gun mountings would not. Tex got a perfect alignment as the *Gannet*'s bows dipped into a trough, and he yanked the trigger cord. The tempered steel of the mounting snapped off short just below the crutch, and the big pistol-like butt of the gun catapulted back into his chest with a sickening thump. He remained on board, very surprisingly, and by a further miracle he had no bone broken, but he was winded and badly bruised, and the *Gannet* was once more out of action as a catching vessel.

But the shark had been fairly struck, and, despite the confusion, the barrel had been thrown overboard at the right moment, and there for the first time was a barrel moving slowly and half submerged along the surface with a flag on top of it and a harpooned shark two hundred feet below.

We brought Tex aboard the *Sea Leopard* and left Neil Cameron and a deckhand aboard the *Gannet* to haul up the barrel while we killed more sharks. I had two successful shots in quick succession, and each time the barrel and flag went over without a hitch. There was an interval of a few minutes after the second shot, and we had time to evolve a further improvement in technique which remained practically unchanged for several years. From the harpoon the eighteen-foot steel trace hung down free over the ship's side; the first few fathoms of the rope to which it was attached were coiled down just below the gun, and behind that the remainder was tied in coils along the outside of the ship's railing. These coils were fastened to the railing with string which would snap and pay out the rope as soon as the shark took the strain. In calm weather the barrel could be tied outboard in the same way, but when there was much movement on the water a man would stand ready to throw it overboard as soon as the string on the last coil of rope had snapped (photograph 23).

My third shot was successful too, and within a radius of half a mile or so were four barrels on the water, sometimes riding high and light, sometimes dipping till only a few inches of them were visible. The flags had snapped off from three of them; they were an idea that we did not afterwards think it worth while to develop.

It was our own special brand of luck that we had chosen for this experiment one of the few spots in the whole Minch where the sea's depth was greater in places than the length of our rope coils. One barrel dipped until it was only just visible; a wave broke over it, and it disappeared altogether. A minute later it was showing a few inches again. We put the *Sea Leopard* full speed ahead, and she came charging up on it with a bone between her teeth, but even as I grabbed with a boat hook at the rope loop it went right under again, and I could see the white strip of sailcloth that was tied to it going farther and farther down into the dim sea until it disappeared. A second later a big belch of aerated water broke the surface, and we knew that the steel drum had collapsed. Another barrel went the same way before we could reach it. We were not only losing nearly a hundred pounds' worth of shark each time, but each was carrying away with him fifteen pounds' worth of gear that it was not easy to replace.

We hauled the two remaining barrels simultaneously, the *Gannet* taking one and the *Sea Leopard* the other, and there was a large and securely harpooned shark on each. We left

these fish tied to the pier at Lochboisdale, for the following day
was a Saturday, and we knew that the factory would still be
hacking through the three carcasses we had brought in on
Wednesday.

We fished all the next week between Barra and Uishenish,
and even though the *Gannet* mounted no gun, and we had to
spend a day and a half in the middle of the week carrying barrels and salt to Soay, we killed another eleven sharks from the
Sea Leopard. We became more and more expert in the use of
the barrels, and without them we should not have had more
than a third of that number.

Almost every night that week we towed our catch home to
Soay during the dark hours and were back on the fishing
grounds soon after dawn. The wind remained fresh to strong
from the southwest, and as we lurched and rolled across the
Minch the carcasses would thump and bang against the ship's
sides till it seemed as though they must crash through into my
cabin itself. Both boats were by now beginning to show signs
of surface wear, and near the bows neither had much paint left
within the area that a shark's tail could lash.

It was at some time during that second week in July that I
realized that the fulmar petrels had come to know the *Sea
Leopard* from other boats, and that they had begun to follow
hopefully even when we had no shark in tow. On the first day
of the week we had sailed for home early in the evening while
it was still light. Small pieces of liver began to break loose from
the sharks and drift astern in our wash. The gulls began to
collect, flocking in from all points of the compass where no
gulls had been visible before. With them came fulmars, a few
at first, then more and more, until there were over a hundred.
The gulls were mainly herring gulls and lesser blackbacks,

with a few kittiwakes and a pair or two of great blackbacks, massive and vulturine. A few gannets joined the throng, by now several hundred strong. The fulmars, tamer than the gulls, bickered and quarrelled with grotesque and unavian gestures in the water a few feet from the boat, dropped astern as some morsel engaged their attention, and returned with the full breath-taking glory of their flight to join others who had taken their places. Beside them in the air the gulls looked clumsy and inept, old-fashioned landaulettes beside modern racing cars, their flight lacking grace and style in comparison. To me the flight of the fulmar is the most beautiful of all bird flight, and has a strange and precise individuality. Even the take-off from the water is unlike that of the gulls. If there is enough breeze to make it possible, the fulmar takes off as does an airplane, with a short taxiing run on stiff outstretched wings that do not flap. He spreads his wings, runs a few steps on the surface of the water, gives a final kick-off, and lets the wind launch him into the air, usually on a climbing turn. I watched this as the birds that had fallen a few yards astern hurried to catch up with the source of supply, and the same technique again as they dipped to pick up some unexpected fragment on the way. Here the legs are lowered and begin a slightly ludicrous running move- ment before the bird reaches the surface of the water; the wings remain stiffly outstretched, and the legs continue to run while the food is picked up. The act of alighting is accompanied by a fine, almost orgasmic, trembling vibration of the wings; then the long scimitars fold and the airobat is revealed as a dumpy, upright, and very well-groomed little white bird, swimming with quick precise strokes of widely splayed legs. The full characteristic flight is a series of extremely fast alternating div- ing and climbing turns, banking vertically with the long thin wings tensely stretched. At the bottom of the diving turn the tip of the lower wing skims the water with mathematical precision, always appearing to be within an inch of the surface but never breaking it. When these turns follow one another in quick succession at a speed of something like sixty miles an hour the effect is breath-taking, in some way reminiscent of the long swoops and barely held pauses of a lofty trapeze dance.

In their effort to be instantly ready for any fresh piece of liver leaving the sharks' carcasses, the foremost fulmars were flying well inboard the ship, often within arm's length of where I stood against the dinghy on the poop deck. I amused myself by trying to catch one in the air as it hung poised and nearly stationary on the wind. Sometimes the wing tip would almost brush my face, but always as the hand shot out a quick tilt of the wing carried it beyond reach, and the bird would make a steep climbing turn to bring it back to its former position within a yard of my head.

Birds occupy the eye a great deal when one is continuously at sea in Hebridean waters, both because of their numbers and incessant activity, and because for hours at a time they are often the only living things in sight. They were my first love in childhood, and they filled many long empty days on the *Sea Leopard* when there seemed to be no sharks in the sea and I would grow tired of the heat and tobacco smoke of the fo'c'sle or of working through accounts and business correspondence in my cabin. The minute actions of birds, the intimate realization of separate sentient life, have always held for me an almost magic fascination; the herring gull that would alight with an infinitely controlled and delicate poise upon the truck of the wireless mast, smooth white wings folding against a blue sky, the yellow bill with its blood tip gaping a rhythmic wail of defiance to its

companions who hovered above trying to oust it; the migrating
wild geese that would pass high overhead flying northward to
the thawing Arctic wastes during the first week of every shark
season, trailing distant notes of music behind them; the little
dark storm petrels, no bigger than swallows, flitting among the
rearing grey waves of the Minch in the dawn and the dusk; the
kittiwake colonies, appearing against the great rock walls like
a shaken snow scene in a glass paperweight; and, best of all, the
golden eagles soaring above the sea cliffs. Besides all these and
the ubiquitous guillemots, puffins, and razorbills, there were
occasional rarities, such as the great skua, glaucous gull, and
Leach's fork-tailed petrel, which we saw once in daylight near
Barra Head. Tex found another lying stunned on the rocks behind Chinatown in Mallaig. "It sat there on my hand, combing
itself, just the thing," said Tex. He always had some slightly
grotesque and more expressive word to replace the obvious.

The sea and the open sky, the sharks and whales and seabirds,
were the *Sea Leopard*'s background, and my own diary, when
I had leisure to write it, is concerned with each almost equally,
so that when I read those pages now an effort of memory is
needed to recall that the writing of each was an almost conscious escape from the nagging worry of an experimental project already in debt and struggling on insufficient capital.

A long entry on the Tuesday of that week, July 9, is worth
quoting verbatim, because the latter part of it deals with my
own, perhaps not very subtle, reactions to a question that must
present itself to every averagely sensitive individual who kills
great creatures.

Today I have missed three fish and killed four. There is a disproportionate emotional expenditure in this missing, especially
when fish are scarce or difficult to approach and the shot is the re-

sult of a long and painstaking stalk. The sharks were very unsteady on the surface today, appearing at one moment with the whole dorsal fin clear of the surface and the next moment totally submerged and leaving not so much as a ripple to guide one. Each time they submerged they changed direction, usually to reappear on an opposite parallel course on the wrong side of the boat. In misty weather like this the surface reflection is practically opaque unless one is looking vertically into the water, and one strains one's eyes to make out the great brown shadow under the surface. It is worse when there are several sharks near together, one's attention being constantly distracted by the appearance of a fin-tip in some fresh unattainable position.

A teleological observer today would have said without hesitation that the sharks were coolly, confidently avoiding the gun with an exact and experienced eye to its range and the manœuvrability of the *Sea Leopard*. Time and again the fish suddenly changed course at the last moment, or submerged in a leisurely but entirely efficient way at exactly the distance that made a miss a mathematical probability. Sometimes we followed the same fish for nearly half an hour. Standing at the gun and peering down into the water, one can hear, appraise, and mentally criticize the orders issued from the bridge to the engine-room.

The fish surfaces a hundred yards ahead.

"Half ahead both engines."

The boat surges forward in pursuit, and the eye glances over the gun and ropes; steel-trace outboard, harpoon barbs vertical and tied closed, safety bar out of the gun. The shark swims steadily away on an even course. The ship is rapidly overtaking it; I think, "If he comes up at this speed I shall never be able to take an aim."

Exactly as this thought becomes conscious, I hear, "Stop starboard"; and, a moment later, "Stop port."

The shark is twenty yards away; slowly he begins to submerge. The fin disappears, is invisible, then suddenly reappears travelling to starboard at more than right angles to his previous course.

"Slow ahead port, half astern starboard."

The ship wears round.

"Stop starboard."

The fish has sounded again.

"Stop port."

So it goes on. The whole crew, except Jockie below decks at the engines, are watching. At times like these the gunner feels a miss very acutely. There is the last-moment hesitation over a poor chance; the shark is going down and turning away; only the very tip of the three-foot dorsal fin is breaking the surface and there is a rapid undulation over the whole length of the body.

To the inexperienced eye it is an easy target, more than twenty-five feet long, and at least five feet wide, less than ten yards away. Small markings are visible on the shark's body, light-coloured scars left by parasites, a bold python-like pattern on the flank. But the harpoon will have ten feet of water to penetrate before reaching the target, and bitter experience has taught the odds against the success of this shot.

I killed one fish today that I did not expect to hit. It was just such a shot, the shark turning to right angles away from the ship as I took aim, so that I looked down the length of his body from tail to distant gills. He was submerging rapidly when I fired, aiming at the base of the edge-on dorsal fin. The roar and flash of the gun and the boil of spray always make the point of impact difficult to determine, but as the water cleared I could see the great fish a fathom down, swimming away from the boat with blood pouring in a dark stream from a white-edged hole in his back where the steel-trace entered it. He made off slowly, almost as if unconscious of his deadly wound; the eye could follow him far under the surface, a vast grey shadow with glints of white. When we pulled him up we found that the harpoon had passed clean through him and out at his belly.

Yet I should say that earlier in the day I had taken exactly the same aim on another shark presenting an identical target, and the result had been a miss. The wooden harpoon stick came up still attached to the harpoon and covered with slime, showing that it had rubbed along his flank, and implying a lateral error in aim or a lateral deflection of the harpoon by the water it had to penetrate.

I have no explanation for the incidence of these hits and misses in apparently identical circumstances, and I am as nearly certain as I can be that the human factor is not involved.

All this harpooning has its unpleasant side, no matter how much it may be forgotten in the excitement of the moment. If a warm-blooded animal were concerned, and more especially if it were a warm-blooded land animal, ninety-nine people out of a hundred (of whom I should be one) would hold it to be unthinkable cruelty. Yet is one justified, because this monstrous bulk of flesh and muscle is cold-blooded and directed by a brain which could almost be enclosed in a matchbox, in assuming that the experience undergone by the shark is so widely different from our own? It is extraordinary how few people devote much thought to these subjects of pain and cruelty, extraordinary not because it is easy to reach satisfactory conclusions, but because they hold a uniquely ubiquitous position in every sphere of human activity. Yet few people can explain what they mean by pain in all its senses, let alone the complicated and uncomfortable abstract of cruelty.

The dictionary definition of the word pain is "suffering or distress of body or mind," but to find synonyms for a word is far from understanding the meaning and function of the fact for which that word stands.

The function of physical pain in the animal—including the human species—is entirely easy to understand on an unethical plane. The physical sensation of pain is used mechanically to ensure the continuation of the species, just as plainly as is the physical sensation of sexual desire. In the animal world pain is the only limiting factor to the acceptance of physical injury, inflicted either by the animal itself or by another animal, which would result in the death of the individual and ultimately of the species. If it did not hurt to knock one's head against a stone wall, one might playfully do it so hard that it resulted in death. Similarly, a slight stimulus which is at first perceived as pleasure, will, if it is sufficiently increased in intensity, be perceived as pain; an unequivocal warning that if the stimulus persists physical injury will result. This is an invariable law, and on its account we must accept as axiomatic that all animals perceive pain as disagreeable enough for it to act as the necessary deterrent.

We cannot know the exact degree of pain which animals at different evolutionary levels are capable of experiencing, but we know that in all the higher animals and most of the lower it is strong enough to make its avoidance—usually teleologically condensed as the "instinct of self-preservation"—stronger than any other instinct except the sexual. So we must assume that the shark feels pain strongly enough for it to act as the necessary deterrent to self-destruction. There is an argument, possibly fallacious, which attempts to reduce pain at all evolutionary levels to a common denominator. It is the argument that when an animal or human is suffering as much pain as it can suffer the precise degree of pain measurable by a common standard is unimportant; that the maximum degree of pain sufferable by a fish is as unpleasant to the fish as the maximum that a human can suffer is to the human. How can one reconcile this theory with the authenticated fact of a carnivorous shark, gutted and heaved back into the sea, being caught a few minutes later on a hook baited with its own intestines?

From this muddle of inconsistencies we can at least eliminate one glaring example of woolly thinking: the size of the animal concerned is completely unimportant, and one who is moved to pity by the sight of a stranded thirty-foot shark suffocating on a beach should be moved a thousand times more by the sight of a thousand herring suffocating in the hold of a fishing boat; or one who is revolted by the idea of a ten-pound steel harpoon in a thirty-foot shark should be equally revolted by an inch hook in the jaw of a salmon. And perhaps both those facts can be brought into fair proportion only by the realization that at every moment in the sea millions and millions of fish are being pulled into bloody pieces by millions and millions of other fish.

An interesting, though to me very inconclusive, treatise on pain has been written by C. S. Lewis (*The Problem of Pain*) from the Christian standpoint. Being more an exposition of doctrine than a detached examination of the subject, it is perhaps unfair to expect conclusion; as an exposition it is clear and concise, and in the sphere of human pain it is unconvincing only when it attempts explanation on a human, as opposed to an animal, level. In bold précis, pain in its relation to humans is expounded as a divine weapon used to recall man from the formation of a continuing city on earth—as a rod in the hand of God. This doctrine is softened and made more palatable in the course of an able and rather lengthy discussion.

In the chapter devoted to animal pain the argument, though presented with admirable clarity, remains to me entirely unacceptable. The fact of pain as a deterrent to self-destruction is skirted both in this and the previous chapter. But the theoretical difference between sentience and consciousness (the ability to feel as opposed to the ability to translate it into experience) is well explained in words of one syllable, and it is perhaps here that one should look for the true comparison between shark pain and human pain.

But complex though these problems are that arise from consideration of the fact of pain, they are crystal clear by comparison with its child, cruelty. Here the dictionary gives us "indifference to, or delight in, another's pain." As an abstract, independent of the human factor, cruelty does not exist; it stands as an entity divorced from the simple fact of pain only when the human appears on the scene. A swallow flies into a telephone wire and falls to the ground with one wing practically severed from its body. Pain is there, but no cruelty. A boy passes on a bicycle, sees the bird flopping in the pathos of its destruction, and rides on. The unknown factor has made its appearance, and the problem of cruelty has arisen, without interference by a human being, for he has only been a spectator of pain. The bird must suffer an equal degree of pain whether the injury is self-inflicted, inflicted by a beast of prey or by a human, but the word cruelty can be applied only in the last case. A few, but I think a very small minority, would admit the fact of cruelty, in its most precise meaning, between animal and animal, but probably this same minority would describe cruelty as sin, and an animal without ethical code cannot be held guilty of sin even in its widest sense.

One fact emerges plainly from this: that since the degree of pain remains constant whether or not cruelty exists, the evil effect of

cruelty must be confined to the inflictor, and has no reference to
the sufferer. And here more than anywhere else it seems to me that
all men live by instilled standards of conduct, condoning those
cruelties which the code of their upbringing legalizes, and con-
demning those that are exactly similar but outside the sphere of
their habit. The Japanese thought a kiss indecent but displayed
prostitutes in cages; the sportsman is bound to wound several birds
in the course of a day's shooting but is revolted by the sight of his
son pulling off a butterfly's wings. And who pauses to think how
many wild animals can ever die any but a terribly painful death;
how many fish in the end escape the mangling teeth of some larger
sea creature?

We fished for another two months, but we had had the best
of that season. For four weeks the wind scarcely moderated,
and for the greater part of the time the sea was too rough for
us to tell with any certainty whether or not the sharks were
still in the area. I look down those log entries and see again
the panorama of roaring grey skies and flying scud: "Lay riding out westerly gale at Lochmaddy"; "Gale all round the
compass in twenty-four hours; no shelter anywhere"; "Too
much sea to follow the only fish we saw"; "Sou'westerly gale;
lay two days at Lochboisdale." Throughout that time we averaged about two sharks a week, and it was borne in upon me that
even at this low rate the factory or its staff was apparently
working to capacity. Our export licence had come through, and
we were now shipping all the sharks' flesh salted in barrels to
Hamburg, so that even these small catches were not showing us
an appreciable running loss, but we had a heavy capital deficit,
and it was clear that only a complete recapitalization could
carry the project into a full working stage the following season.
Through correspondence I had been pursuing this idea since
early June, and now I decided to stay with the catchers not

later than mid-August before going to Glasgow to try to raise the necessary capital.

Each individual shark that we killed was still an adventure in itself, as fiercely exciting as the very first, and each could still make me forget for an hour the menace of failure and bankruptcy that swept back on those unceasing winds. "Ay," said one of the crew one day, "the weather always beats you in the end—time and the weather," and in these small fatalistic words lay all that there was to be said.

There were times when the crew were bored and discontented, and privately I made up my mind that I would end the season with the first man who left us. Late one evening, when we had lain in harbour for two days, one of the crew came to my cabin to voice, it seemed, a private rather than a general discontent. He was a man I knew and liked, so I foolishly gave him some rum, although it was obvious that he had had too much already. We sat at opposite sides of the narrow cabin, with the table between us. He grew heated, and I tried to be placatory. This made him angrier still; I became angry myself, and with a sudden reversion to an Army pattern of behaviour I told him to get out and come back when he was sober. There was a very quick movement, and his hand came up on the table in front of him, holding a sheath knife by the point of the blade.

"You're not in the bloody Guards now," he said. "Take your eyes off me, and I'll stap this through your guts."

I didn't know whether to take this seriously or not, but he was drunk enough for anything. I was scared stiff. On the vague principle of a lion tamer, which seemed to be running in his mind too, I did not take my eyes off him, and after a moment or two they began to smart with the smoky atmosphere.

"Put that thing away, and don't be a fool," I said, hoping my voice would not show how frightened I was, and forgetting that he was past noticing.

But he only said, "Take your eyes off me—just take your eyes off me, and see what you'll get."

I had a wonderful idea. "All right," I said; "I'll go on looking at you as long as I can, but we can both have a drink while I'm doing it."

He had one, and I had one—about a tumbler full of rum each. Then we had another; he had a flying start on me, and I felt sure I could outlast him. When the first bottle was finished he became more friendly, though the knife remained conspicuous.

"I like you, you know," he said, "if only you weren't such a bloody fool. I wouldn't really want to put a knife through you. But I'm fou', you see, so don't you go taking a risk on it, not if I was you."

I didn't. We were halfway down the second bottle, and I was beginning to feel pretty hazy myself, when he went gently to sleep and I cautiously removed the knife. It was quite calm when I lugged him up, half conscious, on deck about three in the morning, and the rest of the crew had turned in. I plumped him down on the poop deck and seated myself beside him, staring foolishly at the moon and thinking what a wonderful night it was and what a wonderful life it was. You must have been able to smell the rum a quarter of a mile away on shore.

Presently my companion woke up and staggered off, mumbling, "Wonderful evening, Major; thanks for wonderful evening."

It was two years before either of us referred to the incident.

A few isolated days stand out from the remaining month of the 1946 season that I spent with the catchers. One dull afternoon when we arrived at Uishenish Lighthouse there was too much swell for us to get the *Sea Leopard* close under the rocks and understand what Davidson was trying to tell us. It would be sheltered round the corner in Shepherd's Bight, but that would mean a long walk for him. Suddenly we had the idea of firing a message ashore with the harpoon gun. By gesture we made Davidson understand what we were going to do; then we put about, went half a mile out to sea, and hove to. On a piece of paper I wrote:

If this doesn't hit you, please hold up your right hand if you think we should wait in the Bight until evening. Give us a flat wave of both arms at chest level if we should clear off now. The stick is worth eight shillings so save it if you can.

This we screwed up and pushed into the empty socket of a harpoon stick, where the base of the harpoon should fit, and sealed it over with insulating tape. Davidson watched meanwhile through his telescope. We were rather vague as to what charge of powder should fire this novel form of message, but the cliff was several hundred feet high, and we reckoned that if we aimed the gun at about fifty degrees into the air the message must come down somewhere near to the lighthouse. The stick with its metal-shod end would be as deadly as a rifle bullet, so we aimed for the flat grass a couple of hundred yards north of the lighthouse.

It left the gun far too quickly for the eye to follow, then focused itself high and small against the sky midway between us and the shore. At first I thought it was going to fall short into the sea, then through the field glasses I saw that it had cleared the clifftop, as two gulls following the line of the rocks sheered to avoid it. It began to descend, hit the green grass just at the horizon, and bounced high in the air twice.

We were childishly delighted by our little conjuring trick and watched eagerly as Davidson jumped down from the lighthouse wall and ran towards it. I watched him get the message out and read it; then his right hand shot up and stayed there so long that he began to look like Moses upon the hill of Rephidim. This did not seem a perfunctory invitation to stay; the sharks must be back again in numbers.

We waited in the calm water of Shepherd's Bight, and as the sun sank below the hills behind us and left the bight in shadow we saw Davidson take up a position on the headland from which he could watch us. Presently Manson's boats came in from the south and began to "feel" for herring. The weighted piano wire with which this was done has now been generally replaced by echo-sounding devices which record shoals of fish with greater certainty and far less trouble, but these did not become general until the release of the bulk of Admiralty equipment. Manson found mackerel, well up on the south side of the bight, and prepared to ring, with the two boats together and abreast before one set off to drop the net in a wide circle and carry its end back to its stationary partner to haul together.

He had barely started when a big shark's fin showed high out of the water very close in to the rocks between the boats and the shore. The ringer stopped, and Manson came out of the wheelhouse to bawl across the water to us, "Go in and take that damned thing out of it for us."

The shark was right inshore in a narrow cul-de-sac among the rocks; it was a shot for the *Gannet* if either boat could get in there.

The *Gannet* could get in, but there was no turning space for her to get out again, and if we went in and took the shot without room for her to turn, it looked as though she would capsize or be hauled onto the rocks as the shark headed out for the deeper water.

We hung about outside the rocks, not twenty yards from the shark, discussing what we could do, and Manson began to get impatient. In the middle of this the *Sea Leopard*'s gun set the echoes rolling all round the bay, and we looked up to see her half a mile to northward of us, a drench of white spray all round her foredeck and a big black tail churning up the water round her bows in a series of tremendous slaps. We saw the barrel heaved overboard and Bruce at the gun reloading feverishly. There were two more fins moving slowly in line ahead a little to seaward of him.

"Come on," said Tex; "we'll waste all night on this unless we do something. How about we take the boat in stern first and try a shot as he comes out past us?"

We reversed the *Gannet* in very cautiously. The shark had turned and lay practically motionless, head to sea and close in against the rocks; there was only just room for him and the boat, much of a size, in the narrow space. As our propeller drew level with his huge distended gills he seemed to notice us for the first time. A long undulation went through the body as he tried to sound, but his movement carried him forwards rather than downwards.

"Look out, Tex! Here he comes!"

Tex had the gun slewed round to point as far backward as it would go, and he fired as the whole bulk went by him at a range of inches rather than feet. There could be no question of a miss.

What followed was so unexpected that for a moment none of us took it in. As the harpoon struck, the shark must have tried to sound in earnest and hit the bottom. A second later the whole fish, with several tons of water and spray, was in the air level with our eyes. He fell high and dry on the rocks, the great mottled belly towards us, twisted, rolled down into the water under our bows, and shot off at tremendous speed. We were so taken aback that we barely found time to get the barrel overboard before he reached the end of the rope.

The barrel was clear of the ring-netters' area in five minutes, and the men on Manson's boats were waving and laughing as though it was the best joke they had ever seen.

We killed four sharks that evening, but, as always, it was a week-end, and when we got back on Monday Davidson reported that he had seen nothing since we left. But in the mouth of Loch Skipport we met two local fishermen from South Uist, who told us that a shark had carried away two drift-nets that they had set on anchors on Saturday. We waited about the loch, because we had no other reports to follow, and after a time I saw what I thought to be a shark's fin appearing momentarily about a mile to seaward of us. It was never visible when I got the field glasses trained on the spot, but each time as I took them down from my eyes I saw the flash of it again, sometimes much higher out of the water than any part of a shark should be. Someone said it was a killer, someone else said it was something fighting with a shark. We set off to look; the surface was unbroken when we reached the area where it had been, and we cruised around for some time without seeing anything. Then, quite close to the boat, a shark's tail rose high out of the water, dragging with it a heavy black mass of net which trailed just below the surface after the fin had disappeared. Here was the very shark that had carried off the drift-net, and in that helpless condition it did not seem that he could escape us. Again and again some portion of him heaved up well above the water, sometimes the tail, sometimes the head, and all were swathed in those thick black coils of net; he was wrapped up in it like a mummy, helpless, impotent, and illogically pathetic.

An animal displaying *in extremis* an instinctive pattern of behaviour from which no help can come rouses pity in me more easily than in any other way: the mole who seeks escape by movements of digging upon the concrete floor; the hedgehog curling up at the last moment before the oncoming car; the wounded brown hare freezing immobile upon the white snow; the lampreys that when taken from the sharks onto the deck of the *Sea Leopard* would attach their anchoring suckers with terrible avidity even to the boots of their captors.

The shark's very helplessness made him impossible to approach. He was unable to follow a straight course; unable, it seemed, to remain at the surface for long. Those wild flourishes of the tail that tried to free itself of the snake-like constricting net carried him downward without volition; each movement to escape took him on a fresh course. He appeared at the surface perhaps once every minute, but always he had submerged before the boat could reach him. After an hour the appearances became irregular, and finally ceased altogether.

It reminded one of the crew of a story. I wish there was room to write all the stories that were told in that fo'c'sle as we crossed and recrossed the Minch, or lay riding out gales in the Outer Island harbours while the wind howled and the rain battered outside.

"They caught something bigger than they bargained for, those two Uist men," he said: "but not as big as something I once caught," he added with a reminiscent chuckle. "I caught a submarine in a salmon net, and that's the truth.

"It was during the war, and I was on a trawler that had been fitted out as a mine-layer. We were based, along with some other surface craft and two submarines, close to a famous salmon river. Now, I'm as honest as the next man, and as a rule I respect other people's property, but all my life I've never been able to resist poaching a fish. Some people can't resist poaching game, and it's not for the profit of it; it's something in the blood. 'It's my delight on a shiny night in the season of the year.' I'm that way about salmon, and the more difficult it is and the better guarded it is the more's the temptation. Well, I found out that the mate of this trawler was of the same mind as myself, and we began to think about this river. Or rather I should say that we'd both been thinking about it since we first found ourselves there. We did a bit of reconnoitring and found that the best pool was right bang underneath the river-keeper's house. I suppose that's why the house was built there. It was like a challenge, and we made up our minds to have a try.

"We began to make a net in our spare time. It had to be about a hundred and fifty yards long, and materials were a bit difficult to come by in those days; we had to get what we wanted little by little and work at making it in our spare time. It took weeks before we had it finished, and we were as pleased as if we'd built a house.

"Well, the day after we'd finished it at last I was ashore with Jack—that's the trawler's mate—in the pub. It was a great rendezvous, that pub. There were depot ships and all sorts in the harbour, and as soon as every sailor came ashore he made straight for the pub. They didn't go there only to drink, it was a sort of black-market clearing-house—deals in Navy cigarettes, rum, suitcases full of stuff hot enough to burn your fingers, and plugs of black tobacco rolled up in tarry string. There was often a bit of an old shirt sleeve in the middle, to make them look bigger.

"Anyway, I was there that night with Jack the mate, and as we were going back that evening on the liberty boat I said, 'Jack, I'd like to get that net of ours shot tonight.' Now it was finished, after all those weeks, we just couldn't wait to get it in the water, and we agreed that we'd have a go that very night. We had the commander of one of the submarines coming to dine aboard the trawler, but we reckoned we'd be back before that.

"We had a boy—Johnnie—along with us, and we set off up the river as soon as it was dark. We had the tide and the river against us, and it was tough going. When we got to the pool it was as black as pitch—you could hardly see the difference between the sky and the land. It was quiet too, and we had our oars muffled so we wouldn't be heard from the keeper's house. We put the lad ashore on the opposite side of the pool from the house, and we set off to make a sweep of the pool ourselves.

"The tide was too strong for us, and we were making leeway the whole time, getting washed down the river, and after a few minutes we thought we'd give it up and try another night, so we let go our end of the net, thinking the boy Johnnie had a hold of the other end. But Johnnie got a scare and thought he saw someone coming up the bank to him, so he dropped his end in the water, thinking we had a hold of our end, and when we got to the place where he ought to be there's no Johnnie in sight, and no net. It was an hour before we found him, away down the river, striking matches like a fireworks display, and the net we'd spent all that time making was away to sea with the tide. You can guess we weren't best pleased with each other, the way things had turned out, and to make matters worse there was the submarine commander coming to dine aboard the trawler, and we looked like being late.

"And late we were, by a quarter of an hour, but there was no sign of our guest, not even by the time we'd changed our clothes and smartened ourselves up. He was an hour late by the time he did arrive, and mad as a tiger.

" 'We've had one hell of an evening,' he said; 'a bloody great net all wrapped up round our propellers, and we haven't got it free yet. I'd like to get my hands on the silly b—— who let it float away from him.'

"Me and the mate caught each other's eyes just then, and I tell you we had a job keeping our faces straight."

Soon after this, in early August, I was required to attend an Army Medical Board at Inverness. We were fishing the northernmost range of the Outer Island sea lochs—Loch Shell, Loch Seaforth, and Loch Erisort; the *Sea Leopard* put me ashore at Stornoway, and I flew from there to Aberdeen, and from Aberdeen to Inverness. From this flight was born the germ of another idea. From the closed aircraft, flying straight and level, I could not be certain that I saw sharks as we crossed the Minch, but more than once I saw shadows in the water at which I should have liked to have had a closer look, and I determined that if the project was recapitalized we ought to have a spotter aircraft to keep us in touch with the shoals.

When I came back from Inverness the *Sea Leopard* was in Mallaig. I took the secretary and a mass of papers ashore, and nostalgically I watched her sail for Uishenish in response to a message from Davidson. I spent a week ashore, finishing the documents on which we had been working for weeks—detailed statements of our finances and prospects—and set off for Glasgow and London to try to raise the capital for a proper equipment of our venture.

IX

ISLAND OF SOAY SHARK FISHERIES LTD.

Since early that summer my agents had been doing their best to interest likely firms and private individuals in putting up the money necessary to capitalize our experience and to reconstitute the shark fishery in a large way. I still tended to regard the past summer as a working season rather than as an experiment that must necessarily show a loss, and towards the end of June I had written to my nine subscribers, stating our policy as clearly as I was able to see it and asking them to waive the minimum dividend which the form of agreement laid down. They had all replied that they were willing to do so, and I was left free to negotiate our future and safeguard their capital as best I might.

My faith in the commercial possibilities of basking-shark fishing was unshaken, but the supply difficulties, especially in the catching equipment, were so great that I found it difficult to estimate how much more capital might have to be spent on experiment before the fishery could be called a going concern. At the moment we had no attractive balance sheet to lure the invester, not even a hard-and-fast assessment of the amount that must be spent in further investigation. The whole view was fogged by the mist of that original false judgment that every part of the fish must be used, and that the commercial possibilities of all by-products be investigated simultaneously.

Had we ignored these tempting side alleys and drawn up a programme to catch sharks and market their liver oil only, the figures would have been easily computable; other possibilities could have been explored gradually when the business had stabilized itself upon its main product. We had bitten off far more than we could chew.

Our gross revenue for that summer's catching had been a little over three thousand pounds, a third of which was from the sale of salted flesh and the remainder from the oil. We had no established market for any other product, and the time that had been wasted upon preparing and transporting samples of various portions of the fish might have been spent profitably in catching more sharks.

The Soay factory was the narrow channel through which nothing ever seemed to run smoothly, and to which the greater part of our losses could be traced. Whereas we must have some shore base other than a tiny and crowded fishing port, I realized now that Soay must be a base only, and that in any future programme the boats must become more and more independent of it in the routine work of catching sharks and producing barrelled flesh and oil. This was the idea that I had to sell: a floating factory becoming increasingly free, Soay becoming less and less of a factory and more of a harbour and store base. It was clear that to pay our capital debt and our revenue loss, to safeguard the invested money of the nine original subscribers and to carry on, meant selling everything to one man or firm who would then have a controlling interest in the company. I had already set foot on Soay for the last time as its owner.

By this date we had spent a total of rather more than fifteen thousand pounds, still less than a third of what Lord —— had said he would write off to experiment if his firm were undertaking a new enterprise of this kind, but all of it except the value of the boats must indeed be written off unless I could find someone interested in carrying on the idea. Nothing at the factory could be regarded as an asset except in direct connection with shark fishing, for the cost of dismantling and transport to the mainland would be prohibitive; no items of the costly catching equipment would be worth a penny to anyone who did not intend to catch sharks. We had only the boats as directly realizable assets, and they were not worth five thousand pounds between them.

Our creditors were mainly local men from Mallaig and the vicinity, and they agreed to wait for payment until I had had full opportunity to try to form a company and liquidate the debts of the present experimental business.

I sat in the Glasgow train, my briefcases crammed with accounts, receipts, prospectuses, estimated revenue sheets, trade inquiries—everything that I could carry with me in justification of my faith in the possible future of my new industry. Mallaig and the shining sea slid farther and farther behind me; Glasgow, with its drab offices and the sharp cynical brains of those who would smile superciliously as they tore my dream to pieces, filled the whole of my mind.

How many mare's nests I found eggless during those next few months, how many red herrings I pursued avidly to their distant depths, how many oases trembled and dissolved into mirage, I do not know, but they were many. The press had given the Soay project ("Bid to Found New Industry") a wide publicity that summer, ranging from serious features in illustrated papers to the comic-cut type, such as:

Answer.
Doubtful (Duntochter)—The carcass of the average shark

yields, after processing, 7 gallons of oil, 57 lbs fish meal, 9 sq. ft. of shagreen, 3 sets artificial dentures, 2 gold watches, 1 sea boot, 5 wedding rings, 2 golf balls, 7 kirbigrips, and 1 copy (spoiled) of Ella Wheeler Wilcox's *Poems*.

There were also, on days when the daily press was hard pushed to fill its columns, such headlines as "One Man Starts a New War"; and paragraphs in which the subject matter was barely recognizable, such as:

After a thrilling chase of several hours from the coast of Skye to South Uist two basking sharks were captured by Major Maxwell and his crew yesterday. Major Maxwell runs the oil factory at Soay, near Skye.

A school of sharks was sighted off the coast of Skye and after several unsuccessful attempts to harpoon the fish two were eventually struck and set off with the speedboat in tow in the direction of South Uist.

Finally, the big fish were secured and taken to Lochboisdale Pier, South Uist, where they were secured while the hunters left to follow the school which had moved farther up.

Both sharks measured about 10 (*sic*) feet long.

All this had attracted a growing community recently discharged from the Services and restless for adventure. They had savings, varying, usually, between five hundred and a thousand pounds, and were willing to invest it all in a project that offered release from the ennui of peacetime. Some were pathetically specific about the domestic or personal problems from which they wished to escape; one wrote:

I've only got eight hundred pounds in the world, but I'll put it all into your business if you'll give me a job and keep me there. I thought the war was hell and I had a breakdown and then I looked forward to getting home. Now I've got there it's back to a wife who I never wanted and never wanted me—I guess you shouldn't get married that young; I'm only twenty-two now. She's younger, but she's been around these years and I haven't and don't want to. Perhaps I could raise a thousand pounds if that's the minimum. I did all right in the Army and I'll learn anything I have to quick enough if you'll give me the chance.

Whatever the outcome, whether or not the business could be adequately capitalized, it looked as if I at any rate had begun by losing all my own money in it, and I could not with a clear conscience take these widows' mites at the present stage. From those who specified their available capital exactly I could at that time have floated a company with a capital of nineteen thousand pounds, of which every share would be taken up, but if that company failed, each invester would have lost all that he had, and I could not face the responsibility. I declined them all and waited for the man of my pipedreams, who would sink more money in experiment and be patient if the venture went on showing a loss for a season or two.

At this time I was approached by a Mr. Charles Osborne, who wished, in return for an advisory fee, to collect from me enough information to start a basking-shark fishery on the west coast of Ireland. His principal, Mr. Sweeney, owned various sea salmon fishings in County Mayo, where the sharks were to be found in great numbers throughout the summer and caused heavy destruction among the salmon nets. I realized with a pang that were it not for my island factory I had but to transfer the boats and all the catching equipment to Ireland to feel sure of all the capital support that I required. I had many interviews with Osborne, and in exchange for a hundred pounds I told him all I knew of catching, handling, and processing basking sharks.[1] I was not able to follow closely the

[1] Charles Osborne was drowned in the spring of 1951, when a vessel engaged on making a film of the shark fishery was sunk off the coast of County Mayo.

progress of the Mayo fishery; it continues, I think, in a desultory way under the name of Achill Island Shark Fisheries, operated by various small groups up the coast as an interest subsidiary to other forms of fishing. Judging from articles on the subject that I have since read, they have forsaken the harpoon for some form of ring-net, which takes an age to repair after the capture of each shark, and the photographs show only the smallest of fish upon the beach.

I travelled a lot; I was in Glasgow, Edinburgh, London, Manchester, Birmingham, and Southampton in the same week; I was in constant telephone communication with Bruce, who in September was still catching sharks, and arranged with him the closing of the season on September 17. Bruce had to lay the *Sea Leopard* up in Mallaig, and when the winter fishing began and the harbour became crowded out with ring-netters he must have become as irritable and nervous as I was. He wrote to me of the constant necessity of moving the *Sea Leopard* from pier to pier, of the impossibility of clam fishing with the *Gannet* (which I had arranged with him on a profit-sharing basis so that he and the *Gannet* should not lie idle during the winter months) in these circumstances. He warned me, too, that he must leave the business not later than the end of the following summer, as he and Dan were going into partnership in a hire-boat business. He was beginning already to look for the 1947 crew, whom, I felt miserably, we had no certainty of being able to employ.

I was very nearly in despair when the pipedream came, or seemed to come, true.

After a very brief preliminary negotiation through lawyers, the business registered as Isle of Soay Shark Fisheries was bought in the winter, lock, stock, and barrel, for thirteen thousand five hundred and fifty pounds, and reregistered under the name of Island of Soay Shark Fisheries Ltd., as a subsidiary of a wealthy firm who already had many interests in the Hebrides. The island, the boats, the gear—all that we had—passed out of my possession, and I became managing director of the new company with a share-holding of five hundred pounds, a nominal salary, and a third share of the net profits when they rose over a thousand pounds per annum. The company was formed with a nominal capital of twenty-six thousand pounds, of which sixteen thousand one-pound shares were taken up; my nine original subscribers accepted shares in the new company in full settlement, and our creditors were paid. I had lost all my capital except that five hundred pounds' worth of shares, but I still had the highest hopes for the future.

By the time the new company was formed, and its first informal meeting held in the spring of 1947, it was far too late to add anything but the most minor pieces of equipment to our existing organization. I think in fact that the only additions were extra pairs of field glasses, some new instruments for the *Sea Leopard*, and an experimental coil of nylon rope. We must work the 1947 season with just the same handicaps as before, the same towing difficulties and factory inadequacies, the same necessity for using the catching vessels as factory transport ships. But the relief that we were able to carry on at all took the edge from these disappointments.

The chairman, who was chairman of the parent company too, was naturally disinclined to pursue my idea of a floating factory or to sink further capital until he saw the result of the first season's effort, and it was clear to me even at that early stage that he had too much on his hands to give much thought to the detailed workings of so small a concern. Thereafter a personal adviser accompanied or deputized for him, a Londoner who had little opportunity to appreciate our problems or to learn them at first hand.

I dreaded the repetition of those hours and days wasted by the catchers in towing dead sharks back to Soay from the Outer Hebrides, but I was not yet ready to accept the fact that it was impracticable at the present stage to market any product other than the liver oil.

In retrospect I think, too, that there may have been a sub-conscious feeling that the company could not be expected to find acceptable a programme that involved increasing inde-pendence of a factory which they had so recently bought. The general policy was to explore more and more products as opportunity offered, the tacit goal for some future season being a large floating factory which could produce them all on board. It was one of the major turning points; had we in-vested then in one boat capable of extracting liver oil at sea, and abandoned the sale of all other materials, we should have seen a handsome dividend on our first season.

The Articles of the company provided for five directors, of whom I might nominate one and the parent company three. I nominated Gordon Davidson, of the Glasgow firm of J. N. Davidson, who had helped and advised me with marketing problems since the inception of the project. In common with the rest of the world, he had, unfortunately, no experience of the materials with which he was dealing, and in his failures I used unjustly to forget that experiment by trial and error was perhaps as necessary on shore as at sea.

The parent company nominated only two of the three direc-tors to whom it was entitled, the chairman and his brother, whom I did not meet until the middle of that summer. As a body, the board remained elusive, and we rarely achieved a complete attendance during the life of the company.

We aimed at beginning the season on the usual date, the last week of April, but there was much to be done in that short time. The *Sea Leopard* had not had her annual engine overhaul, and it was only a few weeks earlier that I had been able to confirm to the gunmaker our order for modified catching equipment. We fixed our opening date for April 17, the date by which we expected the material from Birmingham, and began a frenzy of reorganization.

There were major changes in the crew. Dan MacGillivray had left me to begin the preparation of the boat-hiring business in which he and Bruce were to be partners; Bruce was to leave us about the middle of the season or when we had found a new skipper to take his place. Two irreparable losses: Dan with his soft island speech and calm unhurrying competence; Bruce, often dour, uncommunicative and "crabbit," but infinitely dependable.

The ring-net boats had already made up their crews while we were still uncertain of being able to carry on at all, and we counted ourselves lucky to find a mate and engineer at such short notice. Harry and Jamieson had been working a small cargo boat of their own, the *Noup Head*, and came to us together, with the tacit assumption that Harry would succeed Bruce as skipper. He was an Orkney man, whose past was something of a mystery, but who possessed a deep-sea Master's Ticket and a tremendously enthusiastic manner.

Neil Cameron had been called up and joined a parachute regiment, and in his place we took on Duncan McPhail from

Knoydart, who later gained a temporary glare of publicity as one of the Nine Men of Knoydart who rebelled overtly against the land management of their English landlord.

We began the season with Bruce as skipper, Harry as mate, Jamieson as engineer, and Tex and Duncan as basic crew of the *Gannet*. Donald Ritchie, a Soay boy, was cook; the remaining deckhand was changed several times during the season.

We were ready to sail by April 28.

X

THE 1947 SEASON

We were ready to sail, but the weather was unwilling to let us. So bad had it been that I had not dared to cross to Soay myself, lest I might be stuck there for an indefinite time. The winter in the Hebrides had been cold and still, with nearly nine weeks of sunshine. The seasons had become reversed, and it had now settled down to a truer winter of rain and gales. We lay in harbour for another week, and, on the only moderate day in fourteen consecutive days of gale, Watkins' shark-fishing fleet arrived from Carradale in Loch Fyne. There were changes, for the *Gloaming*, the parent drifter with the oil-extraction plant, had been wrecked at the mouth of Lochboisdale during the winter, while acting as a herring carrier. In her place was the *Recruit*, a steam drifter of the same character, and on the deck of the *Perseverance* I noticed a stack of harpoons that appeared to be of an entirely new type. Both fleets were ready, but we both had to wait in Mallaig harbour until the wind dropped.

On the morning of Saturday, May 3, the first herring of the season were caught, but they were "winter herring" —that is to say, herring that were not feeding, and not the kind one might expect to find in association with sharks. We sailed on Monday, leaving the *Gannet* in harbour, called at Soay to make sure that the factory was ready for action, and for the

whole week we searched the coasts of the Inner and Outer
Hebrides without sighting a fin. We had covered more than a
thousand miles when we got back to Mallaig on Saturday;
either the sharks had not arrived, because of the backwardness
of the season, or they were keeping to the deep waters. From
Monday until Friday it had blown unceasingly and near gale
force. The wind came for the most part from a clear sky,
forming mountainous emerald seas with cobalt and purple
shadows, the waves rearing splendid and triumphant, white-
crested and shining against the blue sky. We searched the
Skye shore where we had fished all through May of the previous year; An Dhusgeir was hidden by every wave that broke
on it, and no boat in the world could have followed a shark in
that sea had a hundred fins been showing. We crossed the
Minch and went on down to Barra Head in the lee of the
islands; on Friday, when the wind began to moderate, we
went westward through the channel between Mingulay and
Pabbay, lifting high on the crests of a mighty, slow-rolling
blue swell that heaved in from the Atlantic to surge forty feet
up the cliffs. We could hear it booming like distant artillery
through the fantastic caves and galleries of Mingulay's
thousand-foot bird-whitened precipice, surging on into the
dark, losing colour and form to become something disintegrating and violent like an explosive.

When we returned to Mallaig at the end of that wasted
week, it was nearly calm, and when we berthed we were told
that the first of the summer herring had been caught that
morning and that at least one shark had been seen, at the Binch
Buoy, some forty miles north of Barra Head.

Throughout Sunday there was a bustle of preparation aboard
Watkins' boats, berthed just astern of us at the big stone pier,

and we, too, were checking through every detail of the catching equipment. Bruce came to me in the evening.

"Watkins will have got the same news as us, and he'll be going to the Binch Buoy too. I think we should get away ahead of him, but the way we're berthed now he'll hear our engines the moment we start up. I think we'll shift across to the end of the fish pier late on in the evening and slip out of the harbour before it's light."

I turned in to get what sleep I could, and just before four in the morning I was awakened by the *Sea Leopard*'s engines starting. I came up on deck to find that it was still dark, the water of the harbour reflecting our starboard light in a long zigzag of brilliant emerald, a calm morning with the sky just beginning to pale in the east, and belts of mist lying flat along the hillside above the harbour. There was no light from below decks on any of Watkins' boats; I watched them anxiously as we left the harbour and headed for the open sea, but our manœuvre had succeeded.

As dawn began to break we found ourselves nuzzling into a dense sea mist, so that we could see no more than when it had been dark, and we set a blind course for the Binch Buoy. As we neared the Barra coast after four hours, the mist was thick, white, and enveloping, but bright and translucent, as though brilliant sunlight were shining behind it. It thinned for a second, and through a gap we had a glimpse of the low hills of the Barra shore a mile away in full sunshine. Then the mist settled round us again, so that we could barely see the other end of the ship.

"I think we'll just wait here until the sun takes the mist off," said Bruce. "There's no point in mucking around in this."

The sea was flat calm; with the *Sea Leopard* hove to, one

could look down over her side to a narrow belt of water enclosed by mist and as unrippled as glass.

We had waited for perhaps half an hour when the mist began to furl up quickly, and the sun broke through, brightening the dispersing tendrils to a dazzling white. The Barra hills, hard and brilliant in the early summer sunshine, were streaked with the same white cottony strips, and half a mile away on our port bow was the Binch Buoy, black on a sea of pale blue.

We got out the field glasses; we looked to the north, to the south, and back across the Minch, but the Buoy itself was all that broke that satiny surface. Then the incredible happened; a shark's fin, flashing light wetly from the low sun, came up between us and the Buoy; before we had got the ship under way another surfaced a quarter of a mile to the south of us; then two more farther inshore. We had steered a perfect course, arrived exactly where the sharks were, and they had appeared at just the moment when we wanted them.

It was a glorious beginning to the season. We harpooned four sharks in less than an hour, and there were four barrels at the surface within a radius of a quarter of a mile. We hauled them all up and had the sharks lashed alongside the *Sea Leopard* by nine a.m. We could see a long way now, and there was not another shark in sight. Watkins' fleet came steaming up over the horizon at nine-thirty, and as he came nearer we gave an extra hitch on the tail ropes on each shark, so that the tails should show well above water, and the opposition be in no doubt as to what they had missed. Watkins waited there all day but saw nothing.

We worked up and down that same piece of coastline for the rest of the week, but the sharks still did not seem to have arrived in real quantity, and despite a hundred-per-cent success in attempted kills, we only had a total of nine fish for the week. On Monday morning we returned to the Binch with diminishing hope; from there we sailed south to Barra, north to Uishenish, and back to Lochboisdale, without seeing anything.

I remember the evening in Lochboisdale harbour very clearly. We had friends in most of these ports now, and at Lochboisdale was the owner of the hotel, Finlay Mackenzie. Finlay was the best company in the world, as full of diverse stories as the *Arabian Nights*. He had spent some years in the Canadian Northwest Mounted Police, and grizzly bears and gun fights were part of his stock-in-trade. Besides being a superb narrator, he was also a superlative host, and his large private room on an upper floor of the hotel was the automatic rendezvous for every one of his friends who berthed in Lochboisdale for even an hour or two. Here the profits of his hotel business were poured out in magnificent generosity; Finlay's standard measure of whisky for his guests was the equivalent of about four doubles in one, and many people found that they could remember little of the conversation toward the end of an evening. It was in keeping with the man himself and all that went with him; he was tall, enormously broad, and carried himself so straight that he looked a giant, a silver-haired giant with blue eyes as bright and direct at fifty-five as they had been thirty years before. To complete the picture was his dog, a black Labrador retriever as big as a St. Bernard, which could carry a wild goose at the gallop.

At this time I had staying on the *Sea Leopard* Hamish Pelham Burn, who afterwards led the Northern British Columbia Expedition in 1949. We spent the evening with Finlay and some mutual friends and left the hotel at about one o'clock in the morning. How many of those gargantuan measures of whisky we had drunk I cannot remember, but it was enough to impair judgment. It was a very still clear night with a new moon, just light enough for us to find our way over the odd hundred yards between the hotel and the pier, with a certain amount of wandering among the sheep pens that lay directly between us and the boat.

When we had berthed it had been at full tide, and the *Sea Leopard*'s decks had been level with the pier; now the tide was out and only the truck of her wireless mast was showing. Her decks were an alarmingly long way below us, and I fumbled around in the dark trying to find one of the fixed ladders on the pier. But they were set back under the main baulk of timber, and my questing toes found nothing to rest upon. I was wearing canvas shoes, and I had all the bravado that such an evening can breed. I pulled myself up again, faced the boat, said "Here goes," and jumped. I landed on my feet on the poop deck, but the jar was enough to make me realize what a long jump down it had been. I was just picking myself up when I heard a violent oath above me and saw against the sky a figure hurtling downward in the most extraordinary attitude. Hamish had failed to negotiate the last of the sheep pens as adroitly as I, had been left some twenty yards behind, and had not noticed at all that the *Sea Leopard* had changed her level in relation to the pier. He just stepped off into empty air and came down like a plummet. He hit the deck beside me and bounced; I could never have believed that a human being could bounce so high. He landed on his buttocks, with his knees drawn up to his chin, and shot up again like a tennis ball, so that there were two entirely separate sounds of impact, and while he was in the air between them he loosed a stream of invective without changing his attitude. He sat there groaning and swearing in the dark, and if he had broken every bone in his body I do not think I could have stopped laughing at that moment; it seemed to me to be the funniest thing I had ever seen in my life. He was un-damaged, but he walked like a duck for days afterwards, and it appeared to him obscurely to be my fault.

The following morning we tried the area of the Binch Buoy again, and when we found nothing there we decided to cross to the inner islands and look at the coasts of Rhum and Canna. It was weirdly calm as we started across those thirty miles of usually troubled water; there was not so much as a wrinkle upon the surface, and minute objects were visible miles away. From the bridge of the *Sea Leopard* the field glasses would make out a floating feather at half a mile, and patches of drifting weed showed as clearly as dark islands upon a white chart. We saw, as we often did at great distances from our fishing grounds, small relics of shots we had fired: pieces of broken harpoon stick or floating felt wads that had tamped the powder charges. (Years later, at Sandaig Lighthouse, beside which I now live, I was searching the shore below the house for some object that could conveniently be converted into a breadboard. Half concealed in the gravel I saw the projecting edge of a small barrel top, white, smooth, and sea-worn—exactly the object I required. I pulled it from the shingle in which it was imbedded, and there across the centre of it were the still legible letters ISSF—Island of Soay Shark Fisheries. It had all the nostalgia of a *carnet de bal* tied with faded ribbon; it brought so many half-forgotten scenes so vividly to my mind that I began this book the next day.)

We were fifteen miles from land, almost exactly halfway between Barra and Canna, when a mile ahead of us we saw the tip of a shark's fin. The surface was still flat as a swimming pool, and the fin left a long triangular furrow in the water as it moved. As we drew nearer it submerged sometimes, but it was never far below the surface, for the furrow never disappeared, guiding us to the shark's course like the empty footprints of the Invisible Man. It was Bruce who first noticed that far beyond this fin there were other furrows, and as I trained my field glasses on the place I saw that the whole surface of the water was slightly disturbed over a wide area.

The sharks had begun to surface before we reached them. It was a gigantic shoal, far larger than the pack in Loch Scavaig that had so excited us a year before. At one moment we counted fifty-four dorsal fins in sight at the same time, and that was, as it were, only like looking at the topmost branches of a tree that has been almost entirely submerged. We could see the fish down below us in the green water as a practically continuous mass, crossing and recrossing, ponderous and mighty; only the topmost layer, and not all of them, was breaking the surface.

There was one group that was more often visible than other parts of the shoal, a group of five fish that followed each other almost nose to tail. They changed course often, but always they followed the leader, so we felt that we should have warning of their turns and find them easier to follow than the single fins that were everywhere dotted over the surface. We shot the hindmost fish after ten minutes' manœuvring; the barrel was heaved overboard, and within another quarter of an hour we had the next as well.

This was a male fish, and during a tremendous struggle at the surface just after we had got the tail sling into position, he emitted a great quantity of what we afterwards found to be sperm. It was not a fluid but hundreds of semi-opaque milky globules like golf balls, varying in size and looking as though made of Lalique glass. These, Dr. Matthews later discovered, were the spermatophores, each having a hard casing enclosing a central core of sperm.

The *Gannet* was still winching up the first shark when we shot the third; then, for no apparent reason, the sharks began to go down, and in a few minutes there was not one in sight, just a flat, white, unrippled sea that gave no hint of the great herd of antediluvian monsters that moved beneath its surface.

The story of the rest of that week is best told in the words of a letter that I wrote on Saturday:

This is begun on the way into Mallaig from Soay, with the idea of cutting down the enormous amount of writing that there will certainly be to do this evening and tomorrow. There is just enough motion to make writing a little awkward, but I hope I shall remain legible. . . .

We towed the three carcasses to Soay and were back at the same spot soon after dawn next morning (we had marked the place pretty accurately on the chart). There was nothing in sight, and we all felt sure it had been a moving shoal. We took a wide cast round, and in the late evening we found them again, eight miles north of where they had been on Wednesday. It was so calm, the sea so white and utterly flat, that we could see the fins at about four miles. This time we only got two; we lost three more through having ropes too short for the depth of water, the sharks took the ropes and buoys under and never let them up again. I suppose the steel drums burst—next year we ought to have buoys that will stand far greater pressure, so that once a shark was firmly harpooned and the buoy overboard he would always turn up again.

The shoal didn't go down, and we were shooting at them by searchlight long after it was dark; probably even if the barrels hadn't been taken under they would have been lost in the darkness before we could pull them up.

We haven't tied up or dropped anchor since we found the shoal on Wednesday, and we are all getting a little short of sleep; I've averaged about two hours in each twenty-four, and I think some of us are even worse off than that.

The next day, yesterday, we found the shoal still farther north, about sixteen miles from where we first saw them. They did not show until five in the afternoon, and they were thicker than ever. It was still glass-calm, and a mist began to form after about half an hour, so we didn't dare to let the *Gannet* far from the *Sea Leopard*. It got thicker and thicker, and by the time we had got five sharks (our record to date) you couldn't see fifty yards. We shot six, but we lost one barrel in the mist, and I dare say it was just as well, for I don't see how we could have towed another shark. By using the whole length of the boat we can get three one behind the other, overlapping by a few feet, but only on one side of the ship, as on the other side one has to leave a space clear for the engine's exhaust pipes.

We got these five lashed alongside and started very slowly for home. It was very eerie; you know the way writhing white mist is used in films for an effect of mystery and horror—the mist, right down to the surface, was moving and twisting and re-forming, and out of it would appear again and again those great slippery fins, ahead, astern, and on both sides. Heaven knows how many sharks we could have killed if we hadn't had to think about towing them home; we should certainly never have had to wait for a shot after reloading. There was enough money round about us to make us all rich for life, and we couldn't touch it.

Next week—if we haven't lost the shoal. This year, next year, sometime. . . .

We are only a mile out of Mallaig now, and judging by the gulls in the air we are not the only people who have been catching fish.

Bruce left us that week-end. He left, as it were, on the crest, and I had been so impressed by the new mate, Harry, that I did not then realize the magnitude of our loss.

Harry had attracted attention during his first week with us by extracting one of his own teeth with complete nonchalance. He had had toothache all day, and in the evening he tied a piece of wire round the roots of the molar and, using his whole strength on an upward jerk, wrenched it out without batting an eyelid. He explained that once, in the China Sea, he had pulled out four like that in an hour.

His first action as skipper was to persuade the crew to regard Saturday as a full day's fishing. Before this, Saturday had always been completely wasted (the morning being occupied in reaching Mallaig so that the crew could be ashore by midday), and he could have chosen no better way to make me regard him as already indispensable. He went further; he proposed to organize the crew to work all night, in two shifts, and I looked on him as the answer to all problems, the superman of whom all worried business owners dream.

The factory was working to capacity. There were rows of inflated dead sharks tied up or anchored in the harbour, and the factory hands were all working the long hours of overtime which gradually drained each shark of profit. With these catching opportunities we could no longer afford the time to carry salted flesh to Mallaig, and the icehouse was now given its first test as a bulk salting tank. Into three feet of brine the flesh was tipped through a hatch in the concrete cutting-up stance; load after load went in until there were nearly twelve tons of it, the topmost layer floating at the surface of that dark subterranean lake. Floating—it did cross my mind to wonder whether this was as it should be, but we had followed Gordon Davidson's instructions so exactly that I dismissed the doubt.

Scientific work upon the shark's anatomy had begun at last,

and at the factory and with the small resources of the laboratory hut were working Dr. Matthews, now Scientific Director of the Zoological Society, and Dr. Parker of the British Museum. A summary of their work is appended to this book, and the pure scientist may be inclined to regard the book itself as no more than a lengthy explanation of the circumstances that made it possible, a background to discovery in an entirely fresh zoological field.

Matthews and Parker toiled endlessly. They were no pure laboratory scientists, these two; they worked with axes, saws, and knives, and neither their work nor their dress would have excited adverse comment on a whale-flensing plant. The sight of them lopping off for dissection the two giant claspers of an adult male shark (photograph 60) reminded another guest of mine of a story of a German guide conducting a party of pigtailed *Mädchen* through a provincial museum. On reaching a statue of Priapus possessing a like superfluity of equipment, and hearing the party calling one another's attention to this phenomenon in excited whispers, he boomed sonorously, "*Mädchen, wenn der eine müde ist, dann fängt er mit dem anderen an.*" This, in view of Harrison Matthews' later discoveries, would appear to be equally true of the sharks.

Our luck did not hold into the next week; the wind was at hand to defeat us again, and on Friday I wrote in another letter:

We have had an exasperating week. The big shoal is still far out in mid-Minch; the exasperation began on Tuesday, when we lost in the dark the float buoys of two sharks whose ropes had become entangled, and which we had left a mile away while shooting another shark. Next morning a full gale was blowing, and we could not even look for the buoys, which were fifteen miles out in the open sea. The gale went on blowing right through Thursday, and it was too rough to let us out of Castlebay harbour until an hour or two before dusk last night, when we killed two sharks off Barra Head. We found the big shoal again at four-thirty this morning, but they wouldn't remain steady at the surface, and we never got a shot. For sheer temper-trying I know nothing quite so powerful as being among a lot of sharks that won't allow themselves to be shot at.

We got the two fish off at the factory this afternoon, and are now (evening) on our way back to keep contact with the big shoal, which seems to be moving steadily north, and tends to be at the surface only at night. The great enthusiasm of my new skipper means that we are now virtually never in harbour or at anchor, and steam away the whole twenty-four hours. He seems to let most of the crew get a little sleep, but how he survives himself I don't know. But despite these tremendous efforts it is now Friday evening, and we have only three sharks for the week. We intend to work until late tomorrow night, and don't expect to be in Mallaig until the small hours of Sunday morning, so the answering of the week's mail on Sunday is a nightmare in prospect.

At Soay I found that the new salting tank, converted from the icehouse, is apparently tainted, and the whole sixteen tons of salted flesh which it contains may have to be scrapped.

The letter has a postscript:

I reopen this letter today (Saturday) to add that I got two sharks from the big shoal at midnight last night, with the searchlight, and two more at dawn this morning.

In retrospect the rest of that season seems to be dominated by a single incident; or, more exactly, by a single fortnight that was full of incident.

The period was as isolated geographically as temporally, for we were virtually shore-based on an island nearly eighty miles from Soay. During that time we reached the peak of all our shark catching, and our difficulties in handling the carcasses brought into final focus our original error in policy.

A week of gales followed our last attack on the big shoal, and when it was calm enough to sail again we did not know where to look for them. We crossed from Mallaig to Uishenish, but Davidson had not seen a fin since the weather broke. We kept on up the coast and reached Eillean Glas Lighthouse, on Scalpay Island, fifty miles to the north, late in the evening. We had decided to lie the night at Scalpay pier, at the back of the island, but had to follow its circumference right round and come in from the north, as the southern channel, East Loch Tarbert, is blocked by a mass of small rock islands and hidden reefs.

Scalpay was not quite unknown territory to us, for we had brought the *Dove* here two years before, but so far we had had no reason to regard it as an especial shark haunt like Uishenish or Moonen. Rather I had thought of it as a place of beauty so great as to distinguish it even among that long chain of which each individual island is a brilliant jewel. I was never there for long enough to know well the community that inhabited it; they must, like other human herds, have had their ugliness, their strifes, and their despairs, but these were not evident to the outside eye. Here was a small pastoral community, every visible phase of whose life had a minute and individual beauty, whose every activity enhanced rather than detracted from the wider beauty of their surroundings. Much that the cynical might dismiss as having primarily the shallow appeal of the "picturesque" is recognizable as something deeper by an eye already long accustomed to these archaic forms of architecture, dress, and speech, so that they in themselves have no intrinsic allure or novelty.

Wool is the industry of Scalpay's tiny village—wool for dyeing, weaving, and spinning on the island; no great flocks here, but single individual sheep on tether, tended with as much individual care as the milch cows that are tethered in the same way on the short flower-covered turf. Swathes of brilliantly dyed wool hang drying in the sun, and on the hillsides one may see hundreds of yards of bright woven tweed stretched like rainbow pathways. There must have been many colours of dye, but particularly I remember one of a vivid sky-blue, and the warm red-brown crottle that is made from the rock lichen. The scents are of wool and wool dye, mingling with the smell of the sea and the heather and peat smoke. Here the old women do not drag their spinning wheels from the house for the attraction of the tourist; they sit there naturally in the sun, with a shy and perhaps suspicious glance for the stranger.

Shallow thought might hold that the cultivation, also, has only the appeal of the archaic, but the honest eye must concede a specific grace to the deep ridge and furrow of the traditional "lazy-bed," and to the strange rhythmic patterns that it forms.

The people, too, unless a nostalgic imagination has redrawn them, were for the most part of an unusual beauty. The faces of the old had the serenity, the pencilled lines of experience and adjustment, that suggest resolved conflict superficially improbable in that remote Elysium. "True human beauty," said a man whose opinion I respected, "is to be found only in the faces of the old Chinese and the young Balinese," and I wondered how he would have responded to those sculptured heads of Scalpay. The young did not suffer by comparison; I remember a girl of perhaps seventeen, black-haired and blue-eyed, with small straight features, who ran barefoot down a flowery slope to untether a bleating calf and lead it back to the croft. As it gambolled she danced and played with it, tenderly and exultingly, as though her own ebullience of spirit must find a common expression. There were twin fourteen-year-old boys, too, who often visited the boat and made friends with the crew; they were indistinguishable but for a tiny scar that one had above his left eyebrow, and they would ask us to guess which was which. They would go to elaborate lengths to confuse, changing jerseys or jackets at a moment when no one was looking, so that before addressing either one must look for the confirmation of that minute betraying scar. These two were of a different type from the barefooted girl, fair hair curling like fronds of a fern, and colouring as brilliant as that of the distant Norse stock from which they had probably sprung. The people of Scalpay seemed to me to be like the island on which they lived, serene and beautiful.

We woke on that first day at Scalpay to a glorious summer morning with the sun already up over the hills and the colours dazzling and intense, the sea so smooth and brilliant that the mind rebelled against being able to perceive it only with one sense at a time. We turned out through the narrow channel of Scalpay Sound, and the Minch lay before us, pale, shining and glassy, with the weird basaltic-columned turrets and towers of the Shiant Islands ten miles away. Off the lighthouse point there was usually a jabble of small leaping waves; now, in this intense calm, there was no more than a series of faintly disturbed patches, as though an invisible hand were dragging at the water from beneath.

In the middle of one of these patches, almost stationary, swam a large shark, nose, tail, and dorsal fin all breaking the surface. He was the herald, the outrider, of the great shoal from which, when we left Scalpay eighteen days later, we had killed nearly fifty sharks; and could, I think, have killed three times that number if the boats had had nothing else to do but kill them and bring them in. During all that time there were rarely more than half a dozen fish showing simultaneously, but the supply seemed inexhaustible over those ten miles of water between the two headlands, Rudha Bocaig and Rudha Bhaird, to the south and the north of Scalpay Island.

On that first day, a Thursday, we killed no less than nine sharks, and on the Friday, despite bad weather in the afternoon, we shot another six. The last of these had attached to his back a parasite we had never seen before, a brilliant steel-blue fish, perhaps eighteen inches long, clinging to the mid-line of the back between the two dorsal fins. He remained in view while the shark rolled two or three times at the surface after the tail hawser had been secured to the ship's side, but detached himself and swam clear before any way of catching him had occurred to us. This must have been a species of *Remora* or shark-sucker, not previously recorded from the Hebrides.

We were seventy-odd miles from Soay and the factory, and to tow the sharks there would have meant four full days' ferrying for the *Sea Leopard*. We decided to draw them up on the Scalpay beaches and cut out their livers. The beaching of those fifteen giant carcasses took the whole of Saturday and required the cooperation of both boats. The work had to be done, for there was no pier to which they could be tied without obstructing the berth of the island steamer when she came in; outside, the sea was still full of sharks, but we were not free to hunt them. The beaching could be done only at full tide, and it took two tides before the work was complete.

Between tides there was much else to be seen to. We had to find containers for ten or more tons of liver and somehow organize its transport back to the factory. It was the clearest object lesson we had yet received in the futility of working without some form of factory ship which could perform its own oil extraction on board.

It was a windfall to find that in a store in Scalpay harbour there was a huge quantity of new and unused half-size herring barrels which some firm had left there in connection with a herring-curing project. The barrels were no longer required by their owner, and after an exchange of telegrams and telephone calls with the mainland we were able to buy them all at a reasonable figure.

Next there was the question of transport; the bulk was far too great for the *Sea Leopard* to carry without many journeys, and we hoped, too, to kill at least another thirty sharks during the following week. There was only one thing for it, to hire transport, and I arranged with a Glasgow firm, seeming incredibly distant at its two-hundred-odd miles away, to send up a "puffer"—a small steam cargo boat. It was a gamble but, I thought, a justifiable one; the hire of the boat would cost three hundred pounds, but even if we caught no more sharks, the livers of those that we had would do more than pay the cost.

Scalpay was capable of comedy as extreme as its beauty. When, late in the evening, we had finished moving the barrels from the store to the beach where the sharks lay, and the *Sea Leopard* was once more berthed at the pier, a very old and very tiny man came to ask us if we would give him one barrel so that he could cure some herring for the winter. He enunciated the English words with infinite difficulty, and his voice creaked like some piece of machinery long disused. I conceded his apparently humble request with some reluctance; for, small though the item was, it entailed a disproportionate amount of trouble in book transfer and cash adjustment from fund to fund. In the same laborious and unlubricated voice he expressed his everlasting gratitude, but when I handed him the barrel he said he would "send the boy for it," and moved slowly and painfully off up the pier.

Some half-hour later "the boy" arrived, followed at a distance of some yards by the new owner of the barrel. "The boy" was small and slight, and he carried himself bent double, with his back almost parallel to the ground, moving as slowly as his follower. For he was at least eighty years old. Ages beyond that are difficult to estimate with accuracy, but he was no less. The two of them arrived at the ship's side with an almost ritual similarity of movement.

"Put it on the boy's back," quavered the first gnome, advancing with a piece of string already knotted into some form of harness; and the second gnome was carefully reversed up to the stack of barrels on the pier. His shoulders, bent as though they had borne the entire aggregate of human sorrow since birth, made a perfect resting place for the feather-light barrel; it was knotted into position under his armpits, and in response to a creaking Gaelic sentence he moved off into the dusk.

But the first gnome lingered on. He spoke, but we could not understand him. At last the twins arrived, and between angelic grins they translated. He wanted whisky, just a very little, for his health. It so happened that we had none on board—no alcohol at all, in fact, but some champagne we had been keeping to celebrate the first week in which we killed twenty sharks. We told him so, and it was duly translated, but clearly he did not believe us. He thought we were holding out on him. He argued and pleaded, half in English and half in Gaelic, while the boys became brusque and almost menacing.

Then he played his last card. So slowly that there was a

second's interval between each word, he said, "I—am—ferry —bad—with—the—flumatism"; then, as if seized by a sudden doubt, he added "I think."

It was too much for me; it was too much, too, for a distinguished Cambridge don who was staying with me on the *Sea Leopard*, Walter Hamilton, now headmaster of Westminster, and one of my first subscribers. We fled precipitately to my cabin, where we dissolved into fits of giggles unknown to either of us since childhood, pausing only now and again to say to each other, "Ssh—he'll hear us!" before the convulsions came on again.

How many whose livelihood depends on the sea have thought that if they could control the wind they would ask no more? What proof of divinity more certain to touch the hearts of those early fishermen could Christ have given than the stilling of the waves? Now, when at last we were in sight of fortune, those winds that we could not still sprang up again, and for all the following week they blew and blew, until the calm, shining sea over which we had sailed so few days before seemed a memory infinitely distant.

I pictured the boat that we had hired lying, perhaps, in the Crinan Canal, or in some port far to the south of us, unable to face the open sea, while her bills mounted daily. Fortunately for us, however, the *Moonlight*, as she was called, developed boiler trouble half a day out from Glasgow and did not reach Scalpay until Friday evening. We spent the week working upon the beached carcasses and chasing sharks with the *Gannet* among the rocky islets and reefs of East Loch Tarbert, which separates Scalpay from Harris on the south side. Even in that comparative shelter there was quite a sea running; and between

it and the unknown hazards of the hidden rocks we had all
the excitement we could have wished for, if not all the sharks.
It was a different form of shark hunting from any that we had
known; the channels between the islands were often no wider
than broad roads, and among these winding alleyways we had
to look for shelter as well as sharks, and to judge carefully in
what direction a shark would take the *Gannet* after being harpooned, for we could not use the barrels in these conditions.
We were making, as it were, a series of tip-and-run raids upon
the outliers of the main shoal, and we could never kill more
than one fish without returning to the harbour, for that was
the *Gannet*'s towing capacity. Altogether we killed six in this
way during the week, which was, as one of the crew put it,
better than a slap in the belly with a wet fish.

The beaches where we had drawn up the sharks were a
tremendous and terrible sight. The sharks lay in long rows at
the tide line, black mountains on the pale grey boulders. As
more and more of the carcasses were opened the blood trickled
down among the stones, and the sea behind them became
crimson for hundreds of yards, a true sea of blood. We had
soon acquired a technique for the opening of these carcasses,
from which we required the liver only: we would cut two
long vertical slits in the flank, one at the front and one at the
rear end of the belly, and then connect the tops of these two
incisions with a horizontal line. It was, so to speak, a door in
the shark's flank, with the hinges at the bottom. As the horizontal cut was almost completed the door would begin to sag
outward under the tremendous weight of the liver and entrails that it was holding in, and one had to jump aside to avoid
that ponderous slithery mass as it came rumbling out like an
avalanche. Once I was not quick enough in avoiding it, and

was knocked flat on my back and enveloped by it, struggling free drenched in oil and blood, with a feeling almost of horror.

There were other reasons for the horror; this was not the first contact I had had with that particular shark. He was the fourth in the line, a huge bull of unusually black colouring, and when the working party, moving down the line, had reached him, he was still moving, shuddering and undulating down his entire length, though he had been beached for two days. I told them to go on to the next fish, and went back to the *Sea Leopard* for one of the two eight-bore shotguns which we carried aboard her. At point-blank range I shot the shark between the eyes four times, so that the brain must have been completely obliterated. There was no visible effect; the movement of the body neither accelerated nor slowed. Then, to make certain that the fish was dead, we cut off the entire forepart of the head with axes, but this, too, produced no change. Four days later, when we dragged the carcasses off the beach, the body, now headless and disembowelled, was still twitching and jerking over its whole length.

The removal and barrelling of the liver was light work by comparison with the recovery of the harpoons. When they had passed clean through the body, or come to rest in the body cavity, we had only to remove the shackle that had secured the end of the steel trace to the rope and then draw the harpoon out forwards, as a prolongation of its original flight. But when it had penetrated the vertebræ, or its barbs had become jammed in that mass of cartilage, it was sometimes half a day's work with axes and saws to free one harpoon.

At nightfall, when we were all exhausted, the barrels of liver on the beaches must either be ferried across the harbour to the *Sea Leopard* and lifted onto her decks with the hand derrick, or must in some way be secured against the tide floating them off during the hours of darkness. We thought, the first night, that we had moved them all above the tide's reach, but at the very first light a messenger came to tell us that they had broken loose and were floating all over the harbour, and that some had gone out on the ebb tide and would soon be in the open sea. It took nearly all that day to round them up with the *Gannet* and the *Sea Leopard*, and when we had at last beached them again we roped them in flotillas one to another so that they could not become completely dispersed. Even so, they would some-how slip their ropes when the breeze freshened during the night, and latterly one of us would remain as a patrol on the beach while the others slept.

On Friday the *Moonlight* came in from the south, and by degrees the barrels were ferried over to her and stored in her capacious hold. Her capacity was three times what she was carrying, and we decided to gamble on the weather once more and to keep her with us throughout the following week. If the weather was fair she would provide a solution to another problem, too. The *Sea Leopard*'s winch, on which we had been so long dependent before the *Gannet*'s had arrived, was hand-operated, though with a lever large enough for several men to work at a time. The *Gannet*'s was driven directly from her engine, so that now she could haul up a shark far more quickly than could her parent ship, and when we were in these dense shoals the process of winching up with the *Sea Leopard* had come to seem frustratingly slow. We intended, therefore, to keep the *Moonlight* with us on the fishing grounds, to haul in harpooned sharks while we went on shooting. We hoped to bring off during the following week the slaughter of which the gale had cheated us during the past five days.

Monday dawned calm but dull, and we were out at the very first light, the *Moonlight* having been instructed to come out and find us by eight-thirty a.m. The sea had gone down very quickly, and the air, even at that early hour, was muggy and warm. The tops of the hills were hidden by banks of heavy grey cloud, lying flat and inert as though they had always been there and the hills had pressed upon them and grown up through them.

The sharks were nearly as plentiful as they had been before the weather broke, but now they were more capricious in appearance, the fins often submerging before guns could reach them. We had shot three when the *Moonlight* came punctually round the point, and she began at once to pull up the float barrels. Presently a mist started to form, so that after two hours each boat had little idea of where the others were, and only the boom of a gun in the mist, sometimes startlingly close by, would tell us of the others' activity. The visibility limited our catching power, for a float-barrel was soon lost in the mist, and whereas the *Sea Leopard* could summon the *Moonlight* with her hooter the *Gannet* had to winch up her sharks as she shot them, and sometimes approach the next one handicapped by a carcass lashed alongside, whose heavy drag made the steering inaccurate.

Altogether we landed eight sharks that day, and lost two more float-barrels in the mist. The *Moonlight* and the *Sea Leopard* laboured back into the harbour just before dusk, and it was three o'clock in the morning, and the sky already paling, when we had drawn up the sharks on to the beaches, now cleaned by the tide of all trace of their former carnage.

The weather gave us only one more day's fishing. The next morning was as fair and smiling as the day on which we had arrived at Scalpay, and we killed twelve sharks. The *Moon-light*, unaccustomed by practice to the securing of sharks after they had been brought to the surface, took an age to lasso the tails and to fix the gill slings in position, and by seven in the evening there were still five barrels dotted over a radius of perhaps four miles. Most of the sharks had now submerged; only an occasional fin showed through the field glasses far out towards the Shiant Islands. The *Gannet* drew alongside us to discuss our further action, and in the course of comparing notes on the day's work we discovered that we were a shark short. Up to this time in the evening the *Gannet* claimed to have killed four sharks and lost two: one had pulled the harpoon out after being buoyed for three hours, and the other had gone off with its rope—unfortunately, the nylon rope, worth thirty-five pounds—which had been insecurely fastened to the buoy. From the *Sea Leopard* I claimed to have harpooned seven sharks and lost one through a leaking buoy. The *Moonlight* had four strung alongside her and was now hauling up a fifth, yet there were only five barrels within the most distant view of the field glasses. Each of us stuck to our figures, each was unshakable, and eventually we decided to take the *Sea Leopard* for a wide sweep in the direction of the Shiants to look for the missing shark.

We described one semicircle about five miles from land and found nothing, then another, more than a mile farther out. The sea was white and motionless, and midway in the northern part of our arc I thought I could see something about two miles farther out, almost due north to the Shiants. It did not, on the other hand, look quite as a shark should. There was a large dark object that might be the barrel; there were smaller objects not far from it that might be sharks' fins, but among these there was something longer and thinner, like a spar canted over at an angle. We turned and headed for this indeterminate blot, which looked in the heat-shimmer like a small but significant hieroglyphic upon the unmarked white sheet of sea and sky.

At a mile's distance I could make out that it was indeed the barrel, but what was beyond it still puzzled me. There were sharks' fins, several of them, but among them was this object that seemed to move with the others, straight and thin. We were not more than a quarter of a mile away when I recognized it for what it was, a harpoon stick jutting from the back of a shark that was now feeding in the wake of a second, both fish travelling leisurely eastward. The drag on the floating barrel that the harpooned fish was towing was very slight, and there must have been a great sag of slack rope hanging down in the sea between them.

We argued as to whether we should shoot the more distant shark before recovering the first, but in the end decided to steal a march on the harpooned fish and get most of the rope back before he became aware of our presence and remembered the fact, of which he was now apparently unconscious, that he had more than a foot of heavy steel inside him. We picked up the barrel and kept the boat going slowly ahead while we hauled up the slack rope as fast as we could. We were not more than five yards from him when he felt a slight drag on the rope and began to sound, but by that time we had the rope on the winch and he could not go down. We had him secured alongside the boat in less than twenty minutes, and in another quarter of an hour we had shot the leading shark and were hauling him up, too. I remember that a few miles to the east of us we saw the old whaling-factory ship *Sir James Clarke Ross* steaming majestically northward up the Minch, her fleet of five catchers, red-rusted from stack top to waterline, looking like day-old ducklings beside their parent. Perhaps they saw the gun in our bows and puzzled over it, for each in turn gave a blast upon her hooter.

We had killed twenty sharks in the first two days of the week, and it seemed that at last we were going to make the killing of which we had dreamed, perhaps fifty fish in the week. The price of the oil had now risen to a hundred and thirty-five pounds per ton, so that if we could land that number we should take nearly two thousand five hundred pounds for the week on the livers alone. The first formal meeting of the board of directors had been called for the following weekend in Mallaig, and I felt that such a catch would ensure the factory ship for which I meant to press.

When I heard the gale warning on the wireless that night I could scarcely believe that we were, after all, to be robbed of our chance. "Iceland, Faeroes, Hebrides, Fastnet, Shannon; strong to gale south to southwest, visibility good." It seemed that we were never to have a week of fair weather when the sharks were plentiful, and I felt all the frustration of a child who is denied, capriciously as it appears to him, the desire of his heart.

There was, however, much to do on shore. The beaches were packed again, and once more at slack tide one looked down from the hilltop upon a sea crimson with blood. I had had two of the factory workers sent up from Soay, so we had nine men to work on the carcasses. We had finished barrelling and ferrying the livers by Thursday night, and it was plain that it was no use keeping the *Moonlight* any longer. Until two days ago we had been receiving continuous reports from Davidson of sharks at Uishenish Lighthouse, so we told the *Moonlight*'s skipper to call there on his way to Soay and put off several hundred empty barrels in Shepherd's Bight for our future use. (Of these nearly a third had been stolen by passing boats before we reached Uishenish a fortnight later.)

The island steamer, *Lochmor*, berthed at Scalpay during the time we were clearing the beaches. Her skipper, Captain Robertson, whom Compton Mackenzie described in *Keep the Home Guard Turning* and *Whisky Galore*, had long since become an old friend. A short plump man, red-faced and with protuberant blue eyes, he owned a voice whose natural key was pitched so many octaves above the normal masculine that he was universally known as "Squeak." When *Whisky Galore* was filmed [1] there was a project to secure Squeak himself to act the part of the skipper who, in the novel, represented him; but the idea was abandoned owing to practical difficulties. He retired in 1948 and died a year later; without his weekly visits the ports of the Hebrides seem poorer.

That bat's voice decorated the flattest of sentences with a fictitious but intriguing significance, an individuality so intense that it seemed that Squeak never in fact used the words or phrases of his fellow men. The stories of his dry wit are innumerable and often apocryphal; perhaps, too, he had not remained unconscious of his invariable effect. Once when he berthed at Lochboisdale he was shown by Finlay Mackenzie a telegram received from one of the *Lochmor*'s passengers. The message read: *Arriving Lochboisdale this evening with the aid of God and the skipper of the* Lochmor. Squeak read it with

[1] The film was released in America under the title *Tight Little Island*.

bulging eyes, then laid it aside, saying dreamily in a voice almost beyond the range of the human ear, "God and the skipper
of the *Lochmor* . . . aye, two good men."

On this occasion when he came to Scalpay pier, he leaned
down from his bridge to see my guest, Walter Hamilton, whose
head and shoulders were protruding from the after-hatch of
the *Sea Leopard*. Walter, usually a dignified and staid figure,
wore a week's growth of beard and was dressed in a black-and-
white Faeroese sweater. His beard merged with his hair, which
was standing on end, and he presented an entirely unscho-
lastic appearance. When Squeak had made his acquaintance on
the mainland Walter had been engaged upon a translation of
Plato's *Symposium*, a fact that had made a deep impression
upon Squeak's unclassical mind.

His eyes came out on stalks now as he peered down, crimson
and incredulous, and recognized Walter.

"Whatt are you doing hee-ar?" he shrilled. "You look chust
like a py-rate." Then, following no very apparent train of
thought, "You'll be writing another book, I suppose."

He went on to tell us that he had seen a shark in comparatively calm water in Scalpay Sound as he came in. We took the
Sea Leopard out and shot it, the forty-seventh, and last, fish
that we landed from that one shoal.

We had cleared the beaches by Friday, and we sailed for
Mallaig in appalling weather, a raging grey sea on which the
Sea Leopard lurched and rolled sickeningly, until every unsecured object below decks clattered to and fro in hideous
cacophony. Water poured down the galley chimney and put
out the stove, so that we could not have so much as a cup of
tea during the eight-hour run, and we had used the last of our
solid rations the day before. We towed with us that last shark

we had shot; the tremendous and ominous thump of his body against the ship's side became increasingly disquieting, though it was not until after the end of that season that we knew with how much justification.

We went straight to Mallaig, without calling at Soay, and the shark was still lashed alongside the ship when we berthed. In Mallaig itself the sight of a dead shark was still a novelty, and it began to collect a small crowd of tourists and sight-seers. The fish was drawn well up, so that some twenty feet of his flank was clear of the water, and onto that elephantine skin people began to throw pennies. The next day I counted a total of four shillings and twopence halfpenny, and the money was still coming in.

In the London Zoo I have often seen motionless alligators dotted with coins over their entire length, and supposed that the most obvious and available missile had been used to try to break the sphinx-like calm and produce some movement. Since, however, the shark was patently dead, and no missile in the world could stir it to twitch so much as a muscle, I began to wonder whether the alligator coins, too, had in fact some common and unconscious motive of oblation or propitiation. I got into conversation with an elderly lady who was spending her money particularly freely in this way (she had, to my knowledge, contributed a threepenny piece besides four pennies), and asked her if it did not seem rather a waste of money in these hard times.

"Not at all," she replied briskly. "I don't waste my money on cigarettes and drinks like some folk, and I'm on holiday, and it's my own money."

I pointed out that at dusk I was going to empty the collecting plate, as it were, and buy myself a packet of cigarettes with the proceeds. She was unimpressed. "Well, each to his own pleasures," she said and threw down another halfpenny with a slightly defiant gesture. Later I tackled on the same subject a giggling Glasgow girl, who was throwing her coins down with squeals of delight and anticipation. "Why?" I asked. On a fanfare of giggles she blurted, "Och, I'm sure I dinna ken," and took to her heels. My curiosity was left unsatisfied.

In Mallaig for the week-end was Niall Rankin, one of the first of the early subscribers to my venture. He had come up from Treshnish in his converted lifeboat, the *Albatross*; he and this tiny white boat having just returned from an expedition to the Antarctic island of South Georgia, to which the *Albatross* had been carried on one of the whaling ships. This expedition, from which he brought back a huge number of king penguins for British public collections, he has since described in his book *Antarctic Isle*. He had only recently dispersed his penguins to their destinations, and he described two as it were personal penguins that he had kept aboard his own boat. He spoke of leopard seals and sea elephants and Antarctic blizzards, and sitting in the *Albatross*'s sedate little cabin under the July sun in Mallaig it was difficult to believe that these same bulkheads and portholes had been so recent a foreground to the remote world of which he spoke.

Our first board meeting, which was held in Mallaig that week-end, was long, interrupted, and tedious, beginning in the early afternoon and ending at eleven p.m. There was too much to be explained, too much that in the course of years I had come to take for granted as background knowledge, and which was all virgin territory to the rest of the board. "Have you tried . . ." was a favourite beginning to any question asked me, and I had step by step to go back over that road of experiment and rejection of the past years. I faced the board with a clear conscience, for in the spring I had conservatively estimated a season's catch of fifty sharks, and by now we had already killed eighty-three. I made a lengthy report upon the season's work. My two primary requests, for some form of factory ship to accompany the catchers and make them more independent of a shore base, and for a spotter aircraft to keep us in touch with the shoals, were immediately approved in principle, and it was arranged that a Tiger Moth belonging to one of the other directors should be flown up for spotting tests the following week.

We had the worst possible weather for these tests, but I had come to expect nothing else. The aircraft was flown to Glenbrittle, a bay on the Skye shore not far from Soay, which before the war had been a regular calling point for the Glasgow-Hebrides air service. The field was tiny, but it was one of the very few places in Skye where an aircraft could land at all. In the war, however, the field had been obstructed by cairns of stones during the invasion scare, and was never restored as a landing ground. It was under cultivation now, and a narrow strip at the edge of it, used by the farm carts, was the only space on which an aircraft could touch down. My codirector who brought up the plane was a brilliant pilot; he arrived on schedule despite a strong southerly wind and a bumpy passage over the mainland mountains. The small white Tiger Moth appeared flying low down the glen, the tops of the Cuillins nearly three thousand feet above it; it circled the landing field once and returned to make a perfect landing on that unbelievably short and narrow strip.

We made a long tour of the Skye coast and the whole of the

Outer Hebrides, stopping to refuel at Stornoway and Ben-becula. It was bright and sunny with a strong blustering south wind, and the water below us was of a blue so deep as to be almost black, flecked with brilliant white horses, as beautiful and as useless for our purpose as it could be. I occupied the rear cockpit and had to lean continuously over the side of the open fuselage, for only from a vertical angle could one hope to see anything below that opaque surface. One earflap of my helmet was broken; gradually the ear became intensely pain-ful, and I have been slightly deaf in it ever since. What was worse, however, was that the intercom between front and rear cockpit was out of order; there was no way of communicating with the pilot other than writing notes and passing them over his shoulder, and it was difficult to prevent them being torn from one's hand by the wind.

We saw no sharks on the Skye shore, crossed the Minch, and refuelled at Stornoway. We flew on south down the east coast of the island chain in very bumpy weather, and a few miles to the south of Stornoway I saw the first shark, right below me, in some calmer water sheltered by a headland to the south of us. He looked far larger than I had expected, though he was, I think, a fathom or more under water. He seemed to be stationary, looking pale and enormous in the royal-blue water. I leaned forward and tapped the pilot on the shoulder, pointing down to where the shark was below and now slightly behind me. I immediately wished I had not done so, for the instantaneous result was what seemed to be an almost vertical diving turn in which I was so acutely uncomfortable that I lost the position of the shark and took minutes to rediscover it. After that I became rather cautious about attracting the pilot's attention to any object of which I was not absolutely certain.

We saw only two more sharks before we turned to recross the Minch, but in the evening, flying at a thousand feet north of the Isle of Raasay, we saw five together, heading southward, like a fleet of submarines. They were well down below the surface, but even in that rough water they showed plainly, and we considered the results of this first test to be eminently satisfactory. We closed the 1947 season with approved plans to use both a factory ship and a spotter aircraft the following year.

XI

DECLINE AND FALL
1948–49

Spondet fortuna multa multis, praestat nemini,
vive in dies et horas, nam proprium est nihil.

Through the serious business of the next eight months, through the numerous and sometimes acrimonious disagreements on policy, through the struggles to find some mutually agreeable working basis for the 1948 season, I remember a steady and unvarying background. It could not be called an undertone, for it belonged to the sense of smell rather than hearing. The sixteen tons of shark flesh in the factory pickle-tank had turned rotten. The salt solution in which the flesh had been immersed had, despite the most meticulous adherence to Davidson's directions, been of insufficient strength.

On the flat concrete surface upon which the sharks' carcasses were cut up was a small wooden hatch. When this was lifted one looked down into some fifteen feet of obscurity to which the eye became but gradually accustomed; the only other method of inlet or egress was a door, temporarily sealed to adjust the structure to its improvised use as a salting tank, on the outer wall a little above sea level.

This hatch was raised to allow me to inspect the contents and appreciate the situation with which we had to deal. For a wave of air so noisome, so active and evil, it is difficult to find comparison; indeed, to anyone who has not smelled (how meagre a word) sixteen tons of rotten fish whose essence has had no previous possibility of a wider and gentler diffusion, it is indescribable. Ammonia, dense, suffocating, and almost visible, knocked me back from that trapdoor as completely as a robot fist; the smell of the Blackwall crypt seven years before was no more than a pale presage of what my illusory Island Valley of Avalon had to offer me now.

When I had stopped choking and spitting I raised the hatch for the second time. Holding my breath, I steeled myself to peer down into the dusk of that nightmare cave. To say that the surface was crawling would be an understatement so gross as to defeat its own object. It was alive, heaving, seething, an obscene sea such as Brueghel might have conceived, alive as the sanctuary of Beelzebub himself, with a million million grubs, twisting, turning, writhing, as though beneath that surface layer of putrescence were the struggling bodies of all the wounded but resurrected dragons that we had attacked and that had escaped us.

Those million million grubs would become a million million flies; my mind's eye saw the island darkened with them as with a swarm of locusts, Avalon eclipsed by the Prince of Flies whom I had summoned up.

The grubs were as immortal as the evil dreams of which they seemed a part. We sprayed paraffin upon them; they flinched, as it were, but soon the fumes of the spirit had become displaced by those of the ammonia, and the grubs were as living and virulent as before. Months later we poured quicklime through the hatch, but when those acrid vapours had dispersed the charnel pit seemed still to retain its obscene but now amorphous power of movement. Throughout that autumn the question followed me; by wire, by telephone, by letter; it was repeated, as it were a ritual of hypnosis or the slow drip of the Chinese water torture—"How shall we deal with the tank?"

It pursued me, this question, to London, to the board meetings in Glasgow, where it renewed its strength with the sickening urgency of a gastric ulcer; it pursued me in my dreams and as I travelled to distant ports to inspect vessels for sale. For by now we had much to buy before the beginning of the 1948 season. The *Sea Leopard* had been found to have extensive dry rot throughout her hull and was considered unfit to work another season. We had been lucky indeed that she had withstood at sea the tremendous strain of that summer's work. She lay at Troon, in Ayrshire, and by degrees I removed my possessions from the cabin that had been my home for what now seemed an infinitely long time. Her engines were to be sold separately; and the hull, infected by that deadliest of diseases of wooden ships, was to be sold for firewood. The eye of association lent her dignity as she lay at that squalid wharf, the long scars left by struggling sharks reaching almost to her gunwale, and the echo of "Muldoan" barely stilled from her bridge.

The *Sea Leopard* was to be replaced by two or more smaller vessels of the ring-net or skiff types, and we were to buy a ship capable of acting as an accompanying factory. It was autumn then, and we had all the vessels to buy and to equip before the coming April.

In the purchase of the boats I left the last word to Harry, feeling, as I had felt in the case of the *Dove*, that a man with a lifetime's experience of sea was beter qualified than I, and that if the skipper was allowed to buy what he wanted personally, he would not afterwards grumble at the choice.

Harry and I were separated, pursuing different rumours of

advertised boats, when he telephoned to me to say that a ship of the coaster type had come on the market and that he considered her ideal for conversion to a factory ship. He had known this vessel, the *Silver Darling*, for some years, while she had been in use as a herring carrier; she was modern and sound throughout, and he considered her cheap at the asking price of twelve thousand pounds. Another buyer was after the boat, and we could only secure forty-eight hours' option upon her. Harry was utterly convinced that we should buy immediately.

This placed me in a dilemma; the directors were widely separated, and no meeting could be called to discuss the question in the time available. Besides myself, Harry alone was familiar with all our problems, and of the two of us he had infinitely the better qualification for judging the ship's usefulness to us. I could do no more than forward to the secretaries the urgency of his recommendation. After a great deal of feverish long-distance telephoning and inquiry, the parent company was independently advised that the ship was a good investment and decided to buy her, sending me an unequivocal letter to the effect that this vessel was not in the meantime to be regarded as the property of Island of Soay Shark Fisheries Ltd. either in principle or in fact; that it would remain the property of the parent company, to be resold or chartered to the subsidiary Soay Company as they considered advisable.

The *Silver Darling* joined the *Sea Leopard* in Troon harbour on December 12, and soon afterwards a naval architect, together with technical representatives of the parent company, arrived to advise on her conversion. This conversion was to be extensive, to enable us to draw the fish up over a stern ramp and perform a complete dissection on board. Centrifugal oil-extracting machinery had already been ordered by Gordon

Davidson, and it was only now that he realized that these machines could operate only on a true horizontal base, and were therefore useless at sea.

A meeting was held to discuss the naval architect's report; the parent company decided that the conversion would too greatly diminish the capital value of the ship and resolved to sell her again forthwith. Unfortunately they were not prepared to buy any other factory ship until the *Silver Darling* was sold. The surveyors whom they had personally appointed before her purchase had advised that she should resell at a profit, and she was put on the market at fifteen thousand pounds. We were not back where we started; we had actually lost ground, for we now had no authority to buy a factory ship at all, and I could not see how the small catching vessels for which we were still searching could ever show a profit alone, even at the enormous price of one hundred and thirty pounds per ton that we were now offered for the oil. The whole venture was already tottering; I seemed to detect that strange agitation which moves among the high leaves of a great tree as the saw bites into the heart of the trunk.

Meeting after meeting was held, view after view put forward, but it seemed that no agreement upon our future policy could be reached. A small portion of the correspondence of those winter months occupies the whole floor space of a large room as I write now, and reading those letters again I feel all the frustration and the despair that I knew then. The weeks crept on, and but for the last season's shooting gear we had no shark-fishing equipment at all. The *Gannet* was the only boat we had left.

So many detailed proposals for the working of the 1948 season had now been put forward, clothed in so many different words, that it was becoming difficult to tell at a glance where one scheme overlapped or differed from the others.

Harry's proposal was to use catchers only, beaching the sharks, extracting their livers, and carrying them back to Soay, as we had done at Scalpay the previous year. I could not agree; in the light of the last season's experience I felt that the boats could not satisfactorily undertake so many branches of the work, nor the crew stand up to such long hours throughout a season. I remembered the days wasted in clearing the beaches of the great disembowelled carcasses; remembered the number of barrels that had been necessary to contain the livers of that one catch, and the enormous distances over which a huge cargo might have to be carried in small boats—boats that must stop catching sharks in order to do that carrying. The scheme seemed to me a refusal to acknowledge our own experience. It could be carried out only with the addition to our fleet of a boat capable of extracting the liver oil on the spot. I wrote, "Only in this way can I see the possibility of working at a great distance from Soay without a complete floating factory, and I must stress that I consider it absolutely essential that in any scheme the catchers must be responsible for catching only."

At this stage I cleared my mind finally of a long-standing misconception. I recognized at last that the by-products of the shark could have no significance for us for many years; that the liver was the elephant's ivory, and that we should concentrate upon this alone. I failed completely, however, to convince my co-directors of the wisdom of this, which, at best, they regarded as a temporary or emergency policy.

I felt, too, that we were being cheated of all the advantages that our recapitalization should have given us. Where were the opportunities for experiment that should increase our effi-

ciency? During the 1946 and 1947 seasons there had been
no time for experiment other than that which was incidental
to securing sharks by any available means whatsoever; we had
not dared, by experimenting with one fish, to risk losing the
opportunity of killing another. With my private certainty that
until a very much later stage of development had been reached
the liver was all that was worth handling, it was clear to me
that if we could find some means of extracting the liver at sea,
without beaching the fish, most of our problems would be
solved.

With this major point in mind, I put forward to the company the only proposal that I thought would be acceptable.
We were well into the New Year now, and I saw no possible
chance of our being ready to catch sharks on a profitable scale
before the beginning of May. I wrote:

My considered proposal is that two catchers should be bought
in the immediate future, and that they and the *Gannet* should engage in lobster fishing from, say, March until the end of the year.
. . . It should be well possible for the crew to catch a few sharks
with a particular view to finding some method of extracting their
livers while the fish is still in the water. This point is, to my mind,
the crux of the whole matter. The liver is the pearl in the oyster,
and, while every other part of the fish may be of some value, I think
that a profit can be made upon the livers with far less capital outlay. To remove the liver, it is at present necessary to take the fish
on board or beach him on the tide, and it is this one fact that is responsible for the large outlay estimated for the conversion of the
Silver Darling. . . . The catchers will be already in hand for the
1949 season, and the question of a factory ship can be discussed in
detail with very much more leisure and time than has been available
in the case of the *Silver Darling*.

This proposal was finally chosen from the welter of schemes
that now littered the board-room table, though it was made

clear that the board did not consider any policy that aimed at dealing with the livers only to be of any lasting significance; the possible by-products were what fascinated them.

Harry was entrusted with buying two small boats suitable for the new scheme. At the same time I began inspecting a number of Tank Landing Craft Mark IV, which the board had at last approved as a floating factory for the 1949 season. My inspection, carried out with a naval architect and a representative of the parent company, was encouraging; we each rendered independent reports to the board, and by March a firm of shipbrokers had been authorized to buy the first sound example that was offered at four thousand five hundred pounds or less. Although 1948 was to be a non-shark-fishing year, it seemed that the company still had a future.

Harry bought two catchers in Tarbert, Loch Fyne, in the first week of March. By the time I arrived there in response to his telegram he had already taken both boats to sea and had beached one for an inspection of her bottom. He also had a surveyor's report, couched in characteristically noncommittal language. The board authorized the buying of both boats immediately.

The two had names suggesting, perhaps, a slight element of comedy, but certainly not of disaster. The larger was called *Nancy Glen;* the smaller *Maggie McDougall.* They were overhauled in Ardrishaig and arrived in Mallaig on May 2.

At this stage the *Maggie McDougall* developed serious engine trouble. No one in Mallaig could be found to do the work, and the crews of both boats were kept in Mallaig to carry it out themselves.

The boats sailed on May 24, only the *Nancy Glen* mounting a gun, and for a month I was unable to contact them by any means; they might, for all I could tell, be at the bottom of the sea. I took to spending every week-end in Mallaig on the chance of their putting in, but they called neither there nor at Soay, where we had retained a skeleton factory staff.

During that month the determination was growing in me to tender my resignation as managing director. In the course of informal conversation it had become plain to me that we should never obtain unanimity on future policy, and that the use of a floating factory was far from assured; moreover, the board tended to repose increasing trust in certain employees whom I was convinced were unreliable. I had a suspicion, later confirmed, that one of the directors was in private negotiation with our competitors. I had no employee to whom I could turn for the smallest executive work. If so much as a new boiler-glass or a ton of coal was required for the factory I had to make the purchase and organize its transport myself; if a crofter in the Outer Islands wrote for a barrel of shark flesh for lobster bait there was no one else to answer him or deal with his order. My mind was never free to deal with the major problems that faced us.

I remained long enough to prepare a report upon the season's work, which was so deeply shrouded in mystery that I was glad to think that it was the last time I should have to try to account for the work of the boats when I was not with them. The month had yielded twelve sharks, whose liver oil was badly discoloured and of inferior quality owing to long keeping, and, apparently, only about two dozen lobsters. The remainder of the season was as farcical and mysterious in production, but entirely successful from the point of view from which I had originally urged it. The crew had discovered a way of removing sharks' livers at sea.

My last action as managing director was an urgent warning to my successor against relying too far upon certain of his employees. My resignation was finally accepted on July 12, and for me the adventure that had begun four years before was over.

I was succeeded by a young man from the secretaries' office, though his responsibilities were more limited. He began with the greatest optimism and a flood of letters asking my advice upon a thousand questions whose answering looked as though it would fill my time as completely as had the managing directorship itself.

His first official communication was in the autumn, a document headed "Reasons for expecting a profit in 1949"; and, indeed, had his faith in his subordinates been justified, there seemed every reason to expect a profit, and a large one.

The 1948 season had closed early, and there had been an unwonted leisure for the modification of minor equipment. The muzzle-loading whaling guns had had Martini actions fitted to their breeches, the powder charge now being set off by a sizable blank cartridge in place of the unreliable caps and antiquated hammer; and to the armoury had been added a modern Norwegian whaling gun. The harpoons that had been ordered for the previous season, and had not been delivered until July, were now available in bulk for the next year, and there seemed ample time for overhauling the boats. Only the human factor remained unchanged, and for this reason I could not share the new atmosphere of optimism that prevailed. To my mind, too, there was still an evident and unhealthy insistence upon the exploration of by-products, which by this time I was convinced belonged to a much later stage of development.

So strongly did I feel that sense of impending disaster that

HARPOON VENTURE

in November I wrote a personal letter to the chairman, expressing in confidence my lack of trust in certain of the company's employees, and giving in support some irrefutable instances which had recently come to my knowledge. I never knew whether that letter was received, for it was never acknowledged.

I believed the new manager's optimism to be utterly unjustified; I knew in my heart that the saw was near to the centre of the tree trunk, and a lengthy memorandum from the secretaries' office, of which item no. 6 read: "*Boots*. Liver oil gives rubber boots a short life. Is the company to pay for the boots of —— and —— (two employees), who will hold them as company property: the secretaries request instructions," seemed to me to be the brushing of a caterpillar from a leaf at the last instant before the fall of the tree.

Proposals for fresh experiment during the 1949 season included many that I had explored exhaustively during the very earliest days of shark fishing, and I was by now becoming too weary, and necessarily too occupied with trying to earn my own living, to do more than reply that these methods had received the fullest consideration before their rejection years before.

The story of those last months is a little difficult to unravel, nor do I know whom Harry had with him as crew. Tex had left the company's service when I resigned, and was, in partnership with an Englishman, fishing for sharks as a free-lance.

The *Maggie McDougall* had at the last moment been reported unseaworthy, and Harry had sailed with the *Nancy Glen* and the *Gannet*. During the first days of May, Tex met him in Moonen Bay with five floating barrels about him in a narrow radius, and a sixth shark being hauled up. A few days later the sharks were in quantity at the Isle of Canna, and again Tex, now in open competition, met Harry on the fishing grounds. The *Nancy Glen* was faster than the boat on which Tex was harpoon gunner, and Harry had things all his own way. Between the fishing at Moonen and at Canna he must have killed a great number of sharks before the disaster of a few days later. Harry, that strange, contradictory, unclassifiable character, had the first of three shipwrecks in as many months, and in three different ships.

He must have thinned the shoal at Canna and crossed the Minch to Uishenish. Just inside Loch Skipport is a famous anchorage locally known as the Kettle, the only anchorage from there to Lochboisdale. Here Harry went to anchor for the night. It seems that the crew were inexperienced seamen (said to be students), and that may in part explain what followed.

The ship needed fresh water, and it was hard to see where to get it. They decided to slack the anchor till the boat ran ashore, but apparently no one noticed that they were on an ebb tide. The hull grounded upon a rock, and as the tide left her dry she overbalanced and smashed down, breaking her keel far aft. When the tide returned the hull filled with water, and remained full for several tides, so that the crew had to abandon her. They lived ashore, in a nearby croft. After some time they obtained enough cement to fill the lower part of her scuppers, and eventually got her floated. A Mallaig boat, the *Primrose*, towed her back across the Minch, and everyone concerned seemed to agree that Harry had done a magnificent job in preventing a total loss. Long before, the *Nancy Glen* had been called the *Nil Desperandum*, and now she lived up to her name. But the company was now without a single catching vessel except the tiny *Gannet*, which could not work alone.

I was ill in London at the time, and my first certainty that the tree was indeed falling was a letter from the new manager, written on May 17, 1949, when the wreck of the *Nancy Glen* had been towed home, telling me that with the chairman's authority he was beginning the sale of the company's assets immediately.

It is indeed sad to look on the scene of so much hope and possibility, which will so shortly be left to the gulls and the rain. I still believe that there is money in sharks, but this can now never be more than an opinion.

The wreck of the main catcher had not been the only problem. The sharks had been coming into the factory far too fast for the small oil-extraction plant to cope with the livers as they arrived in bulk. A factory boat to accompany the catchers had been an absolute necessity, but of what use now were the vindications of the views I had expressed so long and so urgently?

The guns and the apparatus for extracting the liver at sea had worked perfectly; the manager added that our finish was all the sadder because the catchers could now haul up any shark in ten minutes and have the liver out in another ten. Only I, he said, could really appreciate what that meant, and in that he was right. The parent company could not.

Though our problems were now all virtually solved, though we knew at last how to land, quickly and efficiently, a huge tonnage of liver containing a valuable oil, nothing could persuade the parent company to sink any further capital in a venture which was, by comparison with their larger interests, both small and very tiresome. Like many before us, we were wrecked on the sheltering rock of our own harbour.

The sale of the assets began. A year later, in Mallaig, I was told:

"It would have broken your heart, Major. It was a free-for-all; what wasn't just about given away was taken, and who could blame the takers? Some of the stuff just lay there until it was finally disclaimed and was public property—half the garden fences in Mallaig are held up by your harpoon sticks."

The tree was down at last, and what the foresters left was gleaned by the passers-by.

The venture was over; in a sense we had failed, in a sense we had succeeded. I hope, anyway, that we paved the way for someone with capital to follow us, and that all our experience was not entirely wasted. I did not blame the parent company for turning back when we were in sight at last of the promised land. Only one thing galled me: their first official reason for giving up—that no suitable replacement could be found after my resignation as managing director. I pressed this question before the company finally went into liquidation, and was unable to satisfy myself that any steps at all had been taken to find a replacement.

Tex bought such quantity of the gear and guns as his slender capital allowed, though much was dispersed in less satisfactory ways before he had time to raise the money. He is now a free-lance shark fisherman, with all the experience of our venture behind him, and he is doing well in a small way. If I again have capital to invest, it is to his business that I shall turn as the foundation stone of a new concern. My faith in the future of the idea I conceived in 1944 is unshaken.

Harry survived several disasters to become one of the several small free-lance shark fishermen whose shoots grew seedily from the stump of my felled tree.

Of Harry I thought, as Prince Hal of Falstaff, "I could have better spared a better man."

As people who own dangerous dogs are apt to say, "He's all right with *me*," I inclined always to trust my employees too far and to neglect danger signs, and when I think of them now it is their virtues rather than their defects that I remember, and the many experiences that we shared as companions.

So, too, when I think of Soay, it is not the stench of the rotting shark flesh nor the myriad clamouring problems of the factory that come to my mind; nor the civil wars and demands, about which a separate book could be written, of its tiny population; nor the days of unhappiness, loneliness, and frustration that those who cut themselves off from their kind must endure. I remember it on those glorious summer days when a smooth blue sea lapped the red rock of the island shore and the cuckoos called continuously from the birch woods; or on bright winter mornings when the Cuillins were snow-covered, hard, intricate, and brittle as carved ivory; I remember it with nostalgia for something beautiful and lost, the Island Valley of Avalon to which there can be no true return, no second spring.

When the taste of failure has been bitter on the tongue, I have remembered the lessons of Lewis and of Leverburgh, where all the capital and acumen of Leverhulme's mighty organization left scarcely more evidence of endeavour than is borne by my pathetic little ruined factory on Soay today.

Only a few of the thousands of Hebridean islands can ever
hope for development, and then only by the State and public
funds. The many such as Soay will remain untouched, with a
dwindling population, until at last they are empty and deserted.

All that remained of Lever's plans
Were some half-built piers and some empty cans,
And the islanders with no regrets
Treated each other to cigarettes.

But far below in the Western Seas
The moors were quiet in the Hebrides,
The crofters gossiped in Gaelic speech
And the waves crept over the lonely beach.

APPENDIX

1. Here Be Dragons

I should preface this appendix by saying at once that during the few years I was at sea I saw no living object that I was not able, perhaps after a moment's doubt, to identify as belonging to a known species, sometimes in an unfamiliar aspect. Although my own experience—and that of my crew—was separated from that of the great bulk of inshore seamen by the fact that as a matter of routine we examined carefully every object appearing at the sea's surface, that we saw nothing inexplicable is quite inconclusive. I have met men of very much longer qualification than myself who have seen phenomena outside their very considerable experience, and it is with the greatest hesitation, and only after the minutest examination, that such records should be dismissed as beyond the boundaries of practical science.

I do not want to trespass upon Commander Gould's preserves; the existence or non-existence of the sea serpent was his preoccupation for many years. If one or more very large marine species does remain unknown to science, it is quite certain that its appearances, like those of the much-exploited Loch Ness monster, are rare, and the fact that we saw nothing during four summers is negative evidence. But this book would be incomplete without some reference to "monsters," if only because our unusual familiarity with basking sharks and the other large marine creatures enabled us to recognize them as such when they might have been mistaken, by less experienced observers, for unfamiliar species.

The belief, factual and unsuperstitious, in the existence of at least one giant sea species at present unrecognized by science is widespread in the Hebrides, and is as strong among some of the educated people as it was among their less-informed ancestors.

To appreciate the basis for this belief, one must understand just how familiar an islander, constantly either in sight of the sea or actually on it, becomes with all its apparent life. His names for the creatures he sees, whether bird, fish, whale, or seal, would be unintelligible to modern taxonomy, but they are constant names, the result of repeated identification, and when he sees for the first time some species unknown to him, he is generally able to give an accurate enough description of it, often resulting in its identification beyond reasonable doubt as a rare visitor to the seas he knows.

As very few people who spend much time at sea in the Hebrides have any particular interest in accurate identification, it is perhaps not surprising that I should find the commonest of all creatures other than the basking shark described in a well-known and reputable textbook as a rare visitor to British waters. Because of these popular misconceptions I shall describe the species with which I became familiar before producing any secondhand evidence of creatures unknown to science.

The *Cetacea*—the whale order—includes everything from the giant blue whale to the common porpoise. Of these I identified seven species positively: blue whale, common rorqual, killer whale, Risso's grampus, white-sided dolphin, common dolphin, and common porpoise.

The first two are the great whales, the whalebone whales,

of the family *Balænoptera*. I may have seen the humpbacked whale also, but would be positive only of the blue whale and the common rorqual or finback. One of the methods of identifying the large whales at a distance is by the shape and height of the "spout," but this aid was denied me, for the air was never cold enough to produce condensation. The "spout" is merely the contents of the lungs, violently exhaled after the breath has been held for a long time, and in the majority of seas where whales are hunted the atmosphere is cold enough for this to appear as a column of white steam whose shape and height vary with the species of whale. But cold as it often seemed during those Hebridean summers, I myself never saw more than the faintest mist of condensation above a blowing whale.

The other methods of identification are by size, colour, and the behaviour of the visible part of the body at the surface. The rorqual, for example, rarely shows his tail flukes above water as he sounds, whereas the blue whale characteristically lifts his tail clear of the sea in the final movement.

I saw only one blue whale (*Balænoptera musculus*) of which I could be certain; the size and colour, together with this characteristic action, left no room for doubt.

The common rorqual (*Balænoptera physalus*) we saw much more often, and usually at close quarters. I would say that a week rarely passed without our seeing one or more, usually singly, but the very fact that the "spout," which is what reveals a whale at a distance, was always absent, makes it probable that the numbers were very much greater than that.

These two species of whale were very much the largest creatures, the blue whale commonly exceeding eighty feet and the rorqual little less. They are, in fact, the largest living creatures in the world, and Millais mentions that even the largest of prehistoric animals could not rival their size.

The killer whale (*Orca gladiator*) I have mentioned on pages 47–49. In each of the summers I was at sea we used to meet small packs of killers perhaps a dozen times in the season, and to me they are the most impressive animals of the sea. As a rule there were between five and ten whales in each pack, and never more than one adult bull with that nightmare sword-like fin. I saw parties, too, that were apparently all females and young males. On July 18, 1946, we were cruising in the *Sea Leopard* about a mile off Uishenish Lighthouse, looking for sharks. A party of four killers appeared close inshore about a mile to the south of us. They did not appear to be "travelling"; they were somewhat scattered and moving very slowly, each individual often changing direction. I am not sure of the exact composition of the party, but I remember that there were two immature males, in which the dorsal fin, though little higher than that of an adult female, was already beginning to lose its recurvature. They were still a little to southward when one of the crew called my attention to a dark object at the water's surface some two miles north of us. It disappeared at the same instant as it caught my eye, but soon after I had raised the field glasses it reappeared, and I saw that it was the dorsal fin of a very large bull killer, travelling towards us at a fair speed, probably about ten to fifteen knots. The fin appeared to be eight or nine feet high (the crew support this apparent overestimate), and the whale was alone and holding a straight course in the general direction of the herd that was moving north. It was clear that they would meet at a point roughly between the *Sea Leopard* and the shore. There were three of us on the bridge at the time—Bruce, Dan, and myself—and we watched with interest to see whether either the bull or the north-going party would reverse course and move off in one direction as a herd. The distance between them decreased rapidly. The foremost of the young ones was zigzagging in an aimless sort of way, and on his last blow he was actually facing a little south of west, when simultaneously the giant fin of the old bull began to rise thirty yards to the north of him. It came towering up out of the water to its full height, the bull blew with a deep, harsh exhalation that sounded very loud from where we stood a hundred yards away, and the fin began to go down again on a forward roll as he sounded. At this instant it appeared that the young one became conscious of the bull's presence for the first time. I say "appeared" because it is very easy to draw false or teleological conclusions; one should only record observed fact. The young whale had just blown; now, instead of sounding, his fin remained for a second stationary before he shot off in a rush whose speed was bewildering. The fin showed above the surface the whole way and left a white wake of foaming water behind it for perhaps a hundred and fifty yards before the whale sounded. Both the speed and the acceleration with which it was reached were beyond anything I had ever seen in the water. The old bull paid no attention; he held his course, passed through the scattered herd and went on down the coast, the great fin thrusting up from the water at regular intervals of about a hundred yards.

We began to speculate about the speed the young whale had attained during that ferocious surface rush. I hazarded twenty knots, but Dan shook his head.

"It would be far more than that, Major."

Bruce was able to provide exact comparison. "Well," he said, "you know I was at a torpedo-testing station for quite a while during the war. I've seen hundreds of torpedoes travelling at thirty knots and more, and I'd say yon whale would beat them every time."

I did not feel sceptical, but I felt that we should not be believed if we repeated this story with a speed of more than thirty knots attached to it. Later I consulted Dr. F. C. Fraser of the British Museum, a leading authority on *Cetacea*, and did not find him unbelieving. He produced instead an authentic Admiralty record, in which a killer, travelling near to the surface and on a parallel course, cleared the ship's length in twelve seconds, giving a calculated speed of twenty-two knots, at a time when there was no overt reason to exert himself.

The killers' prey, the very fast seals and dolphins (attaining speeds of more than twenty knots), to say nothing of the larger whales, make it necessary for the killer himself to be capable of a tremendous maximum. Just as we find that the fastest of the gazelles and antelopes, attaining approximately sixty miles an hour, cannot in a short dash escape the cheetah or hunting leopard which reaches a speed of sixty-five miles an hour or more, it is a fair assumption that the killer is faster than any of his prey. The dynamics of these very high speeds in relation to the size of the animal are discussed by Professor Hill in a paper which appeared in *Science & Progress*, April 1950,[1] but it is a little erudite for the average reader.

I do not know if one can safely draw any inference from the fact that we never saw sharks when killers were in the immediate neighbourhood. Only a few whales ever go very deep under water—probably not more than fifteen fathoms under normal conditions—and it is a tempting conclusion that the sharks take refuge in deeper water. We have no proof that

[1] A. V. Hill, "The Dimensions of Animals and Their Muscular Dynamics."

killers attack adult basking sharks, but habitual attacks on the most voracious of tropical sharks are recorded by Millais,[2] and it is a justifiable assumption that young basking sharks of from six to fifteen feet are eaten by killers. In these small sharks the skin is comparatively smooth and soft; the mass of tiny spines which makes the skin of the adult so painful to handle has not yet developed, and the only probable deterrent to attack by killers is wanting. In temperate waters the basking shark, assumed to be six feet long at birth, could have no other natural enemy. This would tend to produce a numerical unbalance of species, more especially as the shark's own food consists of a proportion of larval forms that are eaten before they can attain their final form and reproduce.

The gigantic and deeply indented healed scars that we found on a few adult sharks may have been due to fouling ships' propellers, which could, according to the position of the fish, leave a wound of almost any shape or length; and the shark's power of recovery from the most terrible wounds is suggested by the comparatively small number of fish from which our harpoons had pulled out that were afterwards washed ashore.

So far I have listed these various sea animals, which we came to know and recognize instantly, in the order of their size. The next, which the only textbooks available to me at the time described as a rarity, was, apart from the sharks, the commonest of all creatures that we saw. This puzzled me for a long time and made me hesitate to give a positive identification. It is yet another example of how few naturalists are at sea in one area for long enough to form a clear conception of the relative numbers of the species in it.

[2] J. G. Millais, *The Mammals of Great Britain and Ireland*, 1904–1906, Vol. III.

"A rare visitor to our shores" is a typical textbook description of Risso's grampus (*Grampus griseus*), nor can I find a single reference to the names by which it is well known to every fisherman—"dunter," "lowper," and "false killer." The last name is a confusion with quite a different species, *Pseudorca crassidens*, but the superficial resemblance between the appearance when blowing of a cow killer and an adult Risso's grampus is very clearly illustrated in photographs 76 and 77. These were taken by *Picture Post*'s photographer, Raymond Kleboe, during a week's stay on the *Sea Leopard*.

It was on one of the *Dove*'s early trips that I first saw Risso's grampus, and I do not think I am exaggerating if I say that during the three seasons I was at sea there were very few weeks in which we did not see several schools of them. The schools would range from about a dozen to forty individuals, the average school being about twenty-five, and were always composed of adults and young, the latter swimming close alongside their parents.

As this has not up till now been regarded as a very common species, I record here all my own observations, even if they contradict recognized authority.

The length of the adults seemed to me to be between ten and fourteen feet; there appeared some variation in size even among parents who were accompanied by young, and the smallest calf was not less than four or five feet. The colour is extremely variable, the back and dorsal fin ranging from pale buff to a dark ochre-brown, the dark form being the commoner, and there were odd individuals that appeared greyish. One of a large school that was playing round the *Dove* off the east shore of the Isle of Harris came up right under where I was standing in her bows. He seemed to come up almost vertically from a considerable depth, and was so pale all over that the effect was almost of albinism. The underside of all the Risso's grampuses I saw was white or almost white, and this seems to extend for a variable distance up the flanks and on to the head, but I saw none with a plain demarcation line between the two colours.

When travelling, they hold a speed of ten or twelve knots and blow about every thirty yards. The sound of the blow is not as harsh or prolonged as that of a killer, but it is audible at a considerable distance—up to perhaps a quarter of a mile in still weather.

Sometimes we would find a bay full of them; scattered, and each one going in a different direction, swimming more slowly, at seven knots or less. These were probably in the middle of a shoal of fish, and feeding, and it was easier then to approach them closely. When they were travelling they seemed very conscious of the vibration of the boat's engines and kept an average distance of forty yards to port or to starboard when blowing, though we could see them under water at closer quarters. With the engines stopped among a feeding school they would blow right alongside, but the blow would seem to be cut short by a scared forward plunge as they saw our movements on deck.

During the time that I was trying to identify them with certainty I tried persistently to shoot one with the harpoon gun, but the only satisfactory chances I had were from the *Dove*, whose gun was not able to hit even a practically stationary shark. Once from the *Sea Leopard* we followed a travelling school for some miles; they did not appear frightened or alter the timing of their "blows," but only one came within range of the gun. I saw it coming up from several fathoms down, a pallid moving blur in the dark water, and I took a firm stance and began to align the gun. But as the grampus shot up to the surface just below me I saw, even as my finger was tightening on the trigger grip, that close alongside her and duplicating her every movement was a tubby young calf not more than half her length. He blew at the exact moment his mother blew; he appeared to be a serious-minded baby, anxious to get everything just right. He looked what Americans call "cute," and I could not bring myself to kill the parent and leave him searching the empty sea for her. This piece of absurdly unscientific sentimentality might have resulted in failure to identify the species at all, had it not been for Kleboe's photographs and the lucky accident of finding a half-grown calf stranded on the sands of Morar estuary.

When travelling, Risso's grampus does not show the tail flukes as he sounds except when he is alarmed, and we learned that a flourish of the tail, often ending with a possibly accidental but audible slap upon the water's surface, was always followed by the complete disappearance of the whole school. I did not time their periods below the surface, but I should say that ten minutes to a quarter of an hour was the maximum, after which they would reappear in the far distance.

Whatever their method of communication, no one who has watched schools of the smaller whales can doubt that it is efficient and instant. Following an alarm such as the report of a gun, a whole school will disappear completely, though some were at the surface and some at the maximum depth of their sounding when the alarm took place.

The possibility that it is an actual communication by sound has been considered by Dr. Fraser,[3] who quotes several in-

[3] F. C. Fraser, "Sound Emitted by Dolphins," *Nature*, Vol. 160, Nov. 1947.

stances recorded as varying between "a shrill ringing sound, not unlike that of musical glasses when badly played" to "high-pitched whistles," both apparently beyond the upper limit of most humans' hearing. One early author whom he quotes mentions that the sound is more audible when the animal passes directly below a small boat, suggesting that the woodwork acts as a sort of sound-box. Dr. Fraser also records having seen an intermittent stream of fine bubbles issuing from the blowholes of common dolphins while they were still a fathom or more below water, and it is possible that this is connected with the production of an extremely high-pitched sound.

When Risso's grampuses are feeding or at play practically no attitude or antic is improbable. The very first one of which I had a clear view was stationary—treading water, as it were, and staring at me with his head vertical and three feet clear of the water. The face looked to me like that of a huge lizard, and, as I was seeing mainly the underside of it, it appeared pure white. I was accustomed, as are the great majority of people, to think of sea creatures as virtual automata, heedless of man except in fear of him, and the impression of sentience, awareness, and curiosity that this weird staring head gave me was alarming; a reminder that the whale family have the most highly developed and convoluted brains of all animals but man—far higher than the anthropoid apes; and it may well be that only their environment and virtual dependence upon a single sense prevent them from reaching the degree of civilization or chaos to which we have attained.

When playing, Risso's grampuses breach like other whales, shooting high out of the water; they make short rushes along the surface; flourish their tails in the air; remain absolutely stationary at the surface for several seconds at a time; seem, in fact, to get their bodies into every possible and impossible attitude. More than once I saw a dorsal fin remain stationary and high out of the water while the tail lashed violently up and down, showing itself just above the surface at each upward movement. This, judging by what is known of other *Cetacea*, may well have been the act of copulation, but I was never near enough to them at the time to say so with any certainty.

It was not until the middle of the summer of 1946 that I was able to secure positive identification for these beasts with which we had become so familiar, as the "rare visitor to our shores," *Grampus griseus*. Berthing at Mallaig pier one Saturday morning, I was told that a small whale was stranded on the sands of Morar estuary below Bourblach, Foxy's croft. It was still alive when we reached it, helpless, and with its blow-hole choked with sand, each breath drawn and expelled with a long agonizing groan through that blocked air channel. Dan reminded me years later of the wounding innocence of its face and the distress of those awful breaths. My own feeling was of pity amounting almost to revulsion; the sound was unbearable, and it was only after I had killed him with a shot through the brain that I was able to focus my interest on the species.

We recognized him at once as a half-grown specimen of the animal whose herds we had come to know so well. He was about eight and a half feet long, of a dark buffish colour which looked pearly grey in certain lights. The skin had dried under a June sun, and I wetted it to see whether this would produce an apparent change of colour, but it remained constant. We took photographs (78), from which Dr. Fraser later made the positive identification over which I had hesitated so long.

Both the killer whale and Risso's grampus are strictly speaking dolphins, a family that embraces a large number of genera and species. The common dolphin (*Delphinus delphis*), six to eight feet long, is one of the beaked species, having a well-defined duck-like bill about six inches long. This animal we saw rarely—not more than a dozen times in the whole period—and I should say that of these the greater number were in the southern part of the Minch near to Barra Head. We met one very small beaked dolphin, not more than four feet long, travelling alone and at high speed, near the mouth of Loch Shell. It was raining at the time, and I could not get a very clear view of it; it may have belonged to a less common species.

The common dolphin's relative, the beakless white-sided dolphin (*Lagenorhynchus acutus*), I saw only once to identify certainly, but in very great numbers. We were about a mile off Rodel Bay in the Isle of Harris, heading south at about ten knots, when, looking back over the *Sea Leopard*'s stern, I saw a disturbance of the sea's surface over a wide area a mile or more to the north of us. With the field glasses I could make out a great school of dolphins covering a front of at least half a mile and travelling at speed on the same course as ourselves. They overhauled us amazingly quickly and began to pass close along each side of the ship. We were to the shoreward side of the school; there were perhaps two hundred yards of it on our starboard side and six hundred on the port side. They swam with the characteristic dolphin leaps, each leap taking them a few feet clear of the surface for twelve or fifteen feet, the distance under water between leaps being about double that. They were travelling at not less than twenty to twenty-five knots; the estimate is, I think, conservative, as is an estimate of five hundred adults in the school. In the bright sunshine it was a glorious sight; to the human eye the impression of this leaping grace is of happiness and rapture abounding, an abandon to the joy of speed that is half in the sunlight and half in the cool shining sea.

If they had been animals that I recognized I should have found it impossible to become their enemy; I would rather have had Arion's cithara in my hands than a harpoon gun. But watching them as they sped along the ship's sides, I knew that this was an animal I had not seen before, and desire for knowledge overcame my sentimentality.

As on an earlier occasion, with Risso's grampus, the first to pass under the gun platform was a female with a calf, the latter not much more than a yard long, but imitating her movements exactly. The next was the same, and the next; I felt like a murderer loosed into a communal nursery. The fourth dolphin was unattended, and as he leaped through the air a few feet below the gun I squeezed the trigger grip. I missed him by feet, if not yards. I reloaded with a fresh rope and harpoon and missed another; it seemed like trying to hit driven grouse with a rifle. At the third try I aimed at a point in the air some six feet in front of a dolphin's nose as he began his forward leap from the water, and the massive harpoon caught him squarely in mid-air, killing him instantaneously. He fell back dead upon the sea, and began to sink in a widening pool of bright blood.

At this instant, and not before, the whole school—even the most distant, by now far ahead of us—submerged practically simultaneously, and it was five or more minutes before they resurfaced far to southward. I can find no satisfactory explanation of the fact that they did not submerge after the previous shots. It occurred to me at the time that the school must have passed below Brollem Light-gun as they came south, that they might even have been fishing there, and so become accustomed to the sound of explosions, but this offered no suggestion as to how or why the death of one of their number had caused an alarm that spread immediately to the farthest parts of the school.

The dolphin we had killed was a male, a little over seven feet long, graceful and streamlined as a swallow, the flared white markings on his side looking as though they had been drawn in conscious design to enhance an image of speed and beauty.

The only other true sea mammals we saw were porpoises— about as often as Risso's grampus, but only on a flat calm are they visible at any distance, so in fact they may be the commoner of the two species. It seemed to me that the porpoises were more easily frightened by the vibration of a boat's engine at close quarters than any of their larger relatives, and from the *Sea Leopard* or the *Gannet* we would see no more of them than does the ordinary seaside holiday-maker—a little, steeply arched black back and tiny triangular dorsal fin as on the circumference of a bicycle wheel held below water and revolved so that its edge just breaks the surface. Among the cetaceans that I saw they share this revolving appearance only with the great whales, whose movement suggests the gentler angle of an elliptical or eccentric wheel, while the porpoise's is round and neat without much feeling of forward movement. Their backs above the surface look mole-like, nosy, and intent.

But to be in the middle of a school of porpoises in a rowing-boat in calm weather—to ship oars and avoid all noise or movement, so that they pass and repass beneath the boat, coming up to breathe with that gentle sigh right alongside the gunwale—is to receive quite a different impression. Here is no tubby little black pig, but a swift, compact, and boldly marked little whale the size of a man, the whole of the underside white and the upper side black. One sees the dive after blowing to be very steep for the first fathom or so, which explains the apparent smallness of the revolving wheel, and the buoyant return to the surface has almost the *élan* of a dolphin's leap. Not even the most enthusiastic passenger on a pleasure steamer can readily be made to take much interest in those discreet little black backs. "Oh, just porpoises," they say, for they have not seen them under water, and the word has none of the romantic association of "shark" or "whale" or "dolphin."

Those were all the *Cetacea* that I saw during those summers of shark fishing in the Hebrides, and anyone familiar with the popular textbooks will perhaps be as much astonished by the implied list of omissions as by the unsuspected commonness of Risso's grampus.

Besides the whale family there were the two species of seal— the great grey Atlantic seal, whose nearest breeding station was at the Treshnish Islands, only forty-five miles to the south of us; and the common or brown seal, which we would see almost every day. While a seal is resting with his head above water, eyes closed, and mouth half open with an expression of infinite *ennui* and lassitude (photograph 73), at a distance he is practically indistinguishable from the fin tip of a stationary shark, and often we turned far off our course before recognizing him.

This, then, is a complete list of the sea mammals that I am aware of having seen in the Hebrides, and in considering the possible occurrence of very rare or completely unknown species it must be remembered that the average Hebridean fisherman, though unaware of scientific names or classification, is very much more familiar with each of the species I have described than I was myself.

A letter which I have before me, dated 2 March 1951, is an example of the accurate recording of a species completely

outside the observer's experience. The writer is Ronald Mur-
doch Macdonald, of Meadowbank, Island of Soay. He was
born on the island and has lived there for the greater part of his
life, being now in his late thirties. He has always been keenly
interested in animal life, and when I heard that he had seen a
strange sea creature in 1950 I sent a message to him asking for
details. His reply is an astonishingly perfect description of an
extremely rare creature, one that has been recorded in British
waters less than a dozen times in the history of natural science,
and only once in the last forty-five years. His letter reads:

I have had a letter from my brother this week saying you were
interested to know what kind of fish Neil Macrae and I saw one
day last year at Rudha Dunain while hauling our lobster creels
there in the *Emerald*.

In the first place I can't say what kind of fish it was as I have
never seen any of that kind before or since.

It was pure white in colour from head to tail and would be at
least twenty feet long, probably more, and travelling I would say
at six knots, following the coastline very closely and swimming
about three feet under the surface.

It came up twice to breathe in one hundred yards' distance, at
least it looked like as if it came to the surface to breathe.

The only queer thing I noticed about it is that it had no dorsal
fin. If it had it wasn't to be seen. Also where it broke the surface it
stopped dead for a second or two before diving again.

It had a long roundish kind of nose or snout, something similar
to the tip of a basking shark's nose when you see it sometimes above
the surface when the shark is feeding and plankton floating at the
surface. Another thing that struck me as rather odd about this fish,
it made no noise like whales or porpoise when it surfaced for
breath. At the same time I do think it was a mammal.

I can't explain the exact shape of the fish as we were about
seventy yards away from it. It seemed to be slender for its length. I
wanted to go after it to get a better view of it, but we were in the

middle of a fleet of lobster creels, and could not go in time unless we cut the creels.

You could easily see it a mile away underneath the surface as it was as white as driven snow.

Maybe you can offer an explanation as to what kind of fish or mammal it was. If so, I would like very much to know, so if you have a spare moment maybe you would drop me a note.

Beyond all reasonable doubt Ronald saw a creature of which he had never even heard, the white whale or beluga (*Delphinapterus leucas*). This is an inhabitant of the polar seas, mainly Siberia and Arctic America now, for towards the end of the last century it had already been driven from the Spitzbergen bays, where the females would come to calve when the ice broke up in midsummer. Here it was hunted by the early English whalers of the seventeenth century, and in 1670 there is a record of a Greenland ship arriving in England with twenty-four tons of oil from "white fish." During the nineteenth century it was fished regularly in Spitzbergen by the same method as the Faeroe Islanders kill the pilot whale—fleets of small boats driving the schools either into nets or aground in shallow water—and the Russian trappers who came to the island used also to be equipped with these nets in case a school of white whales should visit the bays during their stay. By the turn of the century it had become scarce in Spitzbergen and Nova Zembla, and it never reappeared in these waters from which it had been driven by ruthless and excessive hunting. The last comparatively heavy killing in the European Arctic of which there is any record seems to have been in 1901, when half a dozen whaling ships sailing from the east coast of Scotland for Arctic waters killed seven hundred and thirty-eight white whales in the season. (It was part of a mixed bag, for from 1890 till 1898 an average of eleven vessels fishing every year had killed a total of only a hundred and forty great whales, and they were by now ready to turn any living thing to profit. Besides the seven hundred and thirty-eight white whales, these six steamers killed in that year four hundred and twenty walrus, three thousand four hundred and thirty seals, and a hundred and forty-nine polar bears.[4])

The slaughter of the white whales by this wholesale murder of pregnant females might well have resulted in their extermination, had they not had the safer waters of the West Siberian Arctic as sanctuary. In Arctic America they are still killed in large numbers. Millais [5] quotes a terrible description of something like a thousand white whales crammed into a small space of open water in pack-ice, being fired on continuously by Eskimos so that at last there was hardly an unwounded animal among them, and many had been wounded several times.

Before Ronald wrote his description in March 1951, there were only eleven records of the white whale in British waters since 1793, and four of these were hearsay evidence of single specimens being sighted in 1832, 1878, 1880, and 1903. There were six isolated strandings between 1793 and 1905, after which the last British record of any kind is of a calf stranded at Stirling on October 13, 1932; but there is a record from even farther south, in France in 1950, when a white whale was captured on the Loire coast, 47° N.[6]

That there may be discrepancies in descriptions by two people who have in all probability seen the same creature or type of creature is evidenced by the following two statements. I know both these people well; the first is from Bruce Watt, who was for a long time skipper of the *Sea Leopard*, and the second from

[4] J. T. Jenkins, *A History of the Whale Fisheries*, 1921.
[5] Millais, *op. cit.*
[6] P. L. Niort, *Bull. Soc. Zool., Fr.* 74, 1950, pp. 244–46.

John McInerney, who was for a time our ship's cook and is, at the time of writing, shark fishing with Tex.

Bruce and Dan MacGillivray share a boat business in Mallaig now, doing both fixed runs with mail and provisions for the islands and carrying large parties of tourists in the summer months. It was on such a trip last year that they saw a fish quite outside their long and wide experience at sea.

Bruce describes the incident as follows:

It was in August last year [1950]—I'm not certain of the exact date. We had a party of twenty-four passengers—trippers—aboard the *Islander* and we were in the mouth of Loch Hourn, on the south side near Crolag. I saw what appeared to be a shark's fin ahead of us—an ordinary shark of perhaps twenty-three or twenty-four feet, I should have said at first. The tourists are interested in that sort of thing, and I thought we would give them a look at it. As we began to approach it, it struck me that somehow it wasn't quite like a shark's fin; it looked kind of quick in movement, although it was the right size and colour. It seemed to be waving from side to side as if it was very flimsy. We approached it from astern; it was going round and round in small circles, and when we came up to it it happened to meet us head on, and started to submerge. It seemed just to sink, without tipping to dive. We were passing it on an opposite course just as it went down, and I expected to see fifteen feet or more behind the fin. Instead of that there was only five or six feet behind it, and in front of the fin it seemed to end off short in a sort of egg-shaped nose, in which I thought I could see a large eye. The tail must have been very small —so much so that at first I thought it was a horizontal tail, and it certainly was not a powerful-swimming fish like a shark. I'd say its depth was at least half its total length—a very squat kind of fish. It looked very dark, darker than a shark, and the whole fish wasn't more than about eight feet or so.

I took this statement down from Bruce, who was quite unaware that anyone else in the neighborhood had seen a fish answering to the same general description and had also mistaken it at first for a basking shark. John McInerney had given me the following statement a few hours earlier, taken down in short-hand and typed by Tex's wife:

On the evening of 12th July we were steaming north from Uishenish Light in flat calm weather looking for sharks. We had reached the tide rip beyond the light when I saw a black fin astern of us; this I took to be a shark and accordingly made preparations to harpoon it. When we were within fifty yards of the fish I observed that though the day was flat calm the fin appeared to be waving or flapping from side to side. Still thinking it was a shark, we approached from the rear preparatory to firing, and then I noticed the fin was paper thin although not at all translucent. There was about two feet six inches of it showing above the water and it was quite as broad at the base as it was high. On seeing this I decided it could not be a basking shark, but I was still prepared to shoot it. As we came within range it sheered off, going at about ten knots. I climbed the mast in order to get a better look at this strange fish and from this vantage point I observed that the fish was approximately fifteen feet long, but unlike a basking shark, where the dorsal fin is situated in the middle of the back this fin was directly over the head which fell away sharply in front of it. The tail was very similar to a shark's tail. I could see no distinctive markings and the fish appeared to be completely black. The proportions were the same as those of the basking shark behind the dorsal fin.

We may take it as reasonably certain that these two descriptions refer to a single species, the ocean sunfish (*Mola mola*), which has a world-wide distribution, though it cannot be described as common. Its appearance in Loch Hourn and at Uishenish is perhaps less surprising than that neither Bruce nor Dan, both widely travelled and with years of sea experience, should have seen the species before.

It is clear that Bruce got a closer and better view of the fish than did John McInerney. The sunfish grows to a length of eight or ten feet and a weight of more than a ton. "They swim," writes Mr. Whitley, quoted by the late Dr. J. R. Norman, "by turning both the dorsal and anal fins to one side at the same time." This is the waving or flapping movement which struck both Bruce and John. The fish is such an entirely improbable shape—Dr. Norman describes it as "having the appearance of an enormous head to which small fins are attached"—that anyone seeing it imperfectly for the first time would subconsciously assume the existence of tail, much as one might assume the existence of legs on a swimming man; and this, I think, accounts for the apparent overestimate of size in John McInerney's description. Minus the tail, which is practically nonexistent in the sunfish, the size of the Uishenish and the Loch Hourn fish would about tally.

Despite the discrepancies, the fish is in both cases recognizable in description; there had been an accuracy of observation sufficient to identify it. Should we necessarily assume that it is the accuracy of observation, rather than our state of knowledge, that is at fault when the description fits no known creature?

Hebridean stories of the "sea serpent," or of some unknown giant of the sea, are common enough to make it pointless for me to quote experiences unconnected with my own island and its vicinity. The stories which follow are of creatures seen by Soay men, of creatures whose description fits no animal known to science, and whose appearance has been exceedingly frightening to these men who know the familiar life of the sea so well.

I am not entirely clear whether there were in fact two or three such incidents at Soay. I have heard Sandy Campbell, eyewitness of the first, tell the story many times, but I found it difficult to remember the details when I came to write it down and asked him to send me an account by letter. The story is arid by comparison with his spoken word, and beyond it I have drawn upon certain details that I well remember but which are not included in his letter. The second incident which he mentions may well refer to the story told to Ronald Macdonald (who saw the white whale) and his brother Harry by their father, who is now dead. The discrepancy between implied dates has inclined me to treat them as separate experiences; Sandy is alive, and I hope will remain so for many years, so that anyone sufficiently interested may check the details.

Sandy's own experience took place when he was a boy. It made a very strong impression upon him; his letter to me ends with the words, "I was only young at the time, but I have never forgotten that night."

It was during the early years of the present century, and Loch Scavaig, in common with all the west coast sea lochs, teemed with herring. It was the custom then for crofters to cure herring for their own use, and scores of boats would congregate where there was a big shoal. One early autumn night Sandy was fishing from a skiff in Loch Scavaig with two men. One, I think, was his uncle, the other was a man called John Stewart; both were elderly and had had a lifetime of experience.

They shot their net well up towards the head of Loch Scavaig, close to the small island. There were a large number .of other boats in the loch, but none very close to them. It was dusk; the sky was still light, but the land was dark—a fine night with a light northerly breeze and a ripple on the water. Sandy and the two old men began to haul their net. He was only a young boy, and his arms tired easily; he rested for a moment, and as he did so he noticed an object rising out of the water about fifty yards to seaward of them. It was about a yard high when he first saw it, but, as he watched, it rose slowly from the surface to a height of twenty or more feet—a tapering column that moved to and fro in the air. Sandy called excitedly to the old men, but at first got only an angry retort to keep on hauling the net and not be wasting time. At last Stewart looked up in exasperation, and then sprang to his feet in bewildered astonishment as he too saw what Sandy was looking at. While this "tail" was still waving in the air they could see the water rippling against a dark mass below it which was just breaking the surface, and which they presumed to be the animal's body. The high column descended slowly into the sea as it had risen; and as the last of it submerged the boat began to rock on a commotion of water like the wake of a passing steamer. Stewart was terrified; they dropped the net and rowed as fast as they could for the shore.

Sandy's letter ends with a paragraph that may or may not refer to Macdonald's story, but Ronald and his brother Harry date the latter as 1917, long after Sandy's experience, and while he himself was at sea during the First World War.

The following summer two old men were fishing lobsters from a coble and rowing towards Rhu when they saw an object about thirty feet in height waving to and fro out of the sea. The day was fine and hot, and they thought they could see the body in the water moving at speed towards them. They got such a scare that they made for the shore at once.

Macdonald was in a boat at the mouth of Loch Brittle on a bright summer's day, when the phenomenon passed, travelling north at about five knots, a mile to seaward of him. It appeared as a high column, said to be a great deal higher than the object Sandy had seen in Loch Scavaig, and light flashed at the top of the column as though a small head were being turned from side to side. There was a considerable commotion of water astern of it, but no other portion of the body was visible above the surface. It submerged slowly until nothing was left showing above the sea, and it seemed to descend vertically and without flexion.

I do not think that the finer details of these stories are important. The points of dissimilarity are fewer than those of similarity, and whereas they correspond to the description of no animal known to science, they do resemble closely a great number of descriptions given by honest and experienced seamen from all corners of the ocean. Sandy and Macdonald describe an object, broadly speaking, corresponding to those recorded by Dr. Matheson at Kyle of Lochalsh in 1893; by Captain Cringle of the *Umfuli*, sailing for Cape of Good Hope in the same year; by the *Valhalla* in 1905; by H.M.S. *Kellett* in 1923; to the description of the Hoy animal in 1919, and to that given by the third officer of *Tyne* in 1920. This is to mention but a few of Commander Gould's generally ignored records.[7]

We have seen how living and unfamiliar objects in the sea are described by people of experience. We have seen that there are often certain inaccuracies and discrepancies, but we have seen, too, that the word-picture is usually complete enough and accurate enough to identify the creature when it is a known species. We may theorize as to the impossibility of the existence of these creatures unknown to us, but we must recognize both the general resemblance between many of the descriptions, and that a number of experienced men of great integrity have be-

[7] R. T. Gould, *The Case for the Sea-Serpent*, 1930.

lieved that they saw very large animals with which they were entirely unfamiliar.

The feelings of men who offer such testimony to find it rejected are summed up in a letter from Captain Cringle (*Umfuli* 1893), quoted by Commander Gould.

Dear Sir,
Re the matter of the Sea-serpent.
I have suffered so much ridicule on this that I must decline to have anything more to do with it.
Whatever unbelief there is in such a monster's existence, I am certainly convinced that what I saw was a living creature capable of moving at the rate of ten knots. I chased it for ten minutes at that speed and had got no nearer to it. I had at that time twenty-three years' experience in Sail and Steam and was not likely to mistake what I saw.

Yours faithfully,
R. J. Cringle.

He believed with absolute certainty that he had seen some entirely strange animal, and the explanations which were forced down his throat seemed to him puerile. If Sandy's story is not believed, I hope it will be of some comfort to him to know that seventy-five years ago Charles Gould wrote: "The west coast of the Isle of Skye is another locality from which several reports of it have been received during this century."

During the centuries when science had not progressed far in the identification and classification of marine species the world had an open ear for stories of strange sea monsters. The general view of natural historians was that anything might exist in the sea, and their efforts were directed to the correlation of descriptions that might build up more or less complete pictures of animals unknown to them. As more and more species were

named and classified (often incorrectly), the tendency by the
nineteenth century was to try to relate "travellers' tales" to
creatures already listed. The rapid growth of science gave it
the intolerance of an adolescent, and the empiricism which had
been one of the most praiseworthy features of the early writers
went temporarily out of fashion.

The positive identification of an entirely new giant sea creature during the latter half of the century was a heavy blow to
many dogmatists. From earliest times a number of "monster"
stories had referred to a dragon with many arms of enormous
length, which could reach into a boat and drag men into the
sea to be eaten at leisure. This creature, almost universally de-
rided by scientists at the time, had become a *fait accompli* by
1875; it was only then that the giant squid (*Loligo architeu-
this*), a ten-armed relative of the octopus, its longest tentacles
having a length of more than thirty feet, was finally recognized
by science.

"One might have thought," writes Commander Gould,[8]
"that, since naturalists had been brought to see that a so-called
myth had a real foundation, and that the sea held at least one
large creature of which they had no knowledge, they might
have gone a step further, and admitted that there might be
others also. Possibly, some did; but the more general attitude,
I think, was that assumed by Lee in his *Sea Monsters Unmasked*—a somewhat optimistic title—which endeavoured to
show that such stories as Egede's, and that of the *Daedalus*,
were distorted narratives of an encounter with a giant squid."

But the giant squid was not the last practical joke that the sea
had in store for scientists. During the winter of 1938 a fish about
five feet long was caught in a trawl net at a depth of forty

[8] *Ibid.*

fathoms off the coast of South Africa. It was not recognized by its captors and was preserved for identification. It was, however, immediately recognized by scientists as *Latimeria*, one of the cœlacanths that were well known from fossils of the Cretaceous Period, which lasted from a hundred and forty million to seventy million years ago. It was believed to have become extinct by the end of that period, which was dominated on land by the great dinosaurs. In other words, it was presumed to have been already extinct for about sixty million years before man appeared upon the earth. How would the scientific world have received an unsupported claim to have seen it in 1938? The species is now recognized by the name of *Latimeria chalumnæ*, and it seems to me that its portraits have a twinkle in the huge eye and an almost audible chuckle in the archaic throat.

Many stories of the "sea serpent" would be treated as barely distorted descriptions of a plesiosaur were this not a prehistoric animal. The plesiosaurs, however—giant lizards of the shallow seas, with a long neck and tail and four paddle-like flippers—are presumed to have become extinct with or before *Latimeria*.

The mososaurs, too, were contemporaries of this Rip van Winkle of the sea, and they were veritable sea serpents; huge rapacious reptiles almost as slender as a snake. So let us "never, never doubt what nobody is sure about."

A proportion of "sea-monster" stories have for a long time been justifiably recognized by scientists as being the result of ill-informed observation of basking sharks. I have several times seen three or more large sharks swimming nose to tail, following each other for long distances and sometimes in circles, and these an inexperienced observer would almost certainly mistake

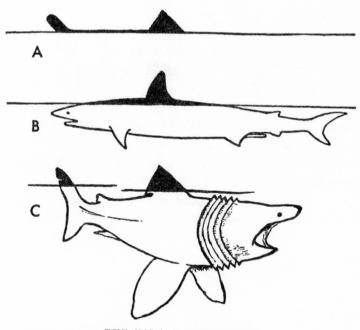

THE *HILARY* "MONSTER"

A: Captain Dean's sketch
B: Commander Gould's explanatory sketch
    (Both from *The Case for the Sea-Serpent* by R. T. Gould)
C: Explanatory sketch by the author

for one creature of great length. It is strange, however, that few who have rightly attempted these explanations seem to have had any idea of what a basking shark looked like, and so have misled the public still further by inaccurate drawings.

For example, on page 213 of Commander Gould's *The Case for the Sea-Serpent* appear two sketches. The first is a rough sketch by Captain F. W. Dean, R.N., of H.M. Armed Merchant Cruiser *Hilary*. The second is Commander Gould's attempt to relate this drawing to a basking shark. (See above.)

Now A, the top sketch, requires only the minutest of modifications to make it into an absolutely typical appearance of a basking shark, while it would take some really heavy reconstruction for B to resemble a basking shark even faintly. If I saw the objects in the top sketch, I should immediately suppose them to be the tail (left) and dorsal fin (right) of an ordinary adult basking shark, and I should be puzzled only by the absence of a "sub-terminal notch" in the tail fin (see photograph 75). The dorsal fin in Commander Gould's drawing suggests an immature bull killer whale, and the body resembles no fish that I have ever seen personally. He carefully tucks the tail below water, whereas a basking shark more often than not shows a foot or more of tail above water when swimming at the surface.

The bottom sketch, C, represents my own explanation of Captain Dean's drawing, nor in his lengthy quoted description can I see anything but my old friend the basking shark.

But not all the sea serpents can be so easily explained away, and with the resurrection of *Latimeria* as so recent a reminder of the folly of dogmatism, we should do well to keep an open mind.

BIBLIOGRAPHY

Gould, Charles. *Mythical Monsters*. London: Allen & Co., 1886

Gould, Rupert Thomas. *The Case for the Sea-Serpent*. London: Philip Allen, 1930

Hawkins, Thomas. *The Book of the Great Sea-Dragons*. London: 1840

Lee, Henry. *Sea Monsters Unmasked*. London: International Fish Exp., 1883

Oudemans, Antonie Cornelis. *The Great Sea-Serpent*. Leiden: E. J. Brill, 1892

2. The Basking Shark

A Summary of Findings by L. Harrison Matthews, Sc. D.
Scientific Director, Zoological Society of London

and H. W. Parker, D. Sc.
British Museum (Natural History)

General. It is remarkable that the anatomy and biology of a fish so large, conspicuous, and common as the basking shark should be practically unknown, especially in view of the fact that it is the subject of a commercial fishery in the British Isles, and consequently is not inaccessible to naturalists. Until 1947 the general anatomy of this fish had been reported on by only four persons: Home (1809, 1813), who examined two adult males; de Blainville (1811), who examined one; Pavesi (1874, 1878), who examined two immature males; and Carazzi (1904, 1905), who examined an immature female. There are numerous observations on the occurrence of the species in various parts of the world, and some authors have described the whalebone-like gill rakers. In the second half of May 1947, Dr. Harrison Matthews and Dr. H. W. Parker visited Major Gavin Maxwell's shark-fishing station and factory on the Isle of Soay, off the coast of Skye. They examined and dissected a number of sharks, and were able to go to sea in hunting craft. The machinery used in dismembering sharks at the factory was an invaluable aid to the work, for sharks are not easy subjects for dissection, the size and weight of the individual organs making handling difficult; and woe betide the anatomist who inadvertently punctures the stomach and releases something like a ton of semidigested plankton over his dissection. A large amount of information was collected and much material fixed and preserved for subsequent examination. A special study was made of reproduction and internal anatomy, food and feeding habits, and of parasites. The results were published in two memoirs presented to the Royal Society and the Zoological Society of London, and printed with many illustrations.

Size and Weight. Though it is often stated that basking sharks reach a length of forty feet or more, few, if any, exceed thirty feet in a straight line from the tip of the snout to the notch of the caudal fin. None of those measured in the Hebrides exceeded twenty-nine feet in this dimension. The weight of a shark twenty-nine feet long would be about ten thousand pounds (roughly four and a half tons), judging from the figures given about two sharks that were weighed piecemeal in America. On the other hand, an estimate of the total weight of such a fish was made at the Soay station as follows: head (estimated by the capacity of a small mobile crane that could only just lift it), one ton; liver (weighed), eighteen and a half hundred-weights; fins (guessed), one ton; tail (guessed), half a ton; skin (guessed), one ton; meat and backbone, one and a half tons; guts (guessed), half a ton; this giving a total weight of nearly six and a half tons, to which may be added half to one ton more for the contents of the stomach and intestines. The general colour is very dark grey, but there is a tendency for lighter and darker areas of grey to form a pattern of longitudinal streaks. Patches of white are generally present on the ventral surface and are sometimes of considerable extent. When basking sharks are seen in the water, however, the impression given to some observers is that the colour in general is a light brown rather than blackish.

Colour and Skin. It is not known whether this appearance represents the true colour of the fish in life, or whether it is produced by the layer of water between the fish and the observer. If it represents the true colour, there must be a rapid change to that described above immediately after death. The placoid scales of simple type cover most of the body, their basal plates forming a complete mosaic. In some parts of the body parallel sulci which appear to correspond with lines of flexure of the skin are almost completely devoid of denticles.

Teeth. The teeth are simple modifications of the placoid scale and, owing to the presence of vestigial secondary cusps, are asymmetrical except near the median line. There are six rows of teeth in the upper jaw, nine in the lower.

Form of Head and Snout in Young. The snout in the juvenile is longer and more pointed than in the adult, but the extreme forms that have been reported may have been produced by post-mortem shrinkage of the ampullary mass above the rostral cartilage. The sudden increase in girth at the level of the pharyngeal region, which has been described as a juvenile character, is probably entirely produced by distortion.

The Digestive System. The skin lining the mouth and pharynx is smooth at the anterior end, but covered with papillæ behind. The papillæ increase in size and complexity from before backwards; they are low and rounded in front, tall and conical farther back, long and branched at the œsophagus, into which they project as a large bunch forming a valve.

The stomach is siphonal in shape, with a large, partly sacculated cardiac portion, and narrow pyloric limb. The mucosa is beset with crypts; into those of the cardiac part numerous large glands open. The semi-liquid contents of the cardiac sac weigh about half a ton and consist of disintegrating planktonic crustacea mixed with a great quantity of mucus. Removal of water at the beginning of the pyloric limb must be rapid, for this limb contains a thick dark-red paste. The distal end of the pyloric limb is expanded to form the bursa entiana before joining the duodenum. The bursa contains a clear red oil derived from the paste in the proximal part of the limb. Histological examination shows that the oil is probably absorbed by the epithelium of the bursa.

The bile and pancreatic ducts open into the duodenum, a chamber proximal to the first turn of the spiral valve, but not externally separated from the mid-intestine. The valve, which is a simple spiral shelf, contains up to about fifty turns. The mucosa of the valve is covered with villi, each closely beset with glands; a stratum of lymphoid tissue lies beneath the glands. The colon and rectum are comparatively short, but there is a large rectal gland lined by a thick glandular mucosa.

The Reproductive System. Practically nothing has hitherto been known of the reproductive anatomy and physiology of the basking shark, no work having been published on the subject since the first incomplete reports over one hundred and thirty years ago.

The testes are embedded in the anterior ends of the epigonal organs, which form an investing cortex round them. The testes are divided into lobes, and these into lobules which contain many ampullæ. Testis tubules lead the spermatozoa from the ampullæ to the vasa efferentia, whence they pass through the ductuli and ductus epididymidis to the enormous ampulla ductus deferentis, where they are incorporated in spermatophores.

The ampulla ductus deferentis contains numerous transverse septa, each with an eccentric perforation; successive perforations form the lumen of the organ as a whole. Spermatic fluid enters the ampulla ductus deferentis and becomes broken up into small aggregations, which pass into the pockets between the septa. Here they are rotated by ciliary action, while the secretion from the deeper epithelial cells is laid down round them in concentric layers. The spermatophores are up to two to three centimetres or more in diameter, and consist of a translucent hyaline cortex surrounding an opaque core of spermatozoa. Several gallons of spermatophores are present in each ampulla.

The skeleton of the clasper is comparatively simple in structure, the cartilages being a few in number and forming a scroll proximally and a groove distally. There is a movable style towards the distal end, armed with a sharp claw. The musculature of the clasper is reduced, the dilator muscle being the largest. The inner surface of the clasper groove within the scroll is covered with a thick layer of glandular tissue, whose secretion is produced by the swelling, degeneration, and detachment of the superficial cells.

The siphons are long and wide sacs lying between the skin and the body wall on the ventro-lateral surface of the abdomen. They are connected by the siphon tubes with the bases of the clasper grooves and are invested by a thin sheet of muscle, part of m. compressor, derived from the pelvic fin. The thick epithelium lining the siphons produces a secretion by the swelling, degeneration, and detachment of the superficial cells. Nothing was found in the siphons beyond a small quantity of mucoid secretion. The siphon is probably used in some way not understood for introducing the spermatophores into the female by way of the clasper groove, but the spermatophores do not enter the siphon sacs.

The epigonal organ in both sexes is alike, and consists of a mass of lymphomyeloid tissue. Its function is hæmatopoietic, and it produces lymphocytes, leucocytes, and erythrocytes.

The ovary of the right side alone is developed; it is large and enclosed in a fibrous tunica. It consists mainly of a mass of small follicles loosely held together by a small amount of connective tissue, and is penetrated everywhere by the ramifications of a system of branching tubes which derive ultimately from a pocket on the right side of the outer surface of the ovary. The ova are discharged from the follicles when they are not more than five millimetres in diameter and pass through the ramifying tubes to reach the exterior through the pocket. The epithelium of the discharged follicle proliferates to form a corpus luteum, the cells of which contain large quantities of lipoid material. Most of the ova, however, are not discharged, but degenerate within the follicles, forming atretic corpora lutea. Great numbers of corpora lutea atretica are present in the ovary. In an average ovary there are at least six million ova 0.5 millimetre or more in diameter, a size at which there is a considerable amount of yolk already present. The ovary is thus unlike that of other elasmobranchs, in which there are usually a few large ova, and in general appearance is more like that of an oviparous teleost. This is remarkable in view of the fact that *Cetorhinus* is almost certainly viviparous.

The unpaired infundibular part of the oviducts opens at the ostium abdominale, and lies shallowly embedded in the liver adjacent to the attachment of the falciform ligament. It follows a course such that the ostium abdominale is brought directly opposite, and into contact with, the pocket on the right side of the ovary. Ova thus pass from the ovary at once into the oviduct, and do not wander in the peritoneal cavity. The paired oviducts are applied to the posterior surface of the septum transversum, and pass to the parietal wall of the abdomen, where they join the nidamentary glands. Their lumina are very narrow, not more than two to three millimetres in diameter, and their walls are thick and inelastic, so that it is impossible for an object larger than an ovum about five millimetres in diameter to pass through them, and even an ovum of this size must undergo considerable distortion.

The nidamentary gland is comparatively small and shows no subdivision into albumen and shell-secreting parts; no stored spermatozoa were found in it. An elongated narrow isthmus leads from the nidamentary gland to the enormous uterus. The greater part of the uterus is lined by innumerable villus-like trophonemata. These are based upon low longitudinal ridges and may be regarded as strap-like prolongations of their free edges. Each trophonema is supported by a central core of connective tissue and is richly vascularized; no separate glands are present upon it, but the epithelial cells increase greatly in number and become swollen with secretion, perhaps trophic in function, which they release by becoming detached and disintegrating. In many places the proliferation of epithelial cells is so great that a solid mass of swollen cells, in which the trophonemata are partly or wholly buried, results. Numerous vesicles up to four or five millimetres in diameter, and containing a clear fluid, may be present in the solid cell mass. It is possible that their secretion may have a solvent action on the cortex of the spermatophores.

The lateral walls of the common vagina bear thick pads of dense fibrous tissue; in adult fish these pads bear scars or lacerations caused by the claw on the clasper of the male. The incidence of the lacerations shows that one clasper only is inserted at a time. A small but distinct hymen marks the lower limit of the common vagina.

The majority of the sharks seen basking at the surface of the inshore waters of the west coasts are non-pregnant females, and pairing certainly takes place during the late spring and early summer; it may possibly also take place at other times of the year. The basking habit, however, is probably in some way connected with the sexual behaviour pattern, as is the annual appearance of the fish near the coast. *Cetorhinus* shows the paradox of having an ovary containing a vast number of small ova and a large uterus thickly lined with trophonemata, the first suggesting that reproduction is by spawning, as in teleost fish, but the second showing that it is undoubtedly viviparous. There is no record of a female fish containing recognizable embryos ever having been examined in modern times. It is evident, therefore, that the female fish, after being inseminated, and before any embryo is recognizable, must refrain from basking, and either swim nearer the bottom or leave inshore waters, or both.

It is impossible to do more than guess at the probable length of gestation. The eggs of small oviparous sharks such as dogfish take as long as a year to hatch, and in some of the small viviparous sharks gestation lasts eighteen months, or even two years. It is therefore probable that gestation in the basking shark is lengthy, especially in view of the small size of the egg when it is released from the ovary; and a gestation of two years or more is probable. It is also possible that many eggs are released at ovulation but that only a few, or perhaps a single one, gives rise to a new shark, the successful embryo developing at the expense of the others.

No young basking shark less than about six feet in length has ever been recorded, and it may therefore be provisionally assumed that sharks of this length are the young of the year. A consideration of the lengths of immature sharks and of the months in which they have been recorded leads to the tentative conclusion that sexual maturity is not attained until at least the third year of life, or perhaps the fourth, when the fish have reached an over-all length of about twenty-three feet. Thereafter growth continues for another two years, until the maximum over-all length of about twenty-nine feet is attained.

Longevity. If the fish are four years old at their first breeding season, and gestation lasts two years, the life span of the individual must be long if the population is not to decrease in numbers. Each female fish must leave at least one daughter that survives long enough to reproduce, and some of them must also leave male offspring: breeding is probably promiscuous, and it would therefore not be necessary, in theory at any rate, for each female to leave a son. But in slowly maturing animals the hazards of life before reaching breeding age are great, and more than this minimum of offspring must be produced if enough are to reach maturity and to breed a further generation. Each female shark must produce probably at least three offspring, and possibly many more, if the population is to be maintained. Further, it is probable that only one young shark is produced at each birth, and the age necessary to produce three offspring therefore is $4 + 2 + 2 + 2 = 10$ years. This is probably an underestimate, and it is quite possible that basking sharks commonly reach their quarter century.

The Brain and Behaviour. The brain is small in proportion to the size of the animal and lies in a voluminous perimeningeal space supported by innumerable fine strands of tissue-like cobweb. The brain is little more than three times the length of that in quite small sharks, such as dogfish, and its small size is possibly correlated with the generally slow movements of the fish and their apparent insensitivity to pain when struck by a harpoon or otherwise injured. There is, of course, a slight reaction if the fish is disturbed, but in common with other elasmobranchs there seems to be little reaction to injuries that would cause great pain in higher animals, and the fish seem to be immune to "surgical shock." It is well known that the brain in some lower animals can be destroyed, but that many of the bodily activities are unimpaired by the operation, a large number of the bodily functions being controlled by the spinal cord; an animal on which this operation has been performed is known as a "spinal animal." The comparison of the basking shark, with its tiny brain and sluggish habits, with a spinal animal needs no stressing. The olfactory tracts are narrow and elongated, exceeding the remainder of the brain in length. The olfactory organ is a modification of the simple type found in many smaller elasmobranchs and is arranged so that a continuous stream of water enters at a scoop-like funnel, passes over the nasal mucosa spread out on a number of plates, and leaves by a backwardly directed exhaust funnel. In the lateral-line system the majority of the ampullæ of Lorenzini are concentrated into a mass which occupies the whole of the space above the rostral cartilage.

Feeding. The gill arches each carry from one thousand to thirteen thousand gill rakers up to ten millimetres long, their free ends directed towards the mouth. When the mouth is opened, the rakers are erected by contraction of a complex of muscle strands connecting the bases of the rakers to the branchial cartilages: when it is shut they are returned to a position flat on the surface of the arches by the action of elastic fibres. It is suggested that plankton filtered off by the rakers is entangled in mucus secreted by the epithelium at their bases, and that the mixture is squeezed out into the mouth when the rakers collapse. The total respiratory surface of the gill filaments in a shark seven metres long is calculated to be of the order of two hundred and seventy square metres.

Among the contents of the stomach it was possible to recognize fish eggs of several species, *Calanus* and other copepods, and larvæ of cirripedes and decapods; there were no indications of organisms larger than *Calanus*. The plankton-remains in the stomach are very fragmentary and appear to have been subjected not only to chemical disintegration, but also to mechanical breakdown, possibly by a churning action of the stomach muscles and crushing movements of the gill rakers. The net weight of solid organic matter in the stomach contents was less than thirty per cent of the total, and mucus accounted for a considerable part of it. The organic solids contain approximately seven to eight per cent of the clear, red astacene-containing oil which is separated out in the bursa entiana.

When feeding, the basking shark swims at a rate of about two knots, and calculation shows that at this speed a shark of average size would filter over two thousand tons of sea water an hour. The fish swims with the mouth widely open and the gills and pharyngeal region greatly expanded, feeding and respiration being simultaneous and almost automatic. The basking habit, in which the first dorsal fin and the tip of the tail project above the surface of the water, is probably adopted when the concentration of plankton is great near the surface; it is likely that feeding also takes place when the fish are completely submerged. The basking habit is probably correlated also with the breeding behaviour of the fish.

All the sharks seen at close quarters at sea carried one or more lampreys attached to the skin, and all dead fish examined bore superficial marks caused by the suckers of lampreys. The denticles appear to form an armouring too hard for lampreys to penetrate, for no wounds attributable to them were seen.

Parasites. The large parasitic copepod, *Dinematura producta* (photographs 70 and 71), was common on the skin of the sharks examined. Comparison of the extensive material collected with that from other hosts shows that here are at least three host forms of the copepod. The differences lie in the organs of prehension and adhesion; they may be ecoptypic in origin, their form being determined by the nature of the host skin on which the larvæ settle. The parasites erode the skin of the host sufficiently to expose the basal plates of the denticles, but examination of the gut contents failed to disclose any recognizable blood corpuscles, and it is possible that the food is no more substantial than mucus.

Another parasitic copepod, *Nemesis lamna*, was numerous on the gills, where it causes extensive though superficial damage to the filaments, the mucosa being cut up by the parasite and hypertrophied to three times its normal thickness.

Two species of cestodes of the genus *Dinobothrium*, one of them new to science, were found in the spiral valve, and have formed the subject of a separate report.

3. Controversial Matters

The detailed findings of Dr. Harrison Matthews and Dr. H. W. Parker are published in the *Philosophical Transactions of the Royal Society*, 234B, 147, 1950 (Dr. Matthews' paper dealing exhaustively with reproduction), and *Proceedings of the Zoological Society of London*, Vol. 120, Part III, pp. 535–76, "Notes on the Anatomy and Biology of the Basking Shark," a joint and more general paper by both authors.

When dealing with a creature as little known as this, points of controversy and disagreement are bound to arise, more especially over questions of field natural history, and I should shirk a scientific obligation if I did not record those points on which I must as a result of personal experience disagree with Dr. Matthews' and Dr. Parker's observations; indeed, Dr. Matthews has urged me to do so. On some of these points they have had occasion to modify their views since the publication of these papers, and in particular they have published a supplementary note on the breaching habit in *Proceedings of the Zoological Society of London*, Vol. 121, Part II, pp. 461–62.

In committing to paper opinions at variance with these authorities, I have not trusted to my own memory alone but have consulted both my written records and all the members of my crew with whom I have been able to get into contact. They have in all cases endorsed my own recollections, and the interested reader should remember how extremely familiar we all became with sharks during those seasons of continuous hunting.

For convenience I treat these controversial matters under separate headings.

Dimensions. As Matthews and Parker justly point out, there appears to have been much exaggeration about the length of the basking shark as recorded in literature, and they fix the adult length at twenty-nine feet. The authority for this limit is the fact that none of the eleven fish that they examined at Soay measured longer than this; and that Watkins, who is quoted as having "been engaged in the shark fishery for many years," stated that "a length of twenty-nine feet is never exceeded in Scottish waters." In my opinion these statements are as bold, and as possibly misleading, as the previous overestimates, and I cannot well understand the misconception over the length of Watkins' experience.

I believe that the *average* adult basking shark in Hebridean waters would measure about twenty-six feet; that in a catch of a hundred sharks landed without one being lost there would be two or three of thirty feet; and, however improbable it may sound, that there are quite definitely a very few fish that would measure upwards of forty feet.

When I began fishing for basking sharks I overestimated their length enormously, and I have no doubt that the majority of people who do not become familiar with them continue to do the same. But when one has caught a great number one recognizes that a shark is either inside the average variation that one knows or is something exceptional and outside previous experience. In 1946 Watkins bet me that I would not catch a shark of thirty feet, a bet which I accepted and lost; for our largest shark, fairly measured, was twenty-nine feet eight inches, and I saw only one fish that year that I considered to be larger. On September 11, however, while I was away in Glasgow, Bruce lost a shark which I myself have no doubt belonged to that extreme outside category of which I saw less than a

dozen individuals during all my time at sea. Bruce's own estimate is that the fish was approximately forty feet, but might
have been a little less. He wrote:

Just a line in haste to catch the *Lochmor*. We have just arrived
in here, and I am very sorry and disappointed to tell you that we
are just after losing the biggest fish of the season. Nobody's fault,
there was nothing we could do about it. He put up a terrific fight
after being three hours on the buoys, and the worst part of it was
we had already got the tail sling on his tail. When he was tied up
he gave two or three terrific heaves and broke everything. You
wouldn't have thought any fish could break one of those slings.

This occurred in the dusk at Courachan. The fish had been
shot in daylight, three hours before, and at the time of the
shooting the crew had agreed that it was the largest shark that
any of them had seen.

A somewhat similar incident took place a year later. There
were two fish following each other closely in line ahead. The
rear fish appeared to be of normal size; the leader, on the other
hand, was what Tex used to call "monsterious," the dorsal fin
appearing half as big again as that of its follower, which was
also riding high in the water. For more than an hour the *Sea
Leopard* manœuvred to get a shot at the leader, before deciding that an average shark was better than none at all and harpooning the rear fish. This shark, which had seemed no more
than average to the crew, was in fact the largest ever brought
in to the Soay factory, measuring thirty-one feet five inches
in a straight line. All are agreed that with this comparison in
mind the leading shark cannot have been less than forty feet,
and all consider this to be a conservative statement.

The largest fish that I remember personally was that which
broke the three-inch yacht manila rope between Uishenish

and Lochboisdale, and which I have described on pages 168–70, and again my estimate is of a full forty feet. I am as certain as I can be that these individuals of much greater length than the average do exist and that I have seen them. The fact that they were always "the ones that got away" is due to cause and effect.

On the question of weight, Matthews and Parker have modified in the present Appendix the impression left by an earlier American observation quoted in their published paper, and I have no doubt that this latest speculative assessment is very much nearer to fact.

Colour. Here my contention is that the fish is not as dark as described in the published papers resulting from the Soay work. Looking down from the foredeck of a boat, the body never looks darker than the water surrounding it, always lighter, and of an umberish colour with darker markings. Only the fins, showing above water, appear blackish, and even these have a distinctly brown tinge. As the shark goes deeper in the water he appears more and more grey, as opposed to brown. I think that on land the mucous secretion from the skin dries to a near-black film, which may have given rise to the present confusion.

Speed and Breaching. The feeding speed is estimated at about two knots, with which I am in general agreement, though where there is a current of water the shark may resist it only sufficiently to remain virtually stationary. It is suggested, however, that a speed of four knots may never be exceeded. I have seen sharks swimming at the surface which the *Gannet*, with a maximum speed of six knots, would not have overhauled had they not changed direction, and I am certain that when alarmed the fish can reach at least fifteen knots for a short distance. Dan MacGillivray, a cautious and reliable man with a great deal of experience, considers that some sharks occasionally reach twenty knots as they sound after being harpooned, though this is exceptional.

On the question of breaching, I read with near-incredulity the following paragraph in the Matthews-Parker joint paper:

It is alleged that the basking shark sometimes leaps from the water, so that the whole body is brought clear, and that it falls back again with a tremendous splash, an action similar to the breaching of whales. From a consideration of the usual habits of this fish, however, it appears very improbable that this statement is correct. . . . It is probable that the stories of basking sharks breaching are founded upon confusion with the larger dolphins or, even more probably, with the thresher shark which breaches in the most spectacular way, and might well cause a mistake if seen at a distance when basking sharks were numerous close to the observer.

To men who had watched this action as often and at such close quarters as we had, this statement seemed simply ludicrous. To us it was as if some scientist wrote that it was alleged that dogs in London sometimes lifted their legs against lamp posts, but that this was probably due to confusion with one of the rarer species of wolf, that did in fact so lift their legs in a most spectacular manner. I am glad to say that combined testimony has now convinced Dr. Matthews that basking sharks really do breach, and he has published a supplementary note unreservedly withdrawing the original statement.

The Basking Habit. From the summary of the same publication (see p. 294) I quote:

The basking habit, in which the first dorsal fin and the tip of the tail project above the surface of the water is probably adopted when the concentration of plankton is great near the surface; it is likely that feeding also takes place when the fish are completely submerged. The basking habit is probably correlated also with the breeding behaviour of the fish.

I must say at once that, tempting though both these theories are, they accord in no way with my own observations. The suggestion that basking is correlated with breeding behaviour is, I think, completely precluded by the fact that sharks appear to bask from birth onward, and during all their sexually immature years. After the most conscientious examination, we could relate the appearance of the sharks at the surface to no constant factor. Had we been able to do so it would have been a major step towards the success of the venture.

Again and again the plankton net returned a concentrated sample from the first fathom when no sharks were visible, though we knew them to be in the area; again and again we would obtain a weak plankton sample from near to the surface when sharks were up. I feel convinced that there is some at present unconsidered determining factor that is responsible for bringing large numbers of fish to the surface over an area of a mile or more and within a few minutes of each other. Further, all our experience tended to show that rarely if ever are all sharks of a shoal visible at once, which may suggest that not all are receiving the same stimulus. We tried in vain to relate these appearances to weather (temperature, wind force, humidity, light), to the state of the tide, to the concentration of plankton in the surface fathom of water, and I must consider that we are not yet in a state of knowledge to offer any explanation of the basking habit.

Form of Head and Snout in the Young. With the permission of the Zoological Society I reprint this paragraph from the "Notes" in its entirety.

Newly born basking sharks have never been examined but immature examples from 5 ft. 5 in. to 15 ft. have been reported upon from time to time. In many of these reports specimens of less than about 12 ft. are described as having a pointed prominence or beak (one author describes it as "a protuberance resembling a small rhinoceros horn") at the tip of the snout, or a narrow rostrum preceding a very broad, flattened pharyngeal region. Examples are to be found in Cornish (1870; 9 ft.), Pavesi (1876; 9 ft. 8½ in.), Pavesi (1876; 10 ft. 8 in.), Gervais (1876; 12 ft.), Carazzi (1904; 11 ft. 2 in.), de Buen (1925; ?), Platt (1937; 12 ft. 7 in.), and Bigelow and Schroeder (1948; 12 ft.). Professor Schroeder has also very kindly informed us (*in litt.* 1950) that both a 10-ft. specimen washed ashore in Massachusetts Bay about 1947 and a 9-ft. specimen seen at Woods Hole in 1948 had the "proboscis-like" form of snout. Pl. VIII, fig. 26, shows this shape in a specimen caught on June 7, 1950, in a mackerel drifter's net in the English Channel at a position 3 miles south of Portobello (50° 44′ N. × 0°2′ E. approx). The exact dimensions of this fish are not available but, to judge from the photographs, it must have measured between 7 and 8 ft. Bigelow and Schroeder (1948, p. 150) state that a transition to the adult type of snout takes place at lengths of 12–16 ft. Other authors, however, make no mention of any such prominence, *e.g.*, the 9 ft. 4 in. specimen caught in Cullen, Banffshire, in 1935 (Anon., *Scottish Naturalist*, 1935), and a sketch made by Dr. Trewavas of a specimen between 11 and 12 ft. long that was stranded near Penzance in 1921 or 1922, also shows no protuberance but a subconical, rather sharply pointed snout. It seems certain that the form of snout in the juvenile is different from that of the adult, but the protuberant appearance appears to be variable and may well be partly produced by shrinkage and collapse of the flabby ampullary mass that lies above the rostral cartilage. That shrinkage can produce such a result is evidenced by the photographs reproduced as Pl. IV, figs. 10 and 11, which show a terminal horn-like prominence on the end of the snout of a young *Squalus acanthias* that had been allowed to become partly desiccated. Text-fig. 3 [reproduced on page 303] shows the outlines of some of the juvenile heads for comparison with this artificially produced condition. The sudden increase of girth at the level of the pharyngeal region, which has also been described and figured

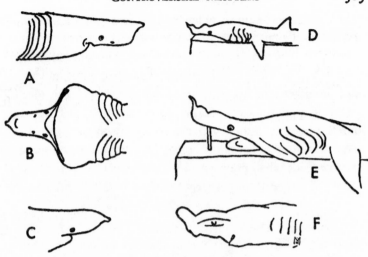

THE OUTLINE OF THE HEAD IN YOUNG BASKING SHARKS
(From *The Proceedings of the Zoological Society of London*, VNRO,
Part III)

as a juvenile character, is probably entirely due to distortion;
when taken from the water these fish naturally sag considerably
under their own weight, and the pharyngeal and branchial regions
are especially distorted; this distortion is clearly shown in Pl. VIII,
fig. 26. Distortions of this nature, together with the juvenile form
of snout, have, in the past, led to the description of different
"species" and "genera." Couch (1868), for instance, was misled in
this way by Pavesi (1874), and Day (1880–84) recognized the
true nature of the described differences; the latter observes that
"should the mouth of one of these fish be left open, by inserting
a piece of wood between the jaws, the peculiar appearance as
described by Couch in *Polyprosopus* is obtained" and adds "this
condition or appearance of the snout has been observed by Sir
T. Browne so long ago as 1662."

Whereas D, E, and F in the illustration are clearly the result of shrinkage and distortion, I should consider A, B, and C

to be all within the range of my own observation of the living or freshly killed fish. The protuberance on the end of the snout varies in inverse ratio to the length of the fish, being most pronounced in the smallest I have seen. These were not measured, but I should estimate their length at seven to eight feet. Photographs 68 and 69 show a smaller proboscis on a fish measuring fourteen feet seven inches, in which any possibility of distortion may be dismissed, since the fish was still displaying muscular movement when photographed. I think that in this connection the evidence of the earlier writers should not be discounted.

"THE ONE THAT GOT AWAY WAS THIS LONG!"
(*From a postcard from Hartley, 1945*)